SADDAM HUSSEIN

THE MAN, THE CAUSE AND THE FUTURE

Fuad Matar

FOR RESEARCH AND PUBLISHING
117 PICCADILLY LONDON W1

ISBN
0-86199 008-0

Printed in Beirut, Lebanon by
EXPRESS INTERNATIONAL PRINTING Co.
FIRST EDITION
1981

CONTENTS

FOREWORD

The date 17 September 1980 will remain a milestone in the history of modern Iraq. On that day the people of Iraq found themselves at war. President Saddam Hussein stood before the National Assembly (the first parliament to be elected in Iraq for twenty-five years) and, in a voice similar to that of the Egyptian President Gamal Abdel-Nasser when he nationalised the Suez Canal, abrogated the 6 March 1975 agreement with Iran and called for the 'return of the Iraqi-Arab Shatt al-Arab with full rights and sovereignty'. On that day Saddam Hussein donned the uniform of Commander-in-Chief of the Armed Forces, and top Iraqi officials donned the uniform of the Popular Army. The 'postponed war' with Iran had begun — 'postponed' war because it had been developing for a long time. Indeed, in order to understand the war, one must go back to the day the agreement of 6 March 1975 was signed, as a quick review of events will show.

In March 1975 Algeria's late President Houari Boumedienne succeeded in bringing about a meeting between Saddam Hussein, the Vice President of Iraq's Revolution Command Council, and Muhammad Reza Pahlavi, the Shah of Iran. The meeting took place behind the scenes at the first summit conference of the Organisation of Petroleum Exporting Countries. The Shah was, at that time, at the height of his power. Saddam Hussein had left behind him a war of attrition in which the Iraqi forces were engaged with the Kurdish insurgents in the North and in which some 60,000 Iraqis (of whom 16,000 were soldiers) had been killed or wounded within one year. The Kurdish insurgents were being financed and armed by the Shah. Boumedienne had succeeded in finding some grounds for negotiation between the two men. However, the Shah, strong as he was, had begun to feel the cold wind of revolution. Revolutionary acts in Iran were being carried out with the backing of Iraq, and Ayatollah Ruhollah Khomeini was leading part of the Iranian revolution from his exile in the Iraqi city of Najaf, revered by the Shia sect of Islam as the burial place of Imam Ali.

Both men had something to gain from an agreement. The Shah wished to be totally secure so as to carry out his chosen role as 'policeman of the Gulf', a role in which he was encouraged and armed by the United States, while Saddam Hussein wanted to secure a breathing space for his country so that it might develop into a modern state with a strong army. The two 'strongmen' finally arrived at an agreement. Saddam Hussein accepted the settlement in spite of what he saw as its bias, and in spite of the doubts some Arab states expressed. It provided for final delineation of the land border between the two countries based on the 1913 Constantinople Protocol and the 1914 Border Committee's minutes. The river was divided according to the Thalweg line. The agreement also provided for recourse to Houari Boumedienne when necessary, and for the removal of all obstacles in the way of normal relations.

Various committees worked actively to implement the agreement after it was signed. Subsequently the Shah was scheduled to pay a state visit to Iraq, but he made it a condition that Imam Khomeini should be expelled from Iraq during his visit as he wanted to tour the holy cities of Najaf and Karbala. Iraq rejected this condition (although there was no co-ordination between the Iraqi regime and Imam Khomeini against the Shah), and the visit did not take place.

Throughout the period of increasing turbulence in Iran and the Shah's overthrow by Imam Khomeini at the head of a popular revolution, little was done by the Iranians to implement the March agreement. Iraq had hoped that the new regime in Iran would take steps to implement the agreement but, instead, relations between Iraq and Iran deteriorated and reached their lowest point. Not only did Iranian officials issue declarations which the Iraqis felt were aimed at arousing sectarian unrest in Iraq, they also claimed that much of the Arab Gulf was Iranian. Several incidents aimed at creating unrest in Iraq followed, the most notable of which was the attempted assassination of Tareq Aziz, who was the target of a bomb hurled by an Iranian at Baghdad's Mustansiriyah University. The attempt on the life of Tareq Aziz, a member of the Revolution Command Council and Vice-President, was seen as particularly despicable because he was a Christian as well as a high-ranking member of the Iraqi Baath Party. The Iranian involved in the failed attempt was a member of the Al-Da'awa Party, the Shia form of the Muslim Brotherhood prevalent in other Arab countries, which is backed and financed by Iran. Moreover, Iran began to back certain Kurdish elements in Iraq, specifically Idris and Massaoud Barzani, sons of Mullah Mustafa Barzani, the late Kurdish leader. Iraq responded by supporting elements opposed to the revolution in Iran as it became increasingly convinced that Imam Khomeini's main aim was to topple the regime of President Saddam Hussein. The Iranian leadership did little to hide its aims. Following the execution of the death sentence passed on Ayatollah Muhammad Bakr Sadr, one of the main leaders of the Al-Da'awa Party in Iraq and a strong supporter of Imam Khomeini, the Iranians called on the Iraqi Army to rise up against the government of President Saddam because it was 'non-

Muslim'. Thereafter it also became clear that Iraq was acting against the Iranian regime, which it considered 'racist and Persian'.

By early September 1980, President Saddam Hussein had learnt that there were Iranian border movements on the joint border and that the Iraqis living in the border area were being exposed to daily shelling. He met the Army Commanders to review the situation, as well as asking the Iraqi Foreign Ministry to send a message to the Iranians through diplomatic channels, requesting them to withdraw from Iraqi territory, the most important occupied area being the border zone of Zein al-Qaus. The Iraqi memorandum was delivered to the Iranian forces on 7 September; far from withdrawing, the Iranian forces were reinforced by jet fighters. Thereupon, President Saddam decided to liberate Zein al-Qaus and other areas. This was clear even during his ordinary meetings with civilians. For example, during a meeting with the Higher Council for Literacy on 8 September he declared, 'Every Iraqi citizen must be prepared to shed his blood for his nation and his principles.' At that moment, the Iraqi forces on the border with Iran were carrying out the liberation plan, which was called 'Operation Saddam Hussein'. It was swiftly executed: two Iranian towns were shelled, two planes were brought down and a number of soldiers were captured. Within hours, on 9 September, the Iraqi Army had settled the matter in its favour; the Iraqi flag fluttered over Zein al-Qaus and a large number of Iranian soldiers, weapons, ammunition and documents were captured. From then on, communiqué succeeded communiqué; more planes were brought down and greater losses were inflicted; the battlefield widened; and the Iraqi Air Force entered the fray.

President Saddam called for a meeting of the Revolution Command Council on 17 September, during which it was decided to abrogate the Algiers agreement between Iraq and Iran. This decision came after it was clear that the Iranians had no intention of abiding by the treaty. The Iranian President Abul-Hassan Bani Sadr had hinted at this when he said, 'Who signed the Algiers agreement? Even the Shah's regime did not implement it.' President Saddam then convened the National Assembly in an extraordinary session and, after reviewing the circumstances of the Algiers agreement, demanded the return of the Shatt al-Arab to Iraqi sovereignty. His message was aimed at the world: 'We assure the world that Iraq administered maritime affairs perfectly well in the days of complete sovereignty before March 1975, showing that it was both capable and responsible. Iraq today is even more capable of carrying out this duty.' A statement was then issued to all ships using the Shatt al-Arab, notifying them that henceforth they would have to fly the Iraqi flag in the area and abide by instructions given by Iraqi officials. The statement noted that the cancellation of the Algiers agreement gave Iraq complete sovereignty over its land, air and waters. The statement also noted that ships would have to pay dues to Iraq for passage through the Shatt and the use of its maritime facilities, and would have to use Iraqi pilots to steer the way through the straits. It was also made clear that any civil or criminal cases that arose in the region fell under the jurisdiction of Iraqi law, and that Iraq was fully responsible for all administrative and maintenance costs, as the water-way was an Iraqi national area.

From the beginning, President Saddam was careful to indicate that he simply wished to restore usurped Iraqi territory and that he had no ambitions over Iranian territory. This was a message to the superpowers to remain outside the conflict. However, the restoration of rights and territory meant war. On 22 September, therefore, the Revolution Command Council issued a statement to the Iraqi Armed Forces instructing them to hit at Iranian military targets. The conflict quickly developed and spread, and it was clear that this was not to be a quick, decisive war.

Iraqi forces penetrated into Iranian territory and conquered a number of positions as well as laying siege to several towns, including Muhammara (the Iranian name for which is Khorramshahr), whose citizens are mostly Arab. Iraq's strategy was as follows: to besiege the city of Muhammara, at whose ports most of Iran's goods were imported; to hit oil refineries and economic installations; to besiege other cities; and to hit airports and military bases in the border area and far into Iran, reaching as far as Tehran. Iraq thus wanted to bring the revolutionary authorities in Tehran to admit defeat and to begin negotiations on coexistence, given the situation on the ground. The revolutionary authorities in Tehran did not admit defeat, however, and instead disseminated information to the effect that the Iranian Army was preparing for a counter-attack. However, the myth of the invincible Iranian forces was severely shaken because tens of Iranian planes and ships were destroyed and hundreds of officers and soldiers captured. On the eighteenth day of the war, Imam Khomeini called on the Iranians to fight the Iraqis on the basis that the Iraqis were 'idolaters' and Saddam Hussein was a 'heretic'. In the meantime President Bani Sadr was busy freeing those army officers who were in Iranian gaols on suspicion of having worked with SAVAK (the secret police) or having plotted against the Iranian revolution, in order to send them to the battlefront. Iranian delegations were scouring the world for equipment, ammunition and spare parts, but this was an attempt doomed to failure because it was not easy to find parts for the modern American equipment possessed by the Iranian Army.

A number of Arabs attempted to mediate between the two warring parties, some secretly and some openly, but these attempts failed from the moment that President Saddam informed the Arabs that they should stand with Arab Iraq and not act as mediators. The most prominent mediator was Yasser Arafat, Chairman of the Executive Committee of the Palestine Liberation Organisation (PLO), who adopted a position of neutrality towards the Iran-Iraq war. At this point all eyes turned to the Algerian President Chadli Ben Jedid who, as Boumedienne's successor and by virtue of Algeria's being a party to the March agreement, was looked upon to play a role as mediator. Ben Jedid did make an attempt, but it was short-lived. Nor were the mediators representing the Islamic world any more successful. Pakistan's President Zia ul-Haq and the Islamic Conference President Habib Chatti visited both countries but in Iran were not able to meet the decision-maker, as had happened to Yasser Arafat. The decision-maker in Iran was Ayatollah Khomeini, and although the mediators met the executive bodies headed by Bani Sadr, the executive in Iran had no power to take decisions. Although Ayatollah Khomeini later met Habib Chatti, the Islamic mediation attempt came to nothing.

It is interesting to note at this point that, although Iraq was victorious on the ground, Saddam Hussein responded to the Islamic mediation and issued orders for a ceasefire. The Iranians rejected the call for a ceasefire, insisting that this could only be met if the military situation reverted to what it had been on the night of 8 September. Some Iranian officials went further: the Iranian ambassador to Moscow, for example, said that Iran would only accept a ceasefire if the Iraqi forces retreated, President Saddam Hussein resigned and the Iraqis gave Basra to the Iranians in compensation for their losses during the war. The ambassador was recalled, but later returned to his post. The ceasefire lasted no more than a few hours, as the Iranians did not abide by it; they replied to the Iraqi penetration by shelling several Iraqi cities without distinguishing between civilian and military targets. This is why Iraq responded with air raids on Tehran and its suburbs on 6 October 1980. They were followed by the destruction of Iran's naval bases on the Shatt al-Arab, which effectively paralysed the Iranian navy.

The chapter on Iraqi-Iranian relations (*see* Chapter 4), and the interview with President Saddam Hussein in which he analyses Iraqi-Iranian relations (*see* chapter 8), show that this war was destined to take place. It was inevitable because Ayatollah Khomeini could not forget that Iraq had extradited him just months before the revolution, and because Imam Khomeini, having toppled the Shah's regime, wished to export the Islamic revolution. This could not happen as long as Iraq was led by Saddam Hussein and enjoyed strength and stability. Imam Khomeini had said on several occasions that 'Iraq is Persian' and that 'Saddam Hussein and the Baathists are heretics.' Four months before the war broke out, Radio Iran broadcast the Imam's statements calling on the 'Iraqi people to liberate itself from the yoke of the aggressors; it is a duty for the Iraqi people and Army to rebel against this non-Islamic party in Iraq.' Moreover, the Iranian Army was kept in a constant state of mobilisation; it was told that it was expected to invade Iraq, whereupon it would be welcomed by the Iraqi people. This was over and above the persistent attempts to incite sectarian unrest in Iraq. The war was inevitable because Iran had wrested certain rights and territory from Iraq at a time when Iran was the stronger country. It was only to be expected that Iraq would seek to regain these lands and rights once it became strong enough to do so.

The following observations will help to clarify the background to the war. In the first place, the decision to go to war can be said to have been taken from the day that the Algiers agreement was signed on 6 March 1975. Iraq's having had to sign an agreement which it saw as infringing its rights can be compared to Gamal Abdel-Nasser's acceptance of the Rogers initiative on the Middle East in July 1970. Abdel-Nasser's acceptance was a tactical move which enabled him to move rocket-launchers to the Suez Canal zone. Similarly, Saddam Hussein, who was Vice-President at the time, was obliged to accept the agreement so that he could have a breathing space in which to build a strong army and a modern state, an army which could one day take on the Shah's army in case the territory and sovereignty over the Shatt al-Arab could not be restored through diplomatic means.

In the second place, the war was not unexpected; it had always been in the background, in the form of a longstanding series of border clashes, with the exception of the time from the signing of the agreement until the overthrow of the Shah. This is the first time, however, that war has broken out directly between the two countries. Previously Iran had conducted its war against Iraq through the Kurds.

From the outset of the war it was clear that Iraq wanted to wage the battles on Iranian territory and did not expect it to be a quick war because of the extent of this territory. The war was not preceded by manoeuvres by the Iraqi Army. It was, however, preceded by true mobilisation of the people: from the moment he assumed full responsibility President Saddam visited almost every single area in Iraq; he laid emphasis on Iraq's destiny in every speech he delivered before the people. Moreover, he adopted a policy of flexibility in his dealings with the other countries of the world, which served its purpose once the war broke out. From the time the President assumed full responsibility there were indications that Iraq was preparing itself for something. This was further clarified by a statement President Saddam repeated over and over again. It was included in a speech delivered in Mosul on 15 April 1980, a speech which was a major step in the conflict with Imam Khomeini. President Saddam declared, 'If you read the history of Iraq you will find that it was either a shining light leading the way, or that it was trampled under the feet of invading armies.'

It should be pointed out that the Iraqi Baath Party had prepared for the eventuality of war some months before it happened. The Party leadership noted on a number of occasions that Iran had no intention of returning the usurped territory. Secret reports and memoranda indicated that if Iraq did not initiate military action, then Iran would go to war with Iraq. These reports were based on documents found on members of the Al-Da'awa Party which included statements such as, 'Iraq is the key to the Arabian peninsula; when we conquer Iraq we will conquer the peninsula.' The Army was also being prepared for the eventuality of war; both the daily Army paper and the weekly Army magazine carried articles analysing Iraqi-Iranian relations some months before war broke out. Courses were organised at the Staff College, telling officers what to do in case of war with Iran or in case Iran declared war on Iraq. When the war broke out it was clear that, although the Shia sect forms the majority in the Iraqi Army, the Army was motivated by nationalism, whereas the Iranian Army had been mobilised along religious lines. The Iranian media concentrated on convincing the people and the Army that the Iraqis were heretics. This had a counter-effect on the Iraqi Army, which went to war believing in God and country.

It was immediately apparent that the kind of war Iraq is waging needs a leader who can plan, take decisions and accept responsibility for his actions, and who has a good deal of self-confidence. The border between the two countries is over 1,000 kilometres long, and the population density is weighted in favour of Iran with its forty million people against Iraq's thirteen million.

Besides, it was clear that the Army the Shah had left behind was still a formidable force, in spite of the fact that it had been weakened by the purges of the Iranian revolution. Its equipment remained sophisticated and the lack of spare parts and maintenance — due to Iran's conflict with the United States over the question of the hostages — had not affected its fighting ability. This was evidenced by the effectiveness of the Iranian Air Force within Iraq, which lessened the impact of the losses suffered by the Iranians during the first two weeks of the war. Iraq has never lived through a full-fledged war in its modern history. The fighting against the Kurdish insurgents in the North was conducted far from the main urban centres, which have not been directly affected by the war.

All these points were taken into consideration when President Saddam took the decision to go to war. President Saddam is a man who is used to taking major decisions: the decision to carry out the 17 July 1968 Revolution; the decision, on 30 July 1968, to expel Abdel-Razzaq Nayef; the decision to nationalise Iraq's oil industry; the decision to take part in the October 1973 war; the decision to solve the Kurdish question; and the decision to counteract the Camp David agreements through the Arab Summit held in Baghdad. Thus the President weighed the possibility of victory and that of defeat, and what the extent of a defeat would be. When he saw that the likelihood of victory outweighed that of defeat he gave the green light.

At the outbreak of the war, Iraq's potential gains and losses can be summed up as follows. Iraq stood to gain the restoration of its territory from Iran. It stood to put an end to Iran's ambitions to topple the regime in Iraq and to export the Iranian revolution. It would make the great powers sit up and take notice of Iraq when they planned their strategies for the Arab world, particularly in the Gulf region, as it would be a strength to be reckoned with. It would be able to find out once and for all who its friends were and who its enemies were. It would force some Arab states to make a choice they could no longer avoid. It would be able to test its Army on the battlefield and evaluate its capacity to handle modern weapons. Iraq's Army was, after all, being prepared for a national duty, the battle with Israel. It is interesting in this respect to note that the weapons of the Iranian Army are the same type as those of the Israeli Army. Iraq also stood to gain from giving its Popular Army practical experience in handling situations when the regular Army was on the battlefield. It would also gain from preparing the people to experience war, and from giving the Baath Party practical experience of a war situation rather than theoretical discussions.

Iraq stood to lose the following. It stood to lose the achievements of eight years of development — but then these achievements were constantly threatened if Iraq could not prove it was a military force. Over the past eight years Iraq has initiated numerous large-scale development projects, which began to be affected as soon as Iraqi troops spread out in Iranian territory. But as long as Iraq's development plans remain carefully studied and the planners avoid prestige projects, it is possible to rebuild with an eye out for protection in case of war. The war with Iran is not going to be the last, and Iraq is in any case preparing for the war for the recovery of Palestine. In this respect Iraq would gain by discovering the stand of the Soviet Union (to which it is linked by a treaty of friendship and co-operation), and by clarifying the extent to which Iraq's independence of action is considered an obstacle by the Soviet Union.

The war has added new dimensions to Saddam Hussein's personality, revealing the fact that he has exceptional ability in directing a war. His other qualities had earlier attracted the attention of the Baath Party founder Michel Aflaq, who made a speech which can be seen as handing over the reins of the Party to Saddam Hussein. As he conducts the war, Saddam Hussein's nerves are made of steel; he is ready for victory, but equally ready to handle any setbacks as they come. President Saddam is not the kind of leader who remains in the operations room day and night, emerging only to go to parliament to announce a ceasefire, as President Sadat did during the October 1973 war, when he stopped the Egyptian Army at the height of its push to liberate its lands. Indeed, President Saddam went so far as to join the crew of the first tank to cross over onto Iranian soil on 22 September 1980, just as he did during the July 1968 Revolution, when he was one of the first in the assault on the Presidential Palace. Had his officers not insisted that he stay behind in order to lead operations, he would have remained fighting on the front throughout the war. President Saddam has always made a point of remaining in touch with the people. As he chats with Iraqis in the streets or pays impromptu visits to various parts of the countryside, he fires the people with his own enthusiasm. Such strolls through the streets, when Iranian Phantom jets threatened overhead, merely served to demonstrate his confidence.

Although President Saddam has not allowed Arab mediation in the war, he has not closed the door to other mediators. At the same time, he has been careful to make it clear that he intends to ensure oil supplies to those countries importing oil from Iraq, which has aroused the admiration of the world. The war demonstrates how the stands adopted by Saddam Hussein since becoming President, and the flexibility he has shown, were in order to prepare the ground for a war he knew was coming (this included the National Charter he proposed on 8 February 1980 to cover relations between Arab states and their neighbours). The war has encouraged Arab and Islamic countries to accept Iraq as a strong state. If they were able to accept an even stronger Iraq, then the war would be settled that much more quickly.

Moreover, President Saddam is not the kind of person to give his people prosperity before a war and then suddenly to have it searching for its basic needs during a war. Iraq stocked up on foodstuffs well before the war and on a large scale. It also stocked up on ammunition, as President Saddam could not forget the experience during the war in the North when the Army was short of ammunition. It is even said that there have been large-scale purchases of gold during the past five years in order to cover the Iraqi currency in the event of war. It is doubtful whether the numerous international studies on armaments have the correct figures regarding Iraq. Iraq has been buying massive quantities of arms over the past five years, but has kept a low profile and not put these arms on display. Iraqi officers have also been conducting careful studies of the weapons held by the Iranians. During the war they have thus been able to use weapons captured from the Iranians, and on some days Iraqi soldiers have fought the Iranians with their own weapons. It should be recalled that, during the past five years, Iraq has extradited large numbers of Iranians, which can now be seen as a preparation for the eventuality of war. The number of Iranians extradited in these years totalled some 100,000. Had Iraq gone to war against Iran with a large population of Iranians in its midst, it would have had to deal with a very powerful fifth column.

It has also become clear that the solid Jordanian-Iraqi relations that have developed during the war were taken into account in planning for it. Since Syria refused to stand with Iraq and Kuwait could not bear the pressure, it was necessary to have a 'strategic depth' that would stand by Iraq's side with courage, and serve as a port for Iraq's needs and a haven for its planes. The Iraqis will never forget King Hussein's stand during the war; nor will they forget the stand taken by some Arabs who have moved a little closer to Iran and so far away from Iraq.

Baghdad itself has stood up well to numerous air raids carried out by the Iranian Phantom jets. Never before had Baghdad had to face air raids; even the British used planes only against military camps, never against the city itself. It is apparent that the Iraqi capital made an easy target and that the radar network was not effective enough to protect it. What helped the Iranian planes is the fact that Baghdad is a sprawling city some fifty-six kilometres wide and some seventy kilometres long. Nevertheless, several Iranian planes were shot down over Baghdad.

From the very first minute war broke out, all eyes turned to the nuclear power station President Saddam had worked so hard to acquire for Iraq, particularly in view of the propaganda campaign Israel had been waging against Iraq's nuclear capabilities before the war. When it was said that a third party had entered the war, it was because Israel had tried to hit the nuclear power station in one way or another; this was confirmed by the French ambassador to Iraq, in his statement on the attack. Iraq had, however, planned for such an eventuality and the strong defences around the station foiled the attempt; the gaps in the defences were soon repaired after the raid.

What is also worth noting about the war is the fact that the Iraqi Air Force has not been brought into play, with the result that while Iran lost 200 out of its 400 planes during the first few days of the war, the Iraqi Air Force lost only a few planes. The Iraqi planes were scattered throughout Iraq and abroad in order to safeguard a force that had battled so effectively on the Egyptian front during the October 1973 war. At that time, Iraqi Hawker Hunters cut through the Israelis' advance lines during the attack on Sinai.

Iraq has made it clear that it is not fighting the Iranian Army or the Iranian people, but Ayatollah Khomeini's rule and the Revolutionary Guards. Thus it treats captured Iranian soldiers very well and explains the reasons for the war to them (captured Revolutionary Guards are treated differently). Iraq is playing on the sensitive nature of the relations between the regular Iranian Army and the Revolutionary Guards, and the resentment felt by the former at what has been done to the Army. It is obvious that the Iranian soldiers are not fighting with the same commitment as the Revolutionary Guards, which explains why so many undamaged vehicles have been captured and so many soldiers have surrendered. The Iraqi war plan involves advancing the armoured units first, without using too many infantrymen, and this is why loss of life has been kept to a minimum. Iraq's Army is the only army in the Arab world which is a fully national army; all the officers are Iraqi, and most are members of the Baath Party.

It seems evident that President Saddam Hussein wanted the war to take place while Imam Khomeini was alive, and that the Imam's critical state of health was what speeded up the decision to go to war. It is true that the war has served Imam Khomeini's regime by unifying the people against an external threat and forcing them to set aside their differences. Once the war is over, however, such differences will loom larger than ever. Moreover, the Iran against which Iraq is waging war was isolated both in the Arab and the Islamic world, and in the wider international sphere. This was a better time to fight than if Iran had gone beyond the revolution to find its Bonaparte, or if it had suffered the same fate as Afghanistan — particularly as there is an effective Communist Party in Iran. Iraq is willing to live with Iran and to deal with it on all levels, but not with an aggressive neighbour such as it has become.

The Iraqi-Iranian war is the first between two members of the Organisation of Petroleum Exporting Countries. It is also the first in which superpower intervention has been kept to a minimum. It is the first in the region between a secular Arab national leadership and a religious leadership. It is also the first war in which American arms are being defeated and Soviet and French arms are proving successful. It is worth noting here that the Brazilian arms purchased by Iraq are also proving effective.

It remains for us to note three points concerning President Saddam's particular brand of leadership. In the first place, it should be remembered that he did not allow the Army to take over on its own during the July 1968 Revolution, but made the Army and the Party work hand in hand, a policy he has followed throughout, thus protecting each institution from the other. The fruits of this policy can be seen in the Iraqi-Iranian war.

Secondly, the President was able to achieve a great many things within a single command which had two leaders (when he was Vice-President of the Revolution Command Council and Ahmad Hassan Bakr was President). He used this time to take major steps such as the nationalisation of oil and the solution of the Kurdish problem, and also to build a modern state backed by a strong army. This has now borne fruit.

Thirdly, Saddam Hussein's flexibility came into operation during the Arab Summit held in Baghdad in November 1978, at which he was able to persuade the Arabs to agree on the bare minimum with which to resist the Camp David agreements. Thereafter, he was no longer just Iraq's 'strongman', he became 'the Arabs' strongman'. The Baghdad Summit was the first occasion for coexistence between the Baath regime in Iraq and the conservative Arab regimes — a coexistence required by national duty. During the brief period from the time he assumed full responsibility until the outbreak of war, Saddam Hussein has strengthened the Arab force within the non-aligned movement.

Indeed, since the last Non-Aligned Summit in Baghdad, most non-aligned leaders have visited Iraq in accordance with President Saddam's preparations for the next summit to be held in Baghdad in 1982. President Saddam has also strengthened Iraq's links with the African states in an unprecedented way. He himself chooses Iraq's ambassadors to Africa, and within three years they will all be first-class ambassadors at the Iraqi Foreign Ministry. Although there is a treaty of co-operation and friendship between Iraq and the Soviet Union, President Saddam Hussein equated the Soviet Union and the United States, as regards the question of superpower intervention in the affairs of others, in his National Charter of 8 February 1980. This has won him the support of Third World and Arab states.

It is important to note at this point that President Saddam Hussein has none of the complexes of a leader who doubts his rightful place in history. This is the complex suffered by, say, Georges Pompidou who followed Charles de Gaulle, or by Anwar Sadat who followed Gamal Abdel-Nasser, or by those who came after Nehru and Mao Tse Tung. President Saddam does not suffer from this complex because he has played a major role from the time the Baath Party came to power in 1968; he led the State side by side with Ahmad Hassan Bakr until Bakr retired and Saddam Hussein assumed full responsibility on 17 July 1979.

President Saddam's leadership qualities are the more pronounced in times of war. He told Iraqi pilots during a visit to the front when the Iraqi Army was on the outskirts of Abadan, 'There are many enemy forces who do not wish Iraq to occupy its rightful position because they know that this will bring good to the Arab nation.' With these words he was summing up many factors that all pointed in one direction: a strong Iraq was one thing, but a very strong Iraq was something which not many powers could accept. From the conclusions I reached during my sessions with President Saddam while I was preparing this book, and from his conduct of the war from the time of its preparation to its most difficult days, I can safely say that President Saddam is seeking to play a major role in world affairs. This role will bring about a very strong Iraq, no matter what the dangers.

Fuad Matar
London
December 1980

INTRODUCTION

A multi-storey building has been erected on a large expanse of land on the banks of the Tigris in Baghdad, not far from the Presidential Palace. This is the headquarters of the National Command of the Arab Socialist Baath Party, directed with ability and vision by President Saddam Hussein. The architect of this building took the Baathist character into consideration in the design and President Saddam Hussein took a great deal of interest in the project. The result is a building finer than that of the Arab League in Cairo and than the new League headquarters under construction in Tunis. President Saddam Hussein, who inaugurated the building shortly after he was entrusted with the reins of leadership of the country and the Party, wanted it to be a symbol of Iraq's future, and this is why he was so closely involved in its construction and design.

On the second floor are the offices of the founder of the Baath Party, Michel Aflaq. Every Arab Baathist who visits Baghdad comes to pay his respects to Michel Aflaq, and members of the Iraqi Command are regular visitors out of respect for their historical leader, whose advice and thoughts they listen to with great interest. Michel Aflaq had suffered a good deal in the service of the Baath Party before coming to settle in Baghdad, with his own offices and home in the Mansour residential district. When he announced the first communiqué of the Baath movement, preparatory to developing the movement into a full-fledged party, he knew that the road would be long and difficult. However, he could not have imagined that it would be one of the most tragic periods of modern Arab history. The tragedy is that the Baath, which calls on the Arabs to unite, is not itself united. The Baath, which should represent the ideal in all things, has been rent by the spirit of revenge. The extent of the tragedy is such that Michel Aflaq, and the other leaders who dedicated their lives to translating the ideals of the Baath into reality, are hunted men. They live in exile under sentence of death by the Baathist regime ruling in Syria.

In the 1940s the Arabs' first concern was independence. The concept of Arab unity could have served to crystallise the struggle for independence, but there were two parties in Syria at that time which were both opposed to Arab nationalism and Arab unity: the Communist Party and the Syrian National Party. After Michel Aflaq had propounded the idea of Arab unity it became clear that many people wanted to define the Arab character and to act accordingly. These people had until then been living in a tormented ideological vacuum. They rejected the Marxist ideology of the Communist Party, and they were not attracted by the concept of Syrian nationalism which would have meant dividing the Arab nation. They remained, however, at a loss as to what action to take. In their search for identity, these people might have been drawn to the Islamic revivalist movement just beginning to surface at that time. But the revivalists sought to resurrect the past, whereas the generation of the 1940s wanted to look to the future. There was nothing extraordinary about what Michel Aflaq and the theoreticians in his circle had to say on Arab history or Arab nationalism. It was simply that Aflaq knew how to convey the need for self-expression and that he defined the road that should be taken.

Between 1943 and 1945 it became increasingly urgent to develop the Arab Baath from a movement into a party to resist the French occupation of Syria and Lebanon. The movement had originally attracted a handful of students, teachers and intellectuals; it then began to draw in civil servants, professional people and workers. The Baath ideas spread beyond Damascus to the other main Syrian towns, where they met a good deal of resistance from the Communist Party. The Communists saw the Arab Baath movement as a dangerous obstacle to the spread of Communist ideas. The Baath was attracting those classes of people that the Communists saw as their natural allies — students, teachers, middle-class merchants and skilled labourers. Thus the followers of the Arab Baath movement found themselves harassed, challenged and hunted at every turn. They decided to bring the confrontation out in the open.

In July 1945 the Arab Baath movement Higher Command, whose members were Michel Aflaq, Salah Bitar and Midhat Bitar, submitted a request to the Ministry of the Interior for permission to establish the Baath Party. They accompanied the request with a list of Baath principles. On 14 April 1947 the conference to found the Baath Party was held in Damascus, and a constitution and structure were adopted. Michel Aflaq was elected Party leader and an executive authority was also elected. The Baath Party was thus able to organise itself on firm foundations and to attract a larger number of members.

On 30 March 1949 the first Arab military coup took place. Led by the Commander of the Syrian Army, Husni Zaim, the coup toppled Shukri Quwatli and his republic. Initially the Party looked on the Zaim coup as a translation of its principles into practice — although the Party Command was well aware that Husni Zaim had been one of the officers in the French Army. This assessment soon turned out to be false, however, and the support for the coup resulted in a division within the Party. Five weeks after the coup, the Party managed to reunify its ranks. The reunification of ranks took the form of a popular march opposing the coup and its leaders. The Party Command then took the unprecedented step of submitting a memorandum calling for a transitional government, the reinstatement of public freedoms, elections and a constitution. Husni Zaim's response was to arrest the Baath leaders as well as the leaders of other parties in opposition.

Having just freed themselves from the yoke of French occupation, the Syrians were not prepared to submit to Husni Zaim's methods of government. In recognition of this fact, the Army organised a coup, led by Sami Hanawi, and Husni Zaim was executed. The Baath Party adopted a favourable stand towards Hanawi, and this was reciprocated. Hanawi allowed the Party to pursue its activities and the Ministry of the Interior gave the Party an official licence. The Party also resumed publication of *Al-Baath*, the newspaper it had set up to disseminate its ideas and principles. The Baath Party took part in the parliamentary elections which were held, but did not register much success; nevertheless the Baath Party leader Michel Aflaq became a member of the Government. He resigned following the parliamentary elections so as to concentrate on the Party's own first elections, which resulted in the formation of the Party Council. The Council held its first meeting during the first week of December 1949. Within a few days of this meeting, Syria witnessed its third military coup, led by Adib Shishakli on 20 December 1949. From the start it was clear that Shishakli was opposed to party activity, and especially to the Baath Party. A series of clashes between the Party and the regime followed.

The most important effect the three military coups had on the Baath leaders was to instill in them a profound wariness of military coups. Thus the Party's first reaction to the 23 July 1952 military coup in Egypt was one of opposition, which continued until March 1955. However, because of the development of the Egyptian revolution during this period, the Party came to see it as its natural ally. The most important development was the growth of Arab nationalism in Egypt, more than in any other country. Gamal Abdel-Nasser even included an article on Egypt's Arab character in the Constitution. Prior to that he had broken the arms monopoly by entering into an arms agreement with Czechoslovakia. Abdel-Nasser also took several steps that demonstrated his belief in unity. The most important were the Arab Covenant between Egypt, Syria and Saudi Arabia, and the bilateral military charters between Egypt and Syria, and Egypt and Saudi Arabia. He also opposed the Baghdad Pact at the

Bandung Conference.

These developments helped the Baath Party to overcome its feeling of wariness and to reassess its stand towards Abdel-Nasser because he himself had changed. The Party began to call for a union between Egypt and Syria. But Abdel-Nasser remained wary of the Baath as a result of its vehement attacks on him between 1952 and 1955. He remained opposed to it in spite of the clear indications that its attitude had changed. Even the telegram of support the Baath Party dispatched from Damascus after Abdel-Nasser was elected President of the Republic, in accordance with the Constitution of 1956, did not change the Egyptian leader's attitude. Although the Baath considered its telegram as a message of support, Abdel-Nasser did not take it as such. The telegram read: 'The Arab people is monitoring your steps taking Egypt towards social justice, sound democracy and the support of the Arab struggle in all areas.' Because of his attitude at the time, Abdel-Nasser stopped at the word 'monitoring'. He would have preferred the Baath to have chosen other words which did not imply a possible lack of confidence in him. As for the reference to the 'steps' he was taking, this might have meant that the Baath had some doubts as to whether these steps would stop or continue. In fact, the only words that Abdel-Nasser would have found acceptable at that critical stage would have been words of praise.

It is necessary at this stage to clarify three points which will explain why the feeling of wariness existed and will shed light on the nature of subsequent relations between the Baath and Abdel-Nasser. In the first place, because of its experience with the three military coups in Syria, the Baath Command voiced its doubts about the Egyptian officers' revolution led by Abdel-Nasser. A man like Abdel-Nasser could not tolerate anyone doubting his revolutionary ability, his Arab stand and his progressive outlook. This was especially unacceptable to those who should have been among the first to support him. Thus it was only natural that he should feel wary, especially as the Baath continued to express its doubts for some three years.

In the second place, the Baath Command's satisfaction that an Egyptian officer could lead a successful revolution was matched by a kind of anger — anger because the Baath had not been able to bring about a similar change in Syria. Moreover, the revolution in Egypt, especially after the first three years, adopted the slogans and principles the Baath had introduced some ten years earlier without any reference to the original source. The Baath Command was beginning to see a picture taking shape, one which it did not like at all: it implied that, after what had happened in

Egypt, the only possibility for revolutionary change was through the military, now that a Nasserite pattern existed whereas a Baathist pattern did not. It is usual for men of principles to feel jealous about their principles, especially when they have fathered them.

In the third place, after Abdel-Nasser had defined his principles of Arab nationalism and unity, he no longer liked to be reminded that the Baath had preceded him by some ten years with the tripartite aim expressed in their slogan 'Unity — Freedom — Socialism'. Rearranging the slogan so that it read 'Freedom — Socialism — Unity' could not hide the fact that it had been borrowed. Abdel-Nasser grew particularly sensitive towards the Baath after he saw that his ideal of Arab nationalism had been fulfilled after the union with Syria and not after his liberation of Egypt; in other words, in the union with Syria, he was following a Baathist line of action and not his own. He decided that the Baath should cease to exist and that major policy decisions should be left to him. This was naturally a matter of life and death to the Baath Party.

The Baath's impact on Iraq was quite different. At the time that it was preparing for its founding conference, a number of publications found their way to Iraq. These pamphlets (such as 'On the Arab Baath' and 'Of Arab Policies') attracted several Iraqi intellectuals. Students from Iskandaroun who went to Iraq to complete their education also introduced and carried with them the ideas of the new party that was being founded in Syria, and helped to spread Baath writings and ideas to a wider audience. Over the next three years, more and more young, educated Iraqis were attracted by the Baath. A number of Iraqi Baathists participated in the national uprising in Iraq, which came to be known as the 'November 1952 Uprising', although they had no organisational structure as yet. After the uprising, they organised themselves into an underground movement. Their existence was revealed by the newspaper *Al-Akhbar*, which said that the Party was playing a major role in organising the demonstrations and troubles prevalent in Iraq's cities at the time. As a result, the Baath attracted still more intellectuals and workers; it also attracted the interest of the security forces and secrecy became even more essential.

By coincidence, the spread of Baath ideas came at a time when the Iraqi Communist Party, until then the strongest and most popular party, was suffering from internal conflicts and splits. Thus the Baathists had an open field, and worked on gaining supporters and members. In 1953 they began to publish an underground newspaper called *Al-Arabi al-Jadid* (The New

Arab), which they later changed to *Al-Ishtiraki* (The Socialist) in order to give a better indication of what the paper was about and to attract the working class. In this way, they were confronting the Communists. Bringing out the newspaper was not an easy task, however. The printing press they had to use was an antiquated machine and it was often difficult to read the print. The newspaper was nevertheless widely read and played an increasingly important role. The paper's popularity convinced the Baathists that there was scope for their ideas and they wanted to express them openly. They decided to try to publish articles in mass circulation newspapers. They published a few articles in a paper called *Al-Horriya* (Freedom), and eventually took over the whole paper. This did not last for long, however, as the authorities threatened to close down the paper if it continued on the same lines. Although they only published openly for a short period of time, the Baathists were able to ascertain the extent of popular support for their ideas.

The visit to Baghdad of the Turkish Prime Minister Adnan Menderes demonstrated the extent of popular support for Baathist ideas (and the continued weakness of the Communist Party). Menderes came for talks with the Nouri al-Said Government about Iraq joining the Turco-Pakistani alliance. The Baathists organised strikes and distributed statements of protest at colleges and factories. The wave of arrests that followed served only to strengthen the Baathists. They became one of the most prominent forces on the political scene, and could afford to propose the unification of all the organisations and forces into one front. The Front of National Unity was thus established and included, in addition to the Baath, the Communist Party, the Istiqlal Party and the National Democratic Party, as well as a number of independent nationalists. The Baath Party's aim in forming the Front was twofold. It wanted to strengthen national action against the regime. It also wanted to pinpoint the strengths and weaknesses of the other parties, which had had more experience of political action than the Baath, in order to penetrate their organisations and to sap their strength. Eventually the Baath was to win the upper hand and become the dominant political force.

The Baath continued to work on consolidating its political presence. Just as the visit by Menderes to negotiate the Tripartite Alliance served as a useful opportunity to demonstrate their strength, so did the 1956 three-pronged attack on Egypt. The protest movements organised by the Party led to further arrests. The extent of their effectiveness was further illustrated by the unified action taken by the Front of National Unity in the spring of 1958, just a few months before the Revolution of 14 July, when parliamentary elections were being held. Although the Baath advocated participating in the elections to obtain the maximum number of parliamentary seats for the members of the Front of National Unity, it abided by the decision of the other parties to boycott the elections. It stipulated, however, that the boycott must take an active form: strikes and demonstrations should be organised and ballot boxes burned to prevent the authorities from imposing their candidates. But the other parties did not abide by the agreement, and contented themselves with a boycott. The Baathists acted alone. They organised strikes and demonstrations and burned ballot boxes, laying the groundwork for the 14 July 1958 Revolution, organised by a hundred officers who had chosen Abdel-Karim Qassem to lead them. Yet the Baath did not profit from the fruits of the revolution; Abdel-Karim Qassem entered into an alliance with the Communist Party against them, cracking down on Baathists and other nationalists. As a result of their experiences at the hands of Abdel-Karim Qassem's regime, the Baathists revised their policies and decided to adopt violence as a mode of action. Previously they had condemned the acts of violence carried out under Nouri al-Said.

The short-lived Revolution of 8 February 1963, which lasted only nine months, was carried out when Saddam Hussein was not in Iraq. After the Party's fall from power, it was marked by internal splits and conflict. It was at this time that Saddam Hussein's leadership qualities came to the fore.

CHAPTER 1

A REBEL AGAINST THE FAMILY: A REVOLUTIONARY AGAINST THE REGIME

'I am the mother, I am the father.'
(Iraqi saying, describing strength of purpose and ability)

Saddam Hussein was nearly eight years old when Michel Aflaq's Arab Baath movement was evolving into a Party in Damascus. He had not yet had any formal education, as his relatives wanted him to become a farmer like the rest of the family. But a cousin on his mother's side Adnan Khairallah (who became Minister of Defence when Saddam Hussein assumed complete responsibility) told him how he had learned to read, write and draw at school. Saddam Hussein decided to travel with his cousin to attend school in the village of Takrit. This was his first act of rebellion against his family, who were then living in Shawish. It had been difficult to convince the family, so Saddam Hussein decided to take them by surprise. When everyone was asleep, he left the house and walked through the dark until he reached a place where some other relatives worked. They were very surprised by his sudden appearance, but understood once he had explained that he wanted to attend school in Takrit against his family's wishes. The young Saddam Hussein was greatly encouraged by these relatives. They gave him a pistol and sent him off in a car to Takrit. There he was welcomed by other members of his family who also applauded his decision. After completing his first year at school, he moved to Baghdad with his maternal uncle Khairallah Talfah, who had looked after him because his father had died before he was born. He completed his primary education at schools in Baghdad and entered the secondary stage.

In 1957 the twenty-year-old Saddam Hussein joined the Baath Party. He found in its principles a reflection of his own nationalist ideals. He had considered himself a nationalist from the time his mother told him stories of how his uncle Talfah had fought against the British during the revolution led by Rashid Ali Kaylani in May 1941. His relatives had been killed by the British and had their houses burned down; his forefathers had fought bravely against the Turks. With this background, Saddam Hussein was all too aware of British imperialism and how the government in Iraq remained a prisoner of the imperialist will. He decided to become involved in political activity. This decision was reinforced because of an incident which occurred after the 1958 Revolution. An official in Takrit was murdered; the authorities accused Saddam Hussein of having killed him and threw him in gaol. At this time the Mahdawi court, set up by Abdel-Karim Qassem after the 1958 Revolution, was striking terror into the hearts of the people. Anyone who appeared before this court was certain to be condemned to death. In gaol, Saddam Hussein met some of his comrades in the Baath Party. They were more concerned about the fate of their comrades outside the prison than about their own fate, as widespread man-hunts and liquidation campaigns were under way. Whoever escaped liquidation would not escape a beating. Saddam Hussein and his comrades were able to win over a few of the prison guards. In order to protect their comrades outside the prison, they persuaded the guards to arrange for their arrest — gaol would afford more protection for them. A number of Baathists were thus brought into the gaol. For many days, they remained in prison until nightfall, when they were released to carry out their activities, returning to gaol before sunrise.

Saddam Hussein was eventually released as a result of national pressure. After he came out of prison he was told that the Party needed him in Baghdad. He travelled to the capital from Takrit. Upon his arrival, he was asked by one of his comrades in the Party if he would be willing to assassinate Abdel-Karim Qassem. He accepted at once as he considered the assignment an honour. He began immediately to train in the use of automatic weapons, having already mastered the use of the revolver. The plan was to shoot Abdel-Karim Qassem as he passed through Rashid Street on his way from his house to his official headquarters at the Ministry of Defence. Saddam Hussein began to explore Baghdad and to familiarise himself with the area in which the operation was to take place. He rented a flat in the area to serve as a base for those involved in the operation. The plan was drawn up, a password was chosen and everything was ready. But the man who was posted to keep a look-out for Abdel-Karim Qassem was slow in transmitting the password, so the operation was postponed to a later date.

Five men participated in the actual operation, which took place some time later. Saddam Hussein's part was to provide cover for the other four when they opened fire on Abdel-Karim Qassem's car. Two were to fire at the front seat, and two at the back. Saddam Hussein was not supposed to fire, just to provide cover for his four comrades as they withdrew. But as the operation got under way, his excitement mounted and he drew his machine-gun from the folds of a long cloak he had borrowed from his uncle Khairallah Talfah, and fired at Abdel-Karim Qassem's car. He withdrew only after covering his comrades' withdrawal. One of them was hit in the chest by a police officer's bullet, and Saddam was wounded in the left leg. Carrying their wounded comrade, the men made their way back to one of the Party's hide-outs in the capital. They assumed that the operation had been successful and that Abdel-Karim Qassem had been killed.

The bleeding in Saddam Hussein's left leg got worse. As it

was obviously impossible to go to a hospital, he took a razor blade and asked one of his comrades to cut into the flesh around the bullet and dig it out, using a pair of scissors and some iodine. He felt faint for a few minutes, but then recovered. When darkness fell, he left the hide-out and returned to his uncle Latif Talfah's house. His uncle surprised him by asking him if Abdel-Karim Qassem had been killed. It transpired that his uncle had watched the operation from a friend's balcony. Saddam Hussein took some medicine to prevent an inflammation developing from the wound in his left leg, pretending that his tonsils were inflamed so that he would not have to give himself away. He learned that the comrades who had taken part in the operation with him had been arrested. He had to do something to escape arrest. The wound in his leg was making him walk with a limp, which would immediately arouse the suspicion of the security forces if they spotted him. He proceeded to burn a number of personal photographs and left the house — not a moment too soon, as the security forces arrived a quarter of an hour later.

Saddam Hussein spent the night at a friend's house. The next day he changed his trousers for a *dishdasheh* (long robe), donned the traditional Arab head-dress and a pair of old shoes, armed himself with a knife and put twenty-three dinars in his pocket. He had decided to leave Baghdad. He tried to hire a car, but after negotiating with the driver, to whom he spoke in a peasant dialect, he felt he could not trust him. He went on foot, but found it difficult because of his wound. Eventually he came across a man on a horse and bought it from its owner for ten dinars. He was thus able to ride along the banks of the Tigris until he reached Takrit. He bought some hay for the horse, and bread and dates for himself as he knew he had a long journey ahead. He was careful not to travel at night, in order to avoid possible danger. At nightfall he came across a bedouin and asked for hospitality. The next morning he resumed his travels, resting from time to time, feeding his horse and eating the bread and dates he had bought. He found nowhere to sleep that night and so, holding the horse's reins, lay down on the ground to await the dawn. On the third night, he was able to make up for the exertions of the two previous nights. Approaching the town of Samarra, he came across a house where an engagement was being celebrated. A sheep had been slaughtered for the occasion, so he ate a hearty meal which made up for the diet of bread and dates, and slept in comfort and security.

The next day he bought some water-melon from one of the farms to slake his thirst and that of his horse during a long day of travel with no water. As he went on his way, he was suddenly overtaken by two cars; the occupants ordered him to stop or they would open fire. He knew they were customs officials; when he tried to spur his horse on, they surrounded him and pointed their machine-guns at him. Saddam Hussein reined in his horse and dismounted, making sure that his cloak covered the bandage on his leg as this was evidence that he was a wanted man. Meanwhile he worked out the best way of handling the situation. Before the officials could ask him any questions, he immediately went on the offensive and asked what they meant by stopping him like that and pointing their machine-guns at him. They replied that they suspected him of being a smuggler. To further win their confidence, he insisted on being taken to their commander to prove that he was not from the area and that he was simply on his way to rejoin his tribe. When they asked for his identity card, he replied haughtily, 'Bedouin do not carry identity cards.' The customs officials beat him and made him swear that he would not tell anyone he met that they were waiting in ambush, and then let him go on his way. He was careful not to look back over his shoulder as he rode on, so as not to arouse their suspicions.

Saddam Hussein next came to a town he had visited four years previously. Finding himself outside the police station, he decided to act calmly and with confidence, and called out a greeting to the police officers. They made no attempt to stop him. He went into a café to ask how he could get from one side of the river to the other. Although he offered to pay the owner of a barge one and a half dinars if he would carry him and his horse across the river, the man refused, saying that there was a curfew. Saddam Hussein could have persuaded the man if he had paid him the seven dinars he had left, but he was worried that such largesse would arouse his suspicions. Eventually Saddam Hussein decided to swim across the river, but he could not decide what to do about his horse. If he took it across, he would arouse the suspicions of the bedouin on the other side. Finally, he left the horse behind. He took off his clothes and tied them in a bundle on his head. Placing his knife between his teeth, he swam across during the middle of the night in the freezing cold. Whenever he felt exhaustion creeping over him, he redoubled his efforts to reach the opposite bank; he had no other choice. He reached the other side in a state of exhaustion, his teeth chattering from the cold. He heard the sound of dogs barking in the distance and decided to make his way towards them, thinking that he might find food and shelter.

The exhausted Saddam Hussein knocked on the door of one of the houses. A woman opened the door and, on seeing him,

General view of Takrit, birthplace of President Saddam Hussein.

Four people occupy a special place in the life of the president: his mother (top right) who brought him into the world when his father had just died, his maternal uncle Khairallah Toulfah (top left) who became his step-father, his paternal uncle Haj Ibrahim Al Hassan (bottom right) who brought him up, and supported him and helped him in particular to escape to Syria after his attempt to assassinate Abdel Karim Kassem, and his elder maternal uncle Adham Ibrahim Hassan (bottom left) who also helped him to escape in 1959.

Saddam Hussein during the 1940s.

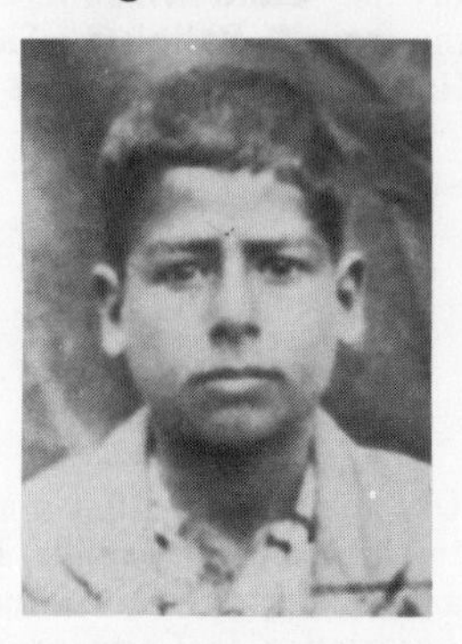

In September 1953

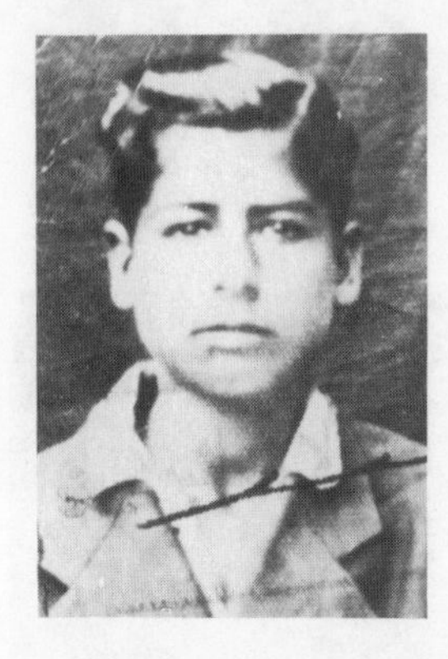

and in 1958

Before escaping to Syria following his attempt to assassinate Abdel Karim Kassem, Saddam Hussein had burnt all his photos. But the authorities of the time found this photo in his school record at the Al Karakh lycée where he pursued his secondary education. It was circulated among all the security forces together with an urgent arrest order.

In disguise, after having escaped across the desert to reach Syrian territory.

In the Cairo villa hired by the exiled Ba'thists. Saddam Hussein is the first on the right.

On the occasion of his marriag to his cousin Sagida Khair allah, the Iraqi Students Association in Cairo organize a reception where Saddam Hussein received the congrat ulations of his Ba'thist com rades, who had, along with many other Arabs, take refuge in Cairo.

Cairo, 1962

Following the revolution of 8 February 1963. A new era in his political life begins. With him was his brother Barzan who shared with him the responsibility for carrying out delicate revolutionary tasks.

Together in a photo taken after the 17 July 1968 revolution.

In this house where the 6th Regional Ba'thist Congress took place . (1966) Saddam Hussein's qualities as a leader asserted themselves: it was he who drew up the resolutions and the closing declaration voted by the congress members.

But he was very soon arrested and imprisoned. These photos show him inside the prison with his comrades.

Surrounded by his comrades, a souvenir photo before leaving prison (standing second right).

شهادة إتمام تدريب

المرحلة الثانوية

١١١٠٩١

وتقدير مقبول .

وتحررت هذه الشهادة بذلك.

والله أكبر والعزة للجمهورية العربية المتحدة

The secondary school diploma gained by Saddam Hussein at the Kasr Al Nil lycée, which enabled him to enrol at the law school of Cairo University.

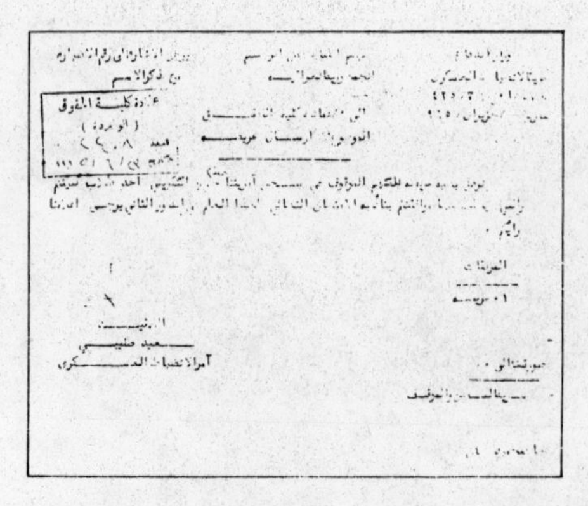
عمادة كلية الحقوق
(الواردة)
الموضوع / ارسال عريضة
المرفقات
آمر الانضباط العسكري

Letter from the military police to the doyen of the Law school, sent with a request from Saddam Hussein when under arrest, requesting permission for the detainee to sit for his Finals in 1965.

Administrative decision of the direction of Baghdad university Law School consenting to a delay in the examination date of Saddam Hussein and two other prisoners of the military police.

بسم الله الرحمن الرحيم

جامعة بغداد
عمادة كلية الحقوق

العدد / ٢٠٧
التاريخ / ١٩٦٦/١/٨

امر اداري

الموضوع / تأجيل امتحان طلبة موقوفين

استنادا الى ما جاء في كتاب آمرية الانضباط العسكري المرقمة ١ع/ق ٣/ ٢٠٥٥٤/١٥ و ١ع/ق٣/٤٢٥/٢٠٥٥٨ و ١ع/ق ٣/ ٤٦١/٤١ والمؤرخة في ١٩٦٥/١٢/٢٨ و ١٩٦٦/١/٣ من أن الطلبة المذكورة اسماؤهم ادناه لايزالون موقوفين في سجن آمرية الانضباط العسكري وانهم قدموا طلبا يرجون فيه تأجيل امتحانهم الفصلي الى الدور الاول ٠

نظرا للعذر المشروع بسبب بقاء الطلبة التالية إسماؤهم موقوفين في سجن آمرية الانضباط العسكري لذلك تقرر تأجيل امتحانهم الفصلي الى الدور الاول للسنة الدراسية الحالية ١٩٦٦/١٩٦٥ واعتبار درجة كل منهم من مائة (١٠٠٪) ٠

الاسماء

٠١	حازم محمد سعيد عبد الرحمن	الصف الثاني
٠٢	صدام حسين التكريتي	الصف الثاني
٠٣	طلال نمر الفيصل	الصف الثاني

م٠ العميد لشؤون التسجيل
محمد طه البشير

نسخة منه الى /ــ
مكتب السيد العميد
آمرية الانضباط العسكري ــ وزارة الدفاع ــ اشارة الى كتابكم المذكور اعلاه ــ يرجى تبليغ الطلبة المذكورين ٠
شعبة التسجيل في الكلية ــ لتأشير ذلك رجاء
لجنة الكتب الصادرة
الملفة الشخصية
الضبا اليومي

screamed, 'Thief!' She had no way of knowing that he was a revolutionary, not a robber, and it was impossible to explain the situation to her. She screamed again, 'A thief; kill him!' A man came to the door ready to beat him up, and Saddam Hussein knew he had to convince him that he was not a thief without entering into explanations about his revolutionary background. He asked, 'Do I look like a thief?' and, after a brief conversation, succeeded in convincing the man that he was not. He was invited in to spend the night, and a fire was lit so that he might dry out his wet clothes. He felt some of his strength returning, but when he got up to leave, the man and other members of his tribe stood in his way and said, 'Where do you think you're going? You have just swum across the Tigris with your clothes on. This means that something is very wrong and we are not going to let you go until we know what the truth of the matter is.' Yet again, Saddam Hussein knew he had to act fast to get himself out of an unpleasant situation. He addressed the man using a bedouin argument he knew the other would understand: 'Supposing I have committed a crime against one of the clans on the other side of the river; supposing they follow me here and kill me in your home. What good will it do you when my clan finds out I was killed among you?' He achieved the desired effect. The man said, 'What you say is true. God protect us.' Saddam Hussein took the head-dress of one of the men, who were now convinced they should let him go, and went on his way. It was after one o'clock at night and bitterly cold, but for the first time he felt a sense of peace because he knew he was approaching the village of Oweinat where his brother Adham worked as a guard at the elementary school. He walked a long way before he reached the school, where his brother welcomed him with tears in his eyes. They both set off to the area of Ouja, where they had family and friends.

A second journey began in Ouja. Saddam Hussein had to travel to Syria with some comrades, in accordance with the wishes of the Baath. A secret journey was mapped out and, after some difficulty, a guide was found who knew the way. They started the journey with a jeep but then had to continue with a donkey. The plan was to travel at night and to hide during the day. They did not stop to rest with any of the bedouin in order not to alert anyone to what was going on. Saddam Hussein and those with him lived through some difficult hours. They drank water polluted by goat droppings, straining the water to remove worms and sand before they drank it. At night, they took it in turns to stand guard in case they were discovered by the security forces doing their rounds. When they reached the border area, they found a cave to hide in and a clean well from which to drink. The guide expressed his relief; he had been complaining ceaselessly although he had been riding the donkey and Saddam Hussein had been walking. Saddam Hussein and his men only realised they were on Syrian soil after they had gone some way into Syria. At this point they relaxed and felt secure, especially as they had run into a night patrol some time earlier. They rested in Boukamal and then in Deir al-Zor, the two main Syrian towns on the border with Iraq, before going on to Damascus where Saddam Hussein spent the next six months.

On 21 February 1960 he left Damascus for Cairo, where a new stage in his life opened. To begin with, he enrolled at a school to prepare himself for the Law School at Cairo University. He also worked hard on strengthening the Baath Party Command in Cairo. In Cairo, Saddam Hussein suffered the fate of all political exiles. He was harassed, kept under observation and had his rooms searched. The harassment stopped after Saddam Hussein informed one of the officials in the President's Office that he and his colleagues were not prepared to suffer such indignities. He was elected a member of the Party Division in Egypt, then of the Branch Command, and then of the Regional Command. After Abdel-Karim Qassem was overthrown in 1963, Saddam Hussein returned to Iraq to take up his Party duties at the Central Farmers' Office. He became a member of a Team Command in 1960 and of a Branch Command in 1961.

At that time the Baath Party was in a very shaky condition and lacked a strong leadership to guide it. Saddam Hussein had not been aware that such problems existed, probably because of his absence from Iraq. The disease was widespread in the Party. After becoming Vice-President of the Revolution Command Council, Saddam Hussein once described these early days as follows: 'There was an atmosphere of terror, and blocs and groupings were formed in the Party; obstacles were placed in the way of those comrades who wanted to work along proper Party lines.' Saddam Hussein began to work to eradicate the disease from the Party. The Party leaders of the time retaliated by setting Party members against him and later by attempts on his life. A military coup against the Baath was led by President Abdel-Salam Aref, who began to hunt down Party members, starting with Saddam Hussein.

It was at this point that the full extent of the difficulties facing Saddam Hussein and Ahmad Hassan Bakr became clear. In Saddam Hussein's view, a strong Party was essential in order to stand up to Abdel-Salam Aref's regime and restore the Revolution. During this time Saddam Hussein had travelled secretly to Damascus to take part in the Seventh National Conference of the Party. In the light of discussions with Michel Aflaq, he decided to work for a strong and integrated Party in Iraq. He returned to Baghdad to carry out this aim. A number of steps were taken as a result, and Saddam Hussein supervised the military organisation of the Party in addition to his responsibility for the Farmers' Office within the new Party Command.

Saddam Hussein began to plan for a Party take-over. The first step towards this goal was to buy the necessary weapons, even if the comrades had to start with hunting rifles. Finances improved, cars were bought and a number of houses were rented and transformed into Party headquarters. Saddam Hussein then asked the Party National Command for more weapons, and some comrades began to make bombs from the dynamite used by fishermen. Preparations were made for an attack on the Presidential Palace, and Saddam Hussein made contact with one of the Palace officials for this purpose, but the attempt failed because the official was suddenly transferred. Saddam Hussein was to have entered the conference room, where the civilian and military leaders were meeting, and machine-gun them all. He had made plans for an overall revolution in September 1964, but this was discovered by the authorities. A wave of arrests followed; every Baathist who was captured was savagely tortured. For the first time, Saddam Hussein refused to obey a Party Command order to escape to Damascus. He remained in Baghdad, and was subsequently arrested and thrown into gaol. He was able, nevertheless, to remain in contact with Party members outside the prison walls, and messages were carried by some of the guards sympathetic to him and his cause. Efforts were made to arrange for Saddam Hussein and other Party members imprisoned with him to escape from gaol. Contributions were collected to hire lawyers to defend them. Saddam Hussein spent his time in prison trying to raise the morale of those comrades whose spirit had been broken by torture. He read a number of books and encouraged the others to read too; he also initiated discussions about the Party and its future. He organised a hunger strike for an improvement in prison conditions, in order to bring outside pressure to bear on the regime, and he was also able to set the prison governor and the guards at loggerheads.

Eventually Saddam Hussein managed to smuggle a number of files into the prison cells, and he and his comrades set about sawing through the prison bars, keeping them in place so as not to attract attention. The escape plan went into action: they captured the guard in the corridor and wrested his rifle from him. Saddam Hussein chose to stay behind with six of his comrades to make sure the others got away safely. The seven who remained behind were taken to another prison, where attempts were made to brainwash them. Then things were relaxed a little and Saddam Hussein was able to see his baby son Adi who was then six months old. Saddam Hussein was able to get several messages to and from Ahmad Hassan Bakr by slipping them under his son's robe when he hugged him. The weekly visits and messages kept him well informed about what was happening outside the prison walls.

While he was sending and receiving messages through his son Adi, Saddam Hussein thought again of escaping from prison. He discussed the matter with Saadoun Shaker, explaining that he could convince the prison guards that they, like him, were victims of tyranny. His resolve grew when he received a message from Ahmad Hassan Bakr telling him of the plans to overthrow the regime. Thanks to the good relations he had established with the guards, Saddam Hussein was able to organise the prisoners' escape. On their way back from the Higher Security Court, where he and seven of his comrades were being tried for attempting to overthrow the regime, he asked the guards to allow them to go to a restaurant in Abu Nuwwas Street, pointing out that two soldiers could accompany them to make sure they did not escape. The guards agreed. The plan was that Saddam Hussein and his six comrades would leave the restaurant by the back door, where a car provided by Saadoun Shaker would be waiting for them. The guards waited in vain for them to come out of the main door by which they had entered the restaurant.

Escape from prison was essential this time, as the Party wanted to prevent a coup by the military. Moreover, the 23 February coup had taken place in Syria, bringing Salah Jedid to power. After escaping from prison, Saddam Hussein patched up Party ranks and prevented the military from trying to take over power alone. At three o'clock in the morning on 17 July 1968 Saddam Hussein, wearing a military uniform, and his comrades led the tank assault on the Presidential Palace and ended the regime of Abdel-Salam Aref, implementing a civilian-military plan to take the reins of power into the hands of the Baath Party. The long period of weakness was over; the second stage had begun.

During the second stage, Saddam Hussein played a major part in preparing the Party for its leadership role. However, he felt that Abdel-Razzaq Nayef's participation was an obstacle in the Party's path. Following discussion of the matter, it was agreed that Saddam Hussein would confront Nayef on his own at the Presidential Palace. Nayef's special guard was drawn off, then, in Ahmad Hassan Bakr's room at the Palace, Saddam Hussein drew his revolver and ordered Nayef to raise his hands. Nayef tried to play on Saddam Hussein's feelings by appealing to him to spare him for the sake of his four children. Saddam Hussein was adamant; he told Nayef that he and his children would be safe only if he left Iraq. Saddam Hussein then said he would appoint Nayef as an ambassador, and asked to which capital he would like to be posted. Nayef chose Beirut, which Saddam Hussein rejected; he also rejected Nayef's suggestion of Algiers, but agreed to send him to Rabat.

Matters did not end here. Once Nayef had accepted, Saddam Hussein ordered a plane prepared to convey him from the Rashid Military Camp to Morocco. Saddam Hussein ordered Nayef to act naturally, to salute the guards when they saluted him, and to walk normally to the official car awaiting him. He warned Nayef that his gun was in his jacket, and that if he saw the slightest sign that Nayef was about to disobey his orders he would end his life there and then. He asked some of his comrades to remain at the Palace to protect President Ahmad Hassan Bakr. Saddam Hussein sat next to Abdel-Razzaq Nayef all the way to the Rashid Military Camp. The plane was waiting. After it took off, Saddam Hussein felt tears come to his eyes. One shot could have aborted the whole operation to get rid of Nayef, but fate decreed that the operation went without a hitch from beginning to end.

Saadoun Shaker, one of those who have Saddam Hussein's confidence, told me during a meeting on 4 April 1980 that Saddam Hussein had decided to remove Abdel-Razzaq Nayef on the first day of the Revolution. Saadoun Shaker said that Saddam Hussein had asked him to have ten committed Party members ready to liquidate Abdel-Razzaq Nayef if Saddam Hussein asked them to. Saadoun Shaker did as requested; Saddam Hussein told him the ten might be called on at any moment and that they were to remain in a state of readiness. Saadoun Shaker, who is now Minister of the Interior, added, 'It was clear that Abdel-Razzaq Nayef had links with foreign forces and that he would have sabotaged the Revolution.' Saddam Hussein went further. He nipped in the bud the plans of some highly-placed Baathist officers in the Revolution Command Council who were hoping to take advantage of the fact that they had taken part in the move to remove Nayef. A brief communiqué announced that Ahmad Hassan Bakr, the Secretary of the Regional Command, was to be Prime Minister in addition to his post as President of the Republic. It added that Bakr was also to be Commander-in-Chief of the Armed Forces.

The new Command of the Baath Party then met and distributed responsibilities. Saddam Hussein chose to be Vice-President of the Revolution Command Council, without this being officially announced. As the second man in the Council and in the Party, this was an effective role to play. Saddam Hussein then surprised Ahmad Hassan Bakr by asking to remain out of power; he considered that he had fulfilled his role in bringing the Baath Party to power. Bakr refused to accept this, which explains why the official announcement of the members of the Revolution Command Council was delayed. Saddam Hussein finally decided to stay after he had uncovered plots against Bakr, and once he realised that Hardan Takriti would continue to try to broaden his influence. He remained to play a special role; he was to remain a long time.

CHAPTER 2

TWO LEADERS, ONE COMMAND

'It has never happened before, either in ancient history (including that of our nation since its dawn) or in modern times, that two leaders have been in power for eleven years within one command, without this resulting in a dangerous moral or practical imbalance in leadership, and without their relationship ending in one of them driving the other out . . .'
(Saddam Hussein in his first speech on 17 July 1979 after being handed overall responsibility by President Ahmad Hassan Bakr)

There are a number of houses for top Government officials and offices for Government departments in the area surrounding the Presidential Palace. Ahmad Hassan Bakr lives in one of these houses. He is one of the Party's first revolutionaries, and he took part in the most important event in the history of the Arab Socialist Baath Party in Iraq, on 17 July 1979. This military man spends his spare time on things that have no bearing on affairs of state. He wakes up early in the morning and goes into his garden; he waters the plants and trims the rose bushes. When he tires, he rests awhile in the company of his grandchildren. He lives with his memories, which are for the most part tragic. His son was killed in a car accident when he was only twenty-three, at a time when Ahmad Hassan Bakr was still recovering from the shock of his wife's death. Then his son-in-law died, and Ahmad Hassan Bakr was left to care for his daughter and her children. Ahmad Hassan Bakr's tragic memories are not only personal; he has lived through the tragedies of the Baath Party and through the difficult stages and setbacks it took to bring the Party to power. Ahmad Hassan Bakr has long suffered from poor health; he was once treated for diabetes in France. He could not travel abroad for this reason, and could not repay official visits. He restricted travel within Iraq to a minimum and went on tours only on the most important occasions. He is a sad and careworn man.

The affairs of state and of the Party did not suffer, thanks to Saddam Hussein's presence at President Bakr's side. But the President felt that the five hours, sometimes less, he devoted to his official responsibilities were not enough and that he was imposing a good deal on his comrade and deputy Saddam Hussein. Bakr could see Saddam Hussein coming to his office at the crack of dawn and staying there until midnight. Although this gave him a feeling of comfort and pride, he also found it distressing because he was a military man and military men do not like to see others carrying out their duties for them. Although Ahmad Hassan Bakr was not seriously ill, he could not bear to see the questions in the eyes of the Iraqis as to how bad his health really was, and why he did not retire in order to rest. Did he want to be like Franco, who chose his successor but remained in power until his last breath? Or did he want to be like Brezhnev, who clung to power ever more vigorously each time his health worsened? There were two scenes Bakr had seen on television which remained vividly in his mind. One was Brezhnev at the Soviet-American Summit — Brezhnev hearing with difficulty, standing with difficulty, sitting with difficulty, even coming down the steps of the plane with difficulty. The official ceremonies were kept to a minimum so as not to exacerbate his poor state of health. Even sadder was the picture of Brezhnev signing the SALT treaty with President Jimmy Carter. The other scene which had affected Bakr was the picture of Soviet Foreign Minister Andrei Gromyko fainting at the United Nations; he resumed his duties regardless and would not step down to make way for any one of the many others suitable for this post.

These two scenes took place only a few months before President Ahmad Hassan Bakr's definitive decision to retire. It is important to point out here that Bakr did not retire because the structure of government restricted his action, or because power politics within the Party had made his role that of a figurehead. He was a strong man in a strong position because of the historic role he had played and therefore there were no restrictions on his movements. He had participated in bringing the Baath Party to power; it was not the Baath that had brought him to power. It is also likely Bakr felt, in addition to the personal matters referred to above, that internal, Arab and international conditions required a young and dynamic leader capable of leading and not just ruling. Ahmad Hassan Bakr would not have retired, no matter how poor his health, had he not felt confident that his successor was fully prepared, and indeed had been playing a leadership role for many years.

President Ahmad Hassan Bakr's retirement and Saddam Hussein's assumption of responsibility was the event referred to earlier as the most important in the history of the Arab Socialist Baath Party in Iraq. The way in which the transition was made was unique in the Third World. Some members of the Party Command were informed of the decision, but no one outside the Command had any inkling that an important announcement was to be made on 16 July 1979, that is, on the eve of the anniversary of the Baath 17 July 1968 Revolution. The matter was surrounded by the utmost secrecy. As the Iraqis sat before their television sets to listen to the President's speech, they thought they would be hearing a speech commemorating the anniversary of the Revolution. But when he said, a few moments after he began his speech, 'I have always been ready throughout my life to bear the responsibilities entrusted to me by the Party and the Command for as long as I could, but I . . .', the Iraqis knew that an important announcement was to be made. He went on to say:

> For some time now I have been telling my comrades, and especially my dear comrade Saddam Hussein, that my state of health no longer permits me to carry the responsibilities the Command has honoured me with, and I have asked them to relieve me of the responsibility. But comrade Saddam Hussein's generous spirit

and that of the other comrades in the leadership led them to reject any discussion of this matter and to insist on lifting some of the burden off my shoulders. But I insisted to comrade Saddam Hussein and my other comrades in the Party Command, based on the ties of brotherhood and comradeship that link us, that I should be relieved of all my responsibilities in the Party and the State. I feel a sense of relief today because they have accepted my request. As I congratulate my brother and comrade Saddam Hussein on his assumption of the responsibility of leadership of the Party and the Revolution, I feel deeply confident that the Command has chosen the right man from the standpoint of his morals, his service to the Party, his bravery and his ability. Comrade Saddam Hussein was a brave and trustworthy comrade throughout the long and bitter struggle before the Revolution. He won the respect and trust of his Party comrades. On the morning of the Revolution, he was in the vanguard of those brave men who launched the attack on dictatorship and reactionary rule. Throughout he has been the leader who was able to face all difficulties and bear all responsibilities, and this is why he has won the love and respect of all the members of the Party Command and the Revolution Command Council, and of all the Party workers and the people at large.

In his speech, President Ahmad Hassan Bakr referred to the previous occasions on which he had insisted that he should be allowed to retire. It is important to review the background to this decision and to his previous attempts to retire.

In May 1979, some two months before President Bakr announced the Baath leadership's acceptance of his resignation, a joint meeting of the Regional and National Commands was held. For the first time they heard President Bakr complain that he had been asking Saddam Hussein to allow him to be relieved of his responsibilities, as he was in a state of exhaustion and his health would not permit him to continue. President Bakr was thus asking the leadership to join him in convincing Saddam Hussein. After the meeting, the rest of the leaders tried to convince Saddam Hussein to comply with President Bakr's wishes, pointing out that it had become difficult for him to continue to bear his responsibilities. Saddam Hussein listened to his comrades' arguments, then went to President Bakr and tried to convince him to stay on. On a number of occasions, Saddam Hussein tried to convince President Bakr to continue as head of state, but without bearing any of the exhausting responsibilities; he, Saddam Hussein, was willing to bear these himself. But President Bakr refused to discuss such an idea, pointing out that he was not interested in the trappings of power. He preferred things to take their normal course and for Saddam Hussein to assume responsibility both in form and in substance. As a result, President Bakr and Saddam Hussein agreed that the President would announce his retirement in a speech to the nation on 16 July, the eve of the anniversary of the 17 July 1968 Revolution.

On 10 July the speech was ready. On 11 July a meeting of the Revolution Command Council was held, at which President Bakr expressed his wish to retire from his responsibilities in the State and the Party. Suddenly Muhie Abdel-Hussein Mashhadi, the Secretary of the Revolution Command Council, stood up and demanded that they vote on the question of President Bakr's relinquishing his responsibilities in the Party and the State to Saddam Hussein. He insisted that the decision be carried unanimously. President Bakr, who was attending the meeting, replied, 'What are you asking for? I have clarified the reasons why I want to resign; why are you speaking on my behalf?' But Muhie Abdel-Hussein continued, 'It is inconceivable that you should retire; if you are ill, why don't you take a rest?' These words annoyed President Bakr and a number of those at the meeting. Muhie Abdel-Hussein was not on such terms with President Bakr as to address him in such a fashion, or to show such concern. Although Muhie Abdel-Hussein was Secretary of the Revolution Command Council (headed by President Bakr) and was therefore one of the insiders at the Palace, he was merely an acquaintance of President Bakr's; he was a relative newcomer in the Baath Party and had not held his position long. Most of President Bakr's special relations were with the old members of the Party. Moreover, Muhie Abdel-Hussein's task was to take minutes, which was not a position that gave him the right to enter into such a dialogue with the President. Indeed, several leaders close to President Bakr had previously expressed doubts about Muhie Abdel-Hussein's character and personality. What was odd was that, in spite of all this, Muhie Abdel-Hussein had remained in his post. After he was found to have taken part in a plot against the leadership, which is described in the following pages, it was said that he had reached his position through devious means and that he was originally Persian.

Most of the Regional Command members had wanted the transfer of power to take place smoothly and in a spirit of trust, confidence and discipline, especially as President Bakr's health was poor and the question of his successor had already been decided by virtue of Party seniority on the one hand and qualifications and ability on the other.

The Revolution Command Council meeting of 11 July ended with a decision to accept President Bakr's resignation. On 12 July 1979 a joint meeting of the Regional Command and the

Revolution Command Council was held, presided over by Saddam Hussein and at which he was unanimously elected President of the RCC and the Republic. Because of Muhie Abdel-Hussein's behaviour, and because Saddam Hussein had his doubts about another Party leader, Muhammad Ayesh, Saddam Hussein decided on two courses of action. In the first place, the transfer of power would proceed as planned. In the second place, he decided to keep under observation those leaders who had looked worried or distressed after the Regional Command had decided that Muhie Abdel-Hussein should be taken in for questioning. The Council then issued decrees on a number of ministerial changes. Some ministries were merged and a new ministry, that of Local Government, was created. The Council also decided to create the post of First Deputy Prime Minister and five posts for Deputy Prime Ministers. These decisions were announced on 16 July, after President Bakr had resigned and Saddam Hussein had become President. Until then, two people had come under suspicion: Muhie Abdel-Hussein, who was replaced as Secretary of the Revolution Command Council by Brigadier-General Tareq Hamad al-Abdallah; and Muhammad Ayesh, who was removed as Minister for Industry in the first Government formed under President Saddam Hussein. Adnan Hussein, who was later revealed as one of the plotters, continued to enjoy the confidence of the Command; he was appointed as Fourth Deputy Prime Minister and head of the President's Office.

On the following day, 17 July 1979, Saddam Hussein delivered his first speech as President of the Revolution Command Council and President of the Republic. During this speech he referred to President Bakr as 'Father and Great Comrade' and said of the transfer of power:

> Yesterday you heard the speech of the Father and Great Comrade Abu Haitham. What he referred to in his speech is unique in history. The transfer of power from one leader to another in such a natural, moral and constitutional manner as has happened in our country, in our Party and in our Revolution is unique in ancient and modern history. It is unique, yet it is not strange because it is drawn from the purity of our Arab breeding, from the greatness of the message of Islam and from the principles of our Arab Socialist Baath Party.

He went on to define the nature of the regime:

> I will not call on my comrades in the Command and in the Party, or on my brothers the people, to do anything I would not do myself, or forbid them anything I would not forbid myself. Our duty is to

> **strive for justice and to struggle against oppression. We will not accept that any comrade in our Party, or any member of the people, be humiliated. We will overcome tyranny in all its forms; we will safeguard justice when called on to do so. Power is not wielded for self-satisfaction; it is a burden we carry in order to translate principles into reality in the service of the people, safeguarding the nation and eradicating injustice.**

President Saddam Hussein then went to pay his respects to President Bakr on the occasion of the anniversary of the 17 July Revolution. Afterwards he went to deliver his speech to the people:

> **Comrade Abu Haitham has given up his official responsibilities in the Party and the State, but he remains in our hearts the father and the leader whose long struggle we admire and look up to, and who has rendered the greatest service to his Party and his nation. I, and my comrades in the Command, pray that God may grant him health and well-being so that he may remain long by our side, our father and our comrade. Comrade Ahmad Hassan Bakr has struggled throughout his life in order to ensure freedom, justice and dignity for our people and did not hesitate to sacrifice all for its sake; the people will always look up to him, in appreciation of his service to the nation.**

Before Saddam Hussein's speech, the Party founder Michel Aflaq had sent President Bakr a telegram in which he said, 'Relinquishing your responsibilities at this time, and now that you are confident about the march of the Revolution and its great achievements on the national and regional levels, will serve as an example to many of the world's leaders . . .'

After he had celebrated the eleventh anniversary of the 17 July 1968 Revolution, President Saddam Hussein resumed investigation of the plot. His brother Barzan participated in the investigations, as he was responsible for the security of the National Council buildings where Saddam Hussein had had his office as Vice-President of the RCC. Barzan had played a major role in the Revolution and had been a comrade for a long time. The participants in the plot tried so hard to act naturally while the questioning of Muhie Abdel-Hussein was going on that they made themselves conspicuous. President Saddam pointed out that Muhie Abdel-Hussein would try to implicate the maximum number of people possible in the plot, in order to weaken the leadership. Even after Muhie Abdel-Hussein began to reveal some of the names of those who had worked with him, it was thought he was trying to implicate others. During the investigation he implied that he had been planning to break with the plotters; they included Muhammad Ayesh;

who was a very close friend of Muhie Abdel-Hussein's and had a great influence over him. Those whose names were revealed by Muhie Abdel-Hussein were not arrested immediately, but their involvement in the plot was confirmed by their guilty behaviour. After Muhie Abdel-Hussein's arrest on 12 July, Muhammad Ayesh behaved in an increasingly guilty manner and he was arrested on 16 July. Ghanem Abdel-Jalil's behaviour was also suspicious, although he had not been investigated, and so too was Adnan Hussein's, although he had been appointed Deputy Prime Minister and head of the President's Office. When President Saddam Hussein and the other members of the new Government visited President Bakr on the evening of 17 July to congratulate him on the occasion of the anniversary of the Revolution, the plotters looked very ill at ease. Adnan Hussein made a point of repeating over and over again, 'I didn't hold meetings with any of them,' in a nervous voice.

On 18 July the top officials were invited to a dinner party at the Presidential Palace; they were told that a meeting of the Party Command would be held after the party. During the meeting, President Saddam Hussein asked each of those present to write a detailed confidential report about any meetings they had held over the past year with Muhie Abdel-Hussein or Muhammad Ayesh. He asked that these reports be presented to him the following day, so that they might help in the investigation.

Saddam Hussein held a meeting with the Revolution Command Council on 19 July; Adnan Hussein, who did not attend the meeting, had already submitted his report to President Saddam. The President read out this report and that of Ghanem Abdel-Jalil, and all those present at the meeting agreed that they raised a number of conflicting issues. The President then said that Muhie Abdel-Hussein had revealed that Adnan Hussein, Ghanem Abdel-Jalil and Muhammad Mahjoub were involved in a plot and were receiving funds from Syria. President Saddam called in the head of the investigation to brief the meeting as to what had been uncovered until then. He also called in Muhie Abdel-Hussein, who confessed that a committee (which he had subsequently joined) made up of Adnan Hussein, Ghanem Abdel-Jalil, Muhammad Ayesh and Muhammad Mahjoub had been meeting since 1975. He said that the committee had been plotting to overthrow the regime and that Muhammad Ayesh had been their liaison with Syria. Muhie Abdel-Hussein also revealed that Ghanem Abdel-Jalil used to summarise the reports reaching the office of the Vice-President (then Saddam Hussein) and send them directly to President Hafez Assad of Syria. When the Joint Charter for National Action between Syria and Iraq was signed in October 1978, the committee's contacts with Syria increased and they began to prepare themselves to take over power, but in May 1979 they discovered that President Bakr was planning to step down.

On 20 July 1979 Ghanem Abdel-Jalil was arrested after he too had confessed. On 21 July Adnan Hussein and Muhammad Mahjoub (who had been abroad and had returned to Iraq on 16 July) were called on to stand before a joint meeting of the Regional Command and the Revolution Command Council. At first they both denied that they had had anything to do with the plot, but they confessed after being turned over to the investigation committee.

On 22 July President Saddam headed the Extraordinary Regional Conference of 'progressive cadres and popular leaders' at Khald Hall in Baghdad. By then he had to hand the names of all those who had taken part in the plot. Those present at the Conference heard the confession of Muhie Abdel-Hussein, and were informed of the steps taken by the Command. The Conference decided to expel Muhammad Ayesh, Ghanem Abdel-Jalil, Adnan Hussein, Muhammad Mahjoub and Muhie Abdel-Hussein from the Regional Command, from the Party, from the Revolution Command Council and from all their posts in Government. The Conference branded them as traitors and left it up to the Regional Command and the Revolution Command Council to take what action they saw fit.

In the light of the resolutions of the Extraordinary Conference, which expressed full backing and support for President Saddam, the Revolution Command Council decided to set up a Special Court to try the plotters; this was announced six days later on 28 July. The Court was headed by Naim Haddad, a member of the Revolution Command Council, and included Saadoun Ghaidan (RCC member and Deputy Prime Minister), Tayeh Abdel-Karim (RCC member and Oil Minister), Hassan Ali Nassar (RCC member and Minister for Trade), Saadoun Shaker (RCC member and Minister of the Interior), Hikmat Ibrahim (RCC member and head of the Youth and Students' Office in the Party) and Abdullah Fadel (RCC member). It was a painful scene: five of the plotters had been members of the Revolution Command Council; they represented a quarter of the Council, which was composed of twenty-one members. It was clear that the choice of Naim Haddad to head the Court had been carefully made; Haddad is a member of the Revolution Command Council, of the Regional Command and of the National Command. The Court had to take a unanimous decision on the fate of those who had been comrades before the plot was uncovered and had participated in running the Party and the State. The tragedy was slightly mitigated by the fact that — with the exception of Unit Commander Walid Mahmoud Seirat and a handful of soldiers — the military had not been involved. This reassured President Saddam Hussein because he attached great importance to Party solidarity within the Armed Forces. The fact that only one officer had participated in the plot proved that this solidarity existed and that the Armed Forces would have stood firm had the plotters gone into action.

The Court was formed on 28 July and went into session on 1 August. On 6 August it condemned twenty-two people to death for high treason, sentenced thirty-three to imprisonment for periods ranging from one to fifteen years, and released thirteen others. It announced that this judgement resolved 'all matters related to the plot and no outstanding matters relating to the plot remain before the Court'. On 8 August 1979 twenty-one of those condemned to death were executed; the twenty-second, Ahmad Karim, had been condemned *in absentia*. The official communiqué issued after the death sentences had been carried out noted that 'comrades from the military together with civilian Party organisations from all over the land carried out the sentence of execution'. After the Court had passed final sentence, it was decided that Party members should carry out the execution since the plotters had all been members of the Party. This would help to boost the Party's morale after it had been shaken to find that conspirators had infiltrated it at such high levels. After this decision had been taken, every Branch was asked to send a delegate armed with a rifle. Hundreds of delegates congregated and carried out the sentence of execution on their comrades who had been found guilty of treason. This way of carrying out a sentence was unprecedented in the history of the Party.

Did Saddam Hussein have an inkling of what was going on before the plot was discovered or was he completely taken by surprise? If he did have some prior knowledge of the plot, why did he not put an end to it then and there instead of starting his rule with such a tragedy in the Party? The reason one asks this question is because intuition and acumen are among Saddam Hussein's qualities — not blind intuition, but that based on the realities of the situation. He had, for instance, had his suspicions about Muhammad Ayesh long before the plot was uncovered, and had discussed this matter with some of the people closest to him. He based his suspicions on the fact that Muhammad Ayesh wanted to play a role in the Party and the Command for which he was not qualified. He had no revolutionary background, although he had risen to a high position in the Party leadership (member of the Regional Command) and in the Government (Minister for Industry). A person in a high position is not, however, always necessarily qualified for it. Muhammad Ayesh reached his position because he had been an active and enthusiastic Party member. It is possible for such a person to reach such a position by being promoted within the Party. But when he assumes that promotion is an automatic process he becomes, if he does not reach the very top, susceptible to corruption. This is the gist of what I was told by some top Iraqis during a discussion of the motives behind the plot. I also asked why the plotters had not wanted Saddam Hussein to take over power, although he had strengthened their position within the Party and the Command (this was especially true of someone like Adnan Hussein). The answer was that as long as there is a revolution, there will be a counter-revolution.

Saddam Hussein was well aware of this fact: in 1976 President Bakr suffered a severe heart attack and Saddam Hussein found himself responsible for all the affairs of state. During this time, Saddam Hussein was upset to hear of certain things that were said by those who later participated in the plot. He responded to these remarks at a closed meeting of the RCC which was not widely reported. At this session, Saddam Hussein answered two questions: when is a problem tackled by the Revolution and when is it tackled by the Party? His reply was:

> An issue is resolved by the Revolution when the error in the State apparatus is simply an error and not a deliberate plan to strengthen the moral and material bases of the counter-revolution. The Revolution's struggle with itself is over once the State apparatus and its relations with the Revolution reach the minimum drawn up by the Party. The Party's struggle with itself is over once there is no longer any danger of a rightist group climbing to power through illegitimate means, and occupying sensitive positions in leadership in order to divert the Revolution from its true path.
>
> I say with full confidence that the fact that these things might come to pass does not frighten us; it simply means that we must be constantly alert and active. We must not be lulled into a false sense of security simply because eight years have passed in the life of the Revolution, believing that this is enough to close the door permanently in the face of counter-revolution. We must strengthen our principles and heighten our powers of observation; we must not relinquish our role of critical observers of the State and of the Party's internal affairs, and we must encourage the people to engage in active supervision of the State apparatus, down to its most minute parts, where reactionary or rightist elements may try to gain a foothold in order to instigate a counter-revolution. We

> must never soften our stand or ease our efforts to purify all the sensitive organs of state where rightist elements have taken up posts. We must block every opportunity of promotion for these elements in the Party, and strengthen the basic principles of Party organisation.

These words indicate that Saddam Hussein was aware of the possibility of a plot two years before it took place. This is why he said, 'The Party's struggle with itself is over once there is no longer any danger of a rightist group climbing to power through illegitimate means, and occupying sensitive positions in leadership . . .'

The Regional Command and Revolution Command Council communiqué issued on 28 July 1979 declared that the plotters were:

> a group of people who had infiltrated the Party leadership and the Revolution and included traitors belonging to the Party. This group had for some years been preparing an ugly plot aimed at hitting the Party, the Revolution and the achievements of our socialist and democratic people, in order to force Iraq to take part in the defeatist plans drawn up by American imperialism in the service of Zionism and the forces of darkness.

Saddam Hussein had spoken of forces climbing to power through illegitimate means; the communiqué spoke of the plotters who had infiltrated the Party and the Revolution leadership. He had described them as a 'rightist group'; the communiqué spoke of the plotters' links with American imperialism.

It is worth noting that some of the plots that took place in Iraq in the period between the 17 July 1968 Revolution and 17 July 1979 were planned within the Party and by Baathists. This can only mean that some Party members' loyalty to the Party is shaky. There was an earlier plot in 1973 which was led by a long-standing Party member, Abdel-Khaleq Samarrai, in collaboration with Nathem Kazzaz, who was responsible for security. This plot actually reached the stage of implementation. First, Nathem Kazzaz arrested the Minister of Defence, Hamad Shehab, and the Minister of the Interior, Saadoun Ghaidan. President Bakr was on a visit to Bulgaria and Poland at the time. The plotters planned to kill President Bakr and his deputy Saddam Hussein when the President returned to Baghdad airport. But because the Bulgarians wanted to hold an official welcoming ceremony during President Bakr's stop-over at Varna, the plane's time of arrival in Baghdad was delayed by two hours. This delay caused confusion among the plotters gathered at Baghdad airport. The security officer attached to Saddam Hussein noticed this and the plot was exposed, but not before the Minister of Defence Hamad Shehab had been killed. Nathem Kazzaz escaped to Iran, which confirmed suspicions about his links with the Iranians, while Abdel-Khaleq Samarrai was thrown into gaol. He was one of those executed after the 1979 plot.

This later plot was overall a more dangerous one, because the plotters all held high positions. Its discovery caused an uneasy atmosphere in Party ranks. To counteract this, President Saddam Hussein met with some of the Party leadership just one week after taking over full authority, and talked to them in a way designed to raise their morale and strengthen their resolution. The meeting took place on 23 July 1979, the day after the Extraordinary Regional Conference was held in Khald Hall to hear Muhie Abdel-Hussein Mashhadi's confession. At Mustansiriyah University, President Saddam Hussein delivered a speech in which bitterness was mingled with self-confidence:

> Comrades. Do not give in to a feeling of defeat. This is a Revolution which aims to destroy the bases of imperialism, to shine over the whole Arab world to make it a new power on the world scene, to involve every Arab and change his life radically to make him a progressive element, to wipe out all vestiges of degradation and backwardness and corruption. Cannot such a Revolution stand up to such despicable plotters? The whole people is with you now and your organisation has over one million members. In this case, where can the plotters come from? Can they arrange a military invasion to overthrow the Revolution? This is impossible now and they will not achieve their goals. Even America cannot carry out such an operation, except by hurling an atomic bomb and then it would take over a land without a people. The only way, then, in which outsiders could hurt us, is to find traitors in Party ranks who occupy sensitive positions and to extend material assistance to them. Therefore, comrades, we must fight back by strengthening our principles and by full adherence to the Party's principles. Our resolve must not be shaken. We must not imagine that placing confidence in the Baathists is wrong; we must not think that the best way to counter such ugly acts is to review our basic strategy or soften our moral belief in our Party's principles . . .
>
> Treason cannot be justified because there are no legitimate reasons for treason. There is no such thing as a level of treason; there may be levels of faithfulness, but not of treason. Treason is an act of sinking into a bottomless pit, a complete and utter breakdown of will. We must not forget the lessons this teaches us; we must reinforce the strength and experience of our Party and equip the Baathists with a will of steel to carry us on the long road we have chosen.

The question that arises at this point is why Saddam Hussein, with his highly developed statesmanlike qualities, had not taken over power much earlier. In answer to this question, one should recall that, after the 17 July 1968 Revolution, Saddam Hussein had expressed a preference for remaining within the Party and not taking over any position of responsibility in the State. He believed that the great efforts to bring the Party to power made it incumbent on him to devote himself to the Party, and that the Government could tackle all problems if it was based on a strong political force. But President Bakr rejected this idea, so Saddam Hussein drew up an unusual role for himself. Because of his great skill in dealing with the issues and problems facing Iraq, he gradually assumed more and more responsibility and was encouraged to do so by President Bakr, so that finally he was in a decision-making role. This made his relationship with his President an extremely sensitive one. Thus, even when Saddam Hussein was successful in tackling one matter or another, he was always careful that this success be attributed to the President, although he himself was responsible for the achievement.

When President Bakr's health worsened and he was unable to preside over the meetings of the Revolution Command Council as President of the Council, or over the Regional Command as Secretary-General, these meetings were presided over by Saddam Hussein as Vice-President of the Council and Deputy Secretary-General of the Command. They were legal meetings of the Revolution Command Council, where decisions were taken on cabinet reshuffles, Army appointments or international agreements. President Bakr's poor state of health lasted for almost a year. It would have been child's play for Saddam Hussein to have issued a simple two-line decree taking over power and assuming responsibility for the State and the Party. He did not do so; he wished to keep the Party safe from conflict and to reassure President Bakr that he remained at the helm although his health was poor.

The transition of power from President Bakr to his deputy Saddam Hussein showed that the relationship between them was very special. One question remains, in order to clarify this relationship: had there, over the previous ten years, been any cause for conflict between the President and his deputy? If not, this would be the first time in history that such a model relationship had existed between a head of state and his deputy. There were in fact sometimes differences of opinion between President Bakr and his deputy, but they never reached the stage of conflict. They were because of the difference in age, on the one hand, and of experience, on the other; because of the military background of the President and the civilian background of his deputy; and, most of all, because neither man based his rule on issuing decrees but on their long, bitter, shared efforts before coming to power. As deputy, Saddam Hussein was also careful not to let the differences of opinion become serious because of the respect he had for President Bakr's position as overall leader and father of the Revolution. He was helped by the fact that both men were equally convinced of the importance of keeping the core of the Revolution and the Party strong and firm, and both were fully aware of the attempts by forces antagonistic to Iraq to destroy the system of 'double leadership' they had adopted. This was a form of leadership unique in the Third World, where the first and second men in power usually live in constant fear of one another and set traps for each other so that only one may rule supreme. Many hostile forces tried to encourage such conflicts, but the two leaders were always fully aware of these attempts and the people who tried to play this kind of game paid dearly for their efforts. Moreover, in spite of his importance in the Party, Saddam Hussein always behaved in an exemplary manner towards President Bakr. The final chapter in this book (which is an interview with President Saddam Hussein) will reveal how he felt and acted towards President Bakr.

One day the Iraqi media began to refer to President Bakr, much to his surprise, as 'President and Commander', whereas previously he had been referred to as 'Comrade Secretary-General of the Regional Command', 'Comrade' or 'Mr President of the Republic'. It transpired that Saddam Hussein had given instructions to this effect. He also instructed the media to refer to President Bakr as 'Father of the Revolution', which became part of his official title before he resigned his responsibilities. Saddam Hussein does not behave in a haphazard manner, and everything he does has a reason. In instructing the media to use the term 'President and Commander' he may well have wanted to abort attempts to make it appear that he, Saddam Hussein, was the leader and not Ahmad Hassan Bakr. President Saddam Hussein has remained in close contact with President Bakr since the latter's retirement. Throughout the ten years they ruled together, they were unaffected by questions of protocol and hierarchy. Their relations have continued to be natural and unaffected since the deputy became President and the President retired to look after his garden and his grandchildren.

Because of his chosen role, Saddam Hussein was able to acquire a great deal of maturity and experience in affairs of state, and the qualities of a statesman crystallised in him. When he assumed overall responsibility for the State and the Party on

17 July 1979, the Iraqi people showed no surprise; it was as though he had been the leader for many years. As for Arab and foreign states, whether friendly or unfriendly to Iraq, they simply said that the 'strongman' of Iraq since 1968 had now become the head of state. Nevertheless, they looked at Iraq with interest to see how Saddam Hussein the President would act. He would not necessarily continue along the same lines as before, they thought, since the previous policies had been imposed by the needs of that stage, and the new stage would bring its own requirements.

Even before he assumed full responsibility for the State and the Party, Saddam Hussein enjoyed the respect of the Arab world. This would have been much greater if unity had been achieved between Iraq and Syria. But the prospect of unity suffered a serious setback when the plotters revealed they had been in contact with Syria, passing on information and receiving money and promises of support if they overthrew the regime. The first steps towards unity had in fact been taken after a Syrian initiative. President Hafez Assad sent a message calling for a new framework for Syrian-Iraqi relations at the end of September 1978. His message came after a series of meetings of the National and Regional Commands and of the Revolution Command Council in Baghdad on how to counter the plans being implemented by President Anwar Sadat of Egypt. By coincidence, when the Syrian President sent his message, the meetings in Baghdad had concluded by adopting Saddam Hussein's proposals, first, that an Arab Summit be held to counter President Sadat's plot, and secondly, that national duty called for the Syrian and Iraqi Armed Forces to be joined — in which case, a new relationship with the Syrian regime would have to be found. We will first examine the matter of a new framework for relations with Syria, in view of its importance to President Bakr's handing over of power to Saddam Hussein, and then we will examine the Arab Summit, its results, and its importance for Saddam Hussein.

Negotiations between Syria and Iraq began immediately and were accompanied by a popular response that was almost overwhelming. In October 1978 the negotiations resulted in the Joint Charter for National Action which was signed during President Hafez Assad's visit to Baghdad. However, in the interval between this date and the time of President Assad's second visit to Baghdad eight months later, the people in both countries began to feel frustrated. They had expected that President Assad would be signing an agreement on unity with the Iraqi leadership, and they wondered what kind of unity it would be. Some thought that the committees set up by the Joint Charter for National Action were working on merging the two states into one, others thought that it would be a kind of confederation, and yet others speculated that it might be a federation. The feelings of enthusiasm were strong because the Joint Charter for National Action was so clear-cut on the issue of unity:

> Having resolved to take relations between the two brotherly regions to a new stage, the Commands of the two regions met in Baghdad between 24 and 26 October, in an atmosphere of full understanding, conscious of the historic responsibility that faces them. Resolving to realise the national aspirations of the Arab peoples, the two Commands have agreed on a Charter for Joint Action between the two regions in all political, military, economic, cultural and information fields within a continuous and practical programme in order to establish the firmest ties of unity between the two Arab regions of Syria and Iraq . . . The decisions adopted by the two Commands during their historic meeting in October 1978 are a clear and prominent milestone on the road to Arab unity . . .

President Hafez Assad's second visit to Iraq did not put an end to the feeling of frustration. The talks held between 16 and 19 June 1979 did not conclude with the announcement of anything approaching unity. At the end of the talks a 'political declaration' was signed by President Bakr and President Assad announcing the formation of a 'united political command for the two regions'. In addition to the 'higher political body' set up by the Joint Charter for National Action, and until such time as a 'constitutional unity' was formed, this 'united political command' was to be responsible for the following:

> drawing up and adopting the foreign policy of the two regions; drawing up and adopting the Arab policy of the two regions; deciding on matters of war and peace and drawing up the defence policy of the two regions; taking decisions and acting in all economic, cultural, educational and information fields so as to complete the foundations of unity between the two regions. The committees set up by the National Action Charter and by the ministries, establishments and institutes concerned in the two regions will execute this under the supervision of the united political command . . .
>
> A Party Committee will be formed in order to discuss the bases and carry out the studies necessary in order to achieve Party unity and constitutional unity . . . A Party Committee will be formed to draw up the final framework for the constitution of the united state in the light of the principles and constitutional bases adopted by the meetings of the higher political committee . . . A united military command will be formed for the Armed Forces in

> the two regions, under the supervision of the united political command, until a united state is established . . .
>
> The committees set up by the Charter have in the intervening period achieved very important results on the road to consolidating relations between the two brotherly Arab regions. They have brought about a fundamental change in relations between them, and the start of a new stage aimed at laying firm foundations and creating the proper conditions for building a union between them as a nucleus for Arab unity.

Despite the desire for unity expressed by the 'political declaration' it was clear that a wide gulf remained between the Syrian Baath and the Iraqi Baath. Statements made by President Bakr and President Assad after the 'political declaration' was announced showed quite clearly that the warmth of the declaration was at odds with the coolness of the atmosphere in which the talks were held. Shortly after the declaration was made, President Bakr said, 'We had all hoped that our steps towards unity would have been greater than what in fact we have achieved.' President Assad refused President Bakr's invitation to lunch and returned to Damascus, declaring:

> There is no doubt that the people in these two countries and in the Arab world in general had expected us to announce unity today not tomorrow. We too look towards this goal, and we shall continue to look towards it, and to act to bring it about as quickly as possible. But we want to build unity on a real, practical, solid foundation.

The points of view and the demands expressed at the meetings of the unified political command committees also showed an incomprehensible gap between the two sides. After the Joint Charter for National Action had been signed, Iraq put forward the idea of a federated state, to be called the 'United Arab State', which would take both Syrian and Iraqi characteristics into consideration and leave room for development into a more advanced form of unity. A Syrian entity and an Iraqi entity would remain on the local government level; in other words, there would be a president and a government for the Iraqi region and one for the Syrian region, but within a federal state and under a federal authority. The Syrians responded with two proposals, the first being a fully unified state (which the Iraqis considered would end up being a union in form but not in practice), and the second being a confederate state, which would maintain two republics, two regimes, two seats at the United Nations and so on, but which would have a confederate authority to co-ordinate matters.

The Syrian side proposed that the united state be called the

'United Arab Republic', as the 1958 union between Egypt and Syria had been called, and proposed articles on the unity of the Revolution and on equal representation in parliament. The Iraqi side agreed, although Saddam Hussein wanted a new name to be chosen, such as 'United Arab State'. The Iraqis also expressed reservations over the question of representation in parliament, on the grounds that as long as there was one Revolution then there was one people. Lukewarm visits were then exchanged by delegations, while the attempts to co-ordinate military action bore no fruit. This was followed by the meetings in Baghdad which resulted in the 'political declaration' providing for a unified political command. It was not surprising that relations were lukewarm: three weeks later came the discovery of the plot aimed at destroying the Bakr-Saddam tandem and preventing Saddam Hussein from taking over power.

Several questions remain. Would the talks on unity between the two countries have failed if the Charter had been signed after the question of leadership in Iraq had been settled and once Saddam Hussein had become head of state and leader of the Party? Would the question of unifying the two countries and the divided Party even have cropped up in this case? Was it really possible to separate the question of unifying the Party from that of constitutional unity, as Syria had wanted, since unifying the Party would have meant resolving the position of Michel Aflaq? An attempt will be made to answer these questions as simply as possible.

The talks on unity would probably not have broken down had Saddam Hussein been head of state when Syria proposed the new framework — 'probably' because Saddam Hussein was adamant about Michel Aflaq's role; although the Party founder had told President Bakr and Saddam Hussein that he wanted to sacrifice himself so that the Party might be united once more and a united state could be set up between Syria and Iraq. In Saddam Hussein's view, Michel Aflaq is not just a member of the Baath Party Command, or an elected Secretary-General; he is the founder of the Party. Saddam Hussein made this clear before going to Damascus on 28 January 1979 to head the meetings of the higher political committee:

> The announcement of unity between Iraq and Syria must be accompanied by the announcement of the unification of the Arab Socialist Baath Party . . . In our modern history, unity has not taken place outside the framework of the Arab Socialist Baath Party, with the exception of some forms of attempted unity which did not succeed in offering a practical basis and a new definition for unity and its aims and goals. The Party was the architect of

> the unity between Egypt and Syria in 1958, just as the Party spirit through its leadership brought about the 1978 initiative for a new relationship between Syria and Iraq and the spirit of unified action.

By the 'leadership [of the Baath Party]' Saddam Hussein meant the Party founder Michel Aflaq. By taking this stand he closed the door in the face of Syria's attempt to separate the question of Party unity from that of constitutional unity. The question of the founder becoming the leader was not a simple matter for the Syrians: Michel Aflaq was under sentence of death in Syria. For the Syrian regime which had passed the death sentence to review Aflaq's position would mean admitting that they had made a mistake, and would necessitate a thorough revision of the Baath Party line in Syria.

The Syrians may have thought that by preventing Saddam Hussein from becoming head of state, they would be able to overcome the 'founder-as-leader complex' and so spare themselves the need to back down on this point. Since it was impossible to overcome the obstacle Saddam Hussein had made of Michel Aflaq, then why not overcome both Saddam Hussein and Michel Aflaq and encourage the group of plotters in their 'corrective movement' under the leadership of Adnan Hussein? Ironically enough, Adnan Hussein had been chosen by Saddam Hussein as a member of the seven-member Iraqi delegation in the unified political command which was announced on 19 June 1979, three weeks before the plot was uncovered. The plot was to have been carried out some time before 19 September 1979, which was the date agreed for the meeting of the unified political command in Damascus.

The discovery of the plot placed President Saddam Hussein in a difficult position and he had to take a quick decision. It may have been the spirit of the Baghdad Summit, or it may have been some remaining shreds of optimism that unity between Syria and Iraq might one day be achieved, but President Saddam Hussein did not accuse Syria directly of complicity. Instead, after informing the Arab kings and presidents of what had happened, he decided on two courses of action. In the first place, Syria was not named in the communiqué issued by the Revolution Command Council and the Regional Command on 28 July 1979. The subject was referred to as follows: 'These plotters had been in contact throughout with a foreign quarter — which the Command does not find it in the national interest to name at present — from which they received money and instructions, and with which they co-ordinated their criminal efforts.' In the second place, a statement was issued reaffirming Iraq's commitments to the Baghdad Summit resolutions, including its commitments to Syria. The statement [1] was announced on 8 August 1979, the day when the Special Courts passed sentence on the plotters.

Thereafter the phrase 'the plotters' links with an Arab quarter' (mentioned in the statement) was not repeated. On 1 January 1980 the sum of 91,618,800 dollars was transferred to the Syrian Central Bank, the first part of Iraq's commitments for 1980 under the Baghdad Summit resolutions. At the beginning of May 1980, Iraq transferred the second part of its commitments to the Syrian Central Bank. The only reference to the transfers was in a brief news item on the front pages of the Iraqi newspapers, to the effect that Iraq was meeting its financial commitments to Syria, Jordan and the Palestine Liberation Organisation in order 'to fulfil all its national commitments to support the confrontation of the Zionist enemy and to foil the treacherous agreement between the Zionist entity and the treacherous Sadat regime.'

President Saddam Hussein continues to work for unity nevertheless. On 29 September 1979, a few weeks after the plot had been uncovered, and in the first interview I had with him after he had assumed overall power, I asked him about his relations with President Hafez Assad. His answer was diplomatic:

> Baghdad has put an end to psychological campaigns — that was one of the strategic aims of the Baghdad Summit. It is obvious that this is not the most exemplary way to destroy the barriers erected by the enemies of the nation; the best way would be

---

1. The statement included the following:

   The responsible authority in Baghdad confirms that the plot aimed at the national regime in Iraq, and what has been mentioned about the involvement of a certain Arab quarter and its links with the plotters, will not affect Iraq's position on the recent Arab Summit resolutions and the positive Arab atmosphere it generated. Iraq considers itself fully responsible for the Summit resolutions and will meet its full commitments as defined by the Summit.

   Iraq has so far paid 346,666,664 dollars of the 520 million dollars decided as its share in the Arab effort by the Baghdad Summit. Syria has so far received 183,237,000 dollars, Jordan 123,808,532 dollars and the Palestine Liberation Organisation 14,857,555 dollars, while 9,905,422 dollars have been paid into the account of the Special Fund in support of the Arab people in the occupied lands, which uses the Jordanian Central Bank as its headquarters.

   Iraq will be meeting the rest of its national commitments on schedule.

The first photo of Saddam Hussein and his wife on their return from Cairo, following the February 1963 revolution in Baghdad.

Facsimile of the civil status of Saddam Hussein. His third daughter was not yet born (the Iraqi president is now the father of two boys and three girls).

وزارة الداخلية – مديرية الاحوال المدنية العامة

مديرية / دائرة الكرخ

صورة قيد للتسجيل العام لسنة ١٩٥٧

السجل ٢١٦ – المحافظ بغداد – القضاء الكرخ

الاسم	الجنس	اسم الاب	اسم الجد الصحيح	اللقب	اسم الام	اسم الجد غير الصحيح	الديانة	المهنة او الحرفة	تاريخ الولادة	محل الولادة
صدام	ذكر	حسين	مجيد	الناصري	صبحه	طلفاح	مسلم	طالب	١٩٣٩ [illegible]	تكريت
ساجده	انثى	خير الله	طلفاح	الناصري	ليلو	وهيب	مسلمه	طالبه	١٩٣٧ [illegible]	تكريت
عدي	ذكر	صدام	حسين	الناصري	ساجده	خير الله	مسلم	/	[illegible]	بغداد
قصي	ذكر	صدام	حسين	الناصري	ساجده	خير الله	مسلم	/	[illegible]	الكرخ بغداد
رغد	انثى	صدام	حسين	الناصري	ساجده	خير الله	مسلمه	/	[illegible]	الكرخ بغداد
رنا	انثى	صدام	حسين	الناصري	ساجده	خير الله	مسلمه	/	[illegible]	الكرخ بغداد

التصحيحات والتأشيرات الثابتة في السجل الاول: [illegible]

توقيع رئيس الدائرة – اسمه الكامل – ختم الدائرة

The first family photo of Saddam Hussein was published (while he was vice-president) in July 1978 in *Al Mar'a*, a magazine edited by the General Union of Iraqi Women. Here he is in the drawing room of his house with his wife Sagida, his two sons Oudai and Louai and his three daughters, Raghd, Rana and Hala.

Saddam Hussein (while he was vice president) with his wife and eldest daughter.

In 1979 Saddam Hussein celebrates his birthday (28 April) with his family a few months before becoming president.

Wearing his 'abaya' (Arab cloak) Saddam Hussein with his son during his official visit to Yugoslavia (in 1976).

Saddam Hussein and his wife in their garden.

Every Wednesday evening Saddam Hussein decides with his children where they will pass the weekend.

The most popular choice in fine weather is a trip on the Tigris for several hours in a motorboat driven by their father.

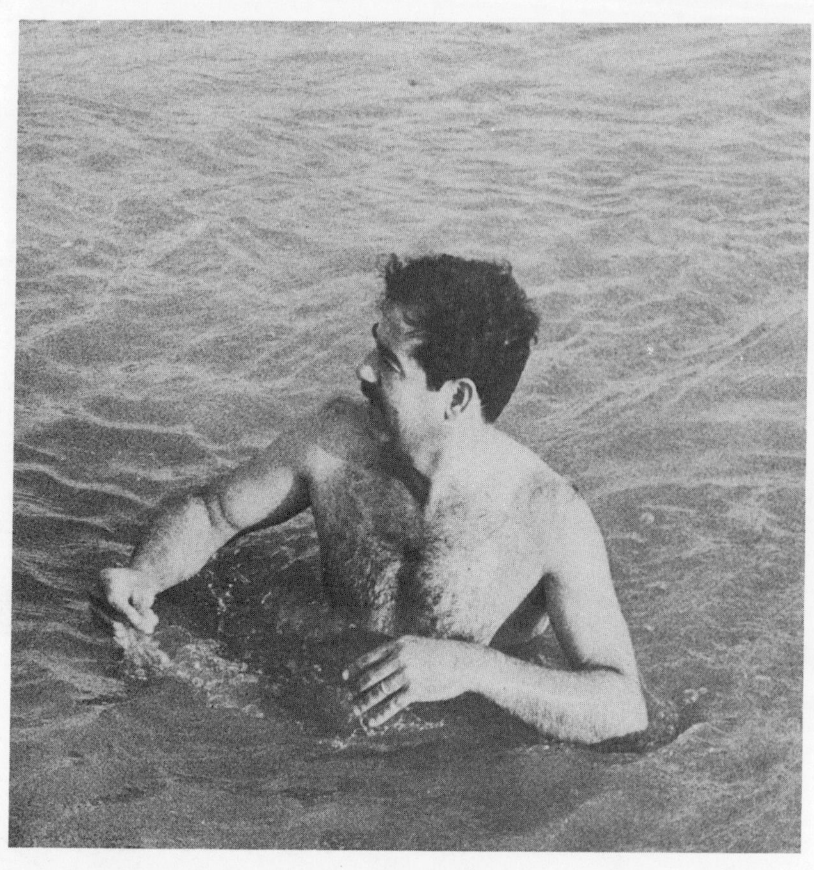

The father tells his children to come and swim.

They play at splashing each other.

The youngest is tired so her father carries her on his back.

They return to the motorboat followed by the others.

But one of the children tries to attract his father's attention.

He stretches out at the river's edge and diverts his daughter with drawings in the sand.

> Iraqi-Syrian unity progressing along the requisite lines and joined by Jordan and the [Palestinian] resistance. We must lead the national struggle to its defined aims, consolidate national unity, and begin a long and bitter struggle independent of any international factors that could abort it before the national objectives have been achieved. I do not mean that Iraq, Syria, Jordan and the resistance should act in isolation from the other Arabs, but that their action should be in the vanguard of Arab strength; that is, the Arabs would back the struggle with traditional means, but the means used by the vanguard should be exceptional.

It is not unreasonable to suppose that the talk of union may well be renewed in the future, albeit in a different form. The following facts add up: Syria was not named in the 'communiqué of accusation' and reference was simply made to 'a foreign quarter'; no propaganda campaigns were waged against Syria; Iraq continued to meet its financial commitments in accordance with the Baghdad Summit resolutions; President Saddam Hussein called for a Syrian-Iraqi unity that would bring in Jordan and the Palestinians; and President Saddam Hussein met President Hafez Assad during the West Asian leaders' talks at the Non-Aligned Summit in Havana. Moreover, although the talks on unity between Syria and Iraq came at a time when relations between the two countries were at their lowest ebb, they went so far as to produce a Joint Charter for National Action and a united political command before the discussions foundered. One must also take into consideration the spirit in which President Saddam announced his National Charter on 8 February 1980 (examined in detail in the last part of this chapter).

First, however, we will examine the Baghdad Summit and its significance for Saddam Hussein. Saddam Hussein knew that the nation would be faced with a tragedy if no action was taken to counter the Israeli-Sadat plan which the United States was about to impose. Thus the Regional and National Commands and the Revolutionary Command Council held a number of meetings during September 1978. At one of these meetings Saddam Hussein proposed that Iraq should call for a summit meeting and announce its readiness to merge Iraqi and Syrian forces. The meeting approved the idea, and President Bakr declared, 'God bless you, Abu Adi [Saddam Hussein], you have found the solution.' After they had adopted the resolution, they prepared to issue the communiqué. At this time, the Iraqi ambassador in Damascus was given a message from President Hafez Assad calling for a new framework for Syrian-Iraqi relations.

Saddam Hussein was not content to let matters take their

traditional slow course and he acted quickly on behalf of President Bakr, whose health would not permit him to do so. He contacted those whose acceptance or refusal to attend the Summit would carry weight. He telephoned Crown Prince Fahd of Saudi Arabia and then flew to Saudi Arabia to meet the Crown Prince, who welcomed the idea. He next went to Kuwait, whose Emir also welcomed the idea, as did King Hussein of Jordan. Saddam Hussein stressed the following point during these talks: if President Sadat's excuse for his action was that Egypt could no longer bear the financial burden of war with Israel, then it was up to the rest of the Arab countries, particularly those who could afford it, to extend enough financial assistance to meet Egypt's needs.

The idea of holding an Arab Summit was accepted, but Saddam Hussein did not think some leaders were willing to go far enough — they wanted to initiate a dialogue with President Sadat and leave it at that. They were concerned about their investments in Egypt and their economic situation. This trend was pronounced even at the Arab Foreign Ministers' conference which was held to prepare for the Summit. Saddam Hussein took it upon himself to try to change this stand before the Summit took place and held bilateral meetings with most of the Arab Foreign Ministers. Before the conference convened, he met the Kuwaiti Foreign Minister, Sabah al-Ahmad. By the time Shaikh Sabah returned to the conference, the opening session had ended and the closed sessions had begun. The results of the Kuwaiti Foreign Minister's meeting with Saddam Hussein were clear at the closed sessions.

During this time, Iraqi defence, protocol and foreign affairs committees worked feverishly to prepare for the arrival of Arab kings and presidents since they expected that the Foreign Ministers' conference would end in a call for an immediate Arab Summit. The kings and presidents were to be accommodated in the building where the conference was to be held rather than in hotels — in any case, there were not enough hotels to hold such a large number of delegations. The Iraqi people participated in the preparations to host the Arab kings and presidents. Many families living in Mansour, one of the most exclusive residential districts in Baghdad, offered their homes as guest houses. The houses were ready to receive the arriving VIPs within two days — some had even been refurnished for the purpose.

The Baghdad Summit began on Thursday 2 November 1978. At the beginning the majority wanted to try to reason with President Sadat. After lengthy discussions and after meetings between the most important participants (Prince Fahd, President

Bakr, King Hussein, President Assad and Shaikh Jaber al-Ahmad), the Arab kings and presidents agreed to send a letter signed by the conference president (President Bakr) to President Sadat, to be delivered by a delegation from the conference. Saddam Hussein remained convinced, however, that President Sadat would not change his stand.

While the heads of state waited in Baghdad, a high-level delegation boarded a special plane at Baghdad airport on Saturday afternoon, 4 November 1978. The members of the delegation were carefully chosen to represent the trends at the Summit: that calling for patient dialogue before condemning Sadat, and that rejecting Sadat's actions on national grounds. The Lebanese Prime Minister Dr Salim al-Hoss was chosen to head the delegation, which included Tareq Aziz, member of the Iraqi Revolution Command Council, the Syrian Minister of Information Ahmad Iskandar and the United Arab Emirates Foreign Minister Ahmad Khalifa al-Suweidi. The message carried by the delegation was responsible and restrained [2]

---

2. The text of the letter is as follows:
   President Anwar Sadat,
   Greetings.
   The Arab Summit Conference convened in Baghdad on 2 November 1978 and attended by their Majesties, Highnesses and Excellencies, the Arab Kings, Emirs and Presidents or their representatives to discuss the agreements you have entered into and which you are about to sign with the Zionist enemy known as the Camp David or Blair House agreements.
   Those present find that these agreements do not serve the Arab nation and its rights in Palestine, Jerusalem, the Golan Heights and Sinai, or the cause of the Egyptian people within the national cause. Indeed, those present find that these agreements will have the worst possible effect on the Arab nation and the interests of the brotherly Egyptian people. Therefore, in the name of the Arab nation's interests and in the name of the principles that tie us to the Egyptian people — those principles that form the basis for our past and our future, for dignity, freedom and prosperity — we call on you in the name of these principles to immediately, openly and definitively reject the agreements and to return to your Arab brothers who have stood by you during the worst of times and at the height of tragedy, who have sacrificed with the Arab Egyptian people and its noble Army, who have shed blood in the trenches of the battle with the Zionist enemy, who have sacrificed all they have to win back our holy Arab land occupied by the Zionist enemy.
   By rescinding these agreements you will offer a great service to the Arab nation and to the future of our Arab people in Egypt,

and addressed Sadat in the language one brother would use to another. It called on him to reject the Camp David and Blair House agreements, and said it would consider this a major service to the Arab nation. Without using threats or warnings, it invited Sadat back into the Arab fold and said it would adhere to Arab aid commitments to Egypt in the name of all the Arab kings and presidents. Even the phrase 'God is our witness that we have acted in good faith' was not used as a warning but as an oath.

The message was in effect a victory for the moderates, who wished to enter into a dialogue with President Sadat before taking any decision to impose sanctions against Egypt. But President Sadat refused to meet the delegation, and would not allow any Egyptian official to meet it either. Although the Egyptian Foreign Ministry had been officially notified before the plane left Baghdad airport, the delegation found no one at Cairo airport except a low-ranking official and a large number of journalists, including some Jewish journalists, who bombarded the delegation with questions. The delegation proceeded to the Sheraton Hotel in Iraqi embassy cars, suspecting that their insulting reception meant President Sadat was not planning to receive them. While still in the cars they heard live excerpts from President Sadat's speech at the opening of the third session of the Egyptian People's Assembly (the parliament) and the insults he addressed to the kings and presidents meeting in Baghdad. This confirmed that their mission was abortive. At the Sheraton Hotel, a low-ranking Egyptian minister came to tell them that President Sadat had replied to their mission in the speech he had just delivered. When Dr Salim al-Hoss asked whether they were to understand that they would not be meeting

---

and you will ward off great dangers from the nation. You will find the Arab nation resolute, capable of defending itself, of recovering its land through joint action, and of safeguarding the basic principles on which it was founded and for which it has struggled against Zionism for thirty years.

The Arab nation, according to the decisions adopted by the Kings, Presidents and Emirs of the Arab countries, is willing to provide Egypt with all it needs to enable it to continue the struggle on the side of its Arab brothers, and all that will protect the dignity of the Egyptian people; the proposal submitted to the Summit Conference will confirm this commitment. God is our witness that we have acted in good faith. Peace be upon you.

Ahmad Hassan Bakr,
President of the Arab Summit Conference,
Baghdad, 4 November 1978.

the President to deliver the Summit Conference's message, the minister nodded and said that even he would not receive the message.

As the delegation returned to Cairo airport in order to fly back to Baghdad, the Arab kings and presidents were handed copies of President Sadat's speech, the answer to their message. The speech was insulting in the extreme, and the Arab heads of state took it as a personal insult. [3] The conference was thus shaken

---

3. Excerpts from President Sadat's speech:
As we build peace, brothers and sisters, there is a great deal of noise and trading with the Arab people's rights. Those voices that are loud today in bargaining with these rights were only yesterday quiet and expressed no will to fight alongside us in the field of peace and honour. We are building peace amidst plots being prepared against us by superpowers, such as the Soviet Union which wants to bring us to our knees. When we countered this and raised our heads these superpowers wished to break the foundations of peace. I tell all these powers from this platform that Egypt cannot be isolated because it is the Egypt of October 1973.

This is Egypt, which will always with God's help have the power to isolate and not be isolated; the Egypt of October which has definitely isolated those petty traders without itself being isolated from the most noble of aims and goals. This is the Egypt of October which restored their dignity and brought them back into existence when they were devoid of life. Who is so deluded as to say that they can isolate Egypt?

This nonsensical pettiness does not deserve a reply. The one who is isolated in his ignorance, hatred and backward mentality is the one who needs rescuing from isolation. We will pay no heed to the hissing of snakes, nor will these childish efforts affect us. We were surprised to hear through foreign news agency services that those meeting in Baghdad have sent a delegation and that it is on its way; they have not requested permission from Cairo. They know that today we are celebrating the opening of the third session of the People's Assembly and that we are concerned with peace and with building the foundations of peace, democracy and freedom. Before their communiqués were issued and before I returned to Cairo I sent all the Arab heads of state (except the Rejection Front) a full analysis. Instead of replying, they resorted to the old way and called for retaliation and the holding of the Baghdad Summit. Until when is the fate of the Arab nation to hang on negative reactions and convulsions? Even if they accept this for their peoples, we do not accept it for Egypt. For the sake of their peoples we shall reply to their message by saying that they will not meet me — or any Egyptian official. And my message, which is being relayed throughout the world and to which they are listening now, is that they cannot buy the will of Egypt . . . they cannot buy our will.

out of its two-day apathy. The members wasted no time discussing details: those who had called for negotiations with President Sadat felt that their consciences were now clear as regards any punishment the Summit might decide to impose on his regime; the others had not suffered such a crisis of conscience to begin with.

The delegation arrived back in Baghdad that night. Tareq Aziz telephoned Saddam Hussein to inform him of what had happened. Saddam Hussein declared that the conference had been a success because Sadat had expelled the delegation. The Baghdad Summit success was in a sense relative. The resolutions adopted were stronger than had been expected, but success was only fully achieved when Saddam Hussein was able to follow through the details the kings and presidents had left to the Foreign and Finance Ministers. They would have been able to resolve these matters at the Summit had there not been some last vestiges of hope that President Sadat would somehow review his actions and return to the Arab fold. Instead of doing any such thing, President Sadat redoubled his attacks on the Arab kings and presidents, thus betraying a complete lack of breeding and good manners. He did not take into consideration the fact that the Baghdad Summit had hoped to help him return to the Arab fold in a manner befitting the leader of the first Arab state. The Arab heads of state had even tried to facilitate his return to the Arab fold by defining a framework for peace in the Summit's final communiqué [4] as follows: 'The Arab conference affirms

---

4. The final communiqué issued at the end of the Baghdad Summit (which lasted from 2 November to 5 November 1978) confirmed:

the Arab nation's commitment to a just peace based on complete Israeli withdrawal from all the Arab territories occupied in 1967, including Arab Jerusalem, and guaranteeing the inviolable rights of the Palestinian Arab people and its right to set up an independent state on its national soil.

It also confirmed that:

the Palestinian cause is the heart of the struggle with the Zionist enemy, and the struggle to regain Arab rights in Palestine and in occupied Arab lands is a national responsibility for all. All Arabs must participate in this, wherever they are and with whatever military, economic, political or other means they possess.

The communiqué called on by the Arab states to back the Palestinian struggle by supporting the Palestine Liberation Organisation in its capacity as the sole legitimate representative of the Palestinian people 'in order to liberate and to regain the national rights of the Palestinian people, including its rights to return and of self-determination and of setting up an independent state on its the Arab nation's commitment to a just peace based on complete Israeli withdrawal from all the Arab territories occupied in 1967, including Arab Jerusalem, and guaranteeing the inviolable rights of the Palestinian Arab people and its right to set up an independent state on its national soil.' This paragraph was the first unanimous Arab stand within a framework designed to resolve the Arab-Zionist struggle. Between the end of the Baghdad Summit on 5 November 1978, and the Extraordinary Meeting of the Arab Foreign and Finance Ministers in Baghdad on 27 March 1979, Saddam Hussein worked on making the ministerial meeting a success in order to translate the Summit's words into action.

The Summit which had condemned President Sadat had also agreed in principle on a number of punitive steps should he refuse to reject the Camp David agreements. In the three months that followed, however, President Sadat redoubled his moves towards peace with Israel, and continued to make declarations insulting to the Arab leaders. There was nevertheless a continued feeling of sympathy for him and this was expressed at the

---

national soil' and declared its 'commitment to safeguard Palestinian national unity and non-interference in the internal affairs of Palestinian action'.

The communiqué reconfirmed adherence to previous summit conference resolutions, especially those of the Algiers and Rabat Summits, noting that:

> One of the basic principles which must not be violated is that no Arab party has the right to act individually or separately to bring about any solution of the Palestinian problem in particular and the Arab struggle against Zionism in general; no solution will be accepted unless it abides by a resolution adopted by an Arab summit conference held for this purpose.

The communiqué registered the Baghdad Summit's rejection of the Camp David agreements and its:

> refusal to accept the results and its rejection of any resulting political, economic, legal and other effects. The Summit calls on the Government of the Arab Republic of Egypt to rescind these two agreements and not to sign any peace treaty with the enemy. It hopes that the Government will return to the ranks of joint Arab action. In this respect, the conference has adopted a number of resolutions to confront the new stage, and it confirms the need to unify Arab ranks in order to counteract the strategic imbalance caused by Egypt's withdrawal from the battlefield. The conference has decided on co-ordination between those states that have the necessary readiness and ability to participate in effective action, and it confirms the need to abide by the Arab boycott rules and regulations.

Extraordinary Meeting of the Arab Foreign and Finance Ministers. In the end, however, the conference adopted the following resolutions: to withdraw the Arab ambassadors from Egypt immediately; to suspend Egypt's membership in the Arab League; and to transfer the Arab League headquarters from Cairo to Tunis. A six-member committee (made up of Iraq, Syria, Tunisia, Algeria, Kuwait and the Kingdom of Saudi Arabia) was given full authority by the League Council to oversee the transfer of League headquarters and employees to Tunis and to take the necessary steps to protect all League property and financial holdings.

The meeting took these decisions because of Saddam Hussein's influence, which was apparent from the moment the conference began. Some of the Arab countries preferred not to break off economic relations with President Sadat's regime. They were content simply to withdraw their ambassadors rather than break off diplomatic relations, and wanted to postpone the decision to move League headquarters from Cairo to Tunis. To counter this, Saddam Hussein called for a joint meeting of the National and Regional Commands and of the Revolutionary Command Council. At the joint meeting, it was decided that Iraq would adopt a stand that the others would find hard to ignore. The stand can be summed up as follows:

> There was no middle course between the road chosen by President Sadat and that chosen by the Summit conference.
>
> The matter was too grave to be resolved through technical or political steps; it was a national matter and no one should falter in his duty.
>
> If the Arab countries were hesitating out of concern for the Egyptian people, they should note that the resolutions adopted by the Baghdad Summit were in fact in the interests of this people. If they were reluctant to honour the financial commitments made at the Summit to each of Syria, Jordan and the Palestine Liberation Organisation (3,500 million dollars annually, of which 100 million dollars was allocated to assisting the struggle in the occupied Arab territories), then Iraq would meet these commitments on its own, postponing its development plans in order to do so.
>
> The conference could be suspended for twenty-four hours, during which time ministers could consult their governments in order to return with a final decision. Iraq would in any case adopt the stand it had outlined, on its own or with anyone else who wished to do so.

This was the strategy drawn up by Saddam Hussein. When the Iraqi delegation announced its stand at the conference, a number of ministers did indeed fly back to consult their governments, and some were annoyed at what they saw as an Iraqi threat. But when they returned to Baghdad with a final decision from their governments, the conference was resumed and achieved its final success.

Two points remain to be discussed as regards the Baghdad Summit and how it increased Arab support for Saddam Hussein. In the first place, during the Summit there was a very strong move to negotiate with President Sadat. However, instead of hardening his stand on rejecting negotiations with President Sadat, Saddam Hussein employed a tactical manoeuvre which enabled him to block the proposal to negotiate with Sadat. This proposal had suggested condemning Sadat while calling on him to return to the Arab fold, setting up a committee to initiate discussions with the Egyptian President, and holding another summit meeting within two weeks to two months after the beginning of talks in order to decide what further steps should be taken. This current was so strong that Saddam Hussein proposed that a committee be formed at once and sent to talk to President Sadat immediately. Had this not been done, the opportunity to adopt a strategy against the Camp David accords would have been lost. It is doubtful whether another summit meeting would have been held.

In the second place, Saddam Hussein was careful to avoid any discussion of the Lebanese situation so that attention could be focused on the main issue. Indeed, Lebanon was not allocated a single dollar of the three billion dollars allocated to Syria, Jordan and the Palestine Liberation Organisation. Saddam Hussein was well aware that if the Lebanese situation were introduced for discussion, this might cloud the main issue and enable some Arab parties to avoid taking a strong and clear stand against President Sadat's regime.

At the Tenth Arab Summit held in Tunis on 20 November 1979, however, President Saddam made up to Lebanon for this lack of concern. In the speech opening the conference, he declared, 'We must all work together to consolidate Lebanon's independence, unity and territorial integrity, and to set up brotherly links between Lebanon and the Palestine Liberation Organisation.' He referred to Lebanon's national role, saying,

> Lebanon has borne a great deal for the sake of the national cause, and it is now up to the Arab nation to bear its responsibilities by finding the appropriate solutions, by defending it against aggression when necessary, and by helping in the reconstruction of Lebanon which has passed through such difficult circumstances.

> The Arabs must participate in healing Lebanon's wounds, suffered because it is Arab in its people, land and responsibilities.

Over and above this, President Saddam Hussein held talks with the Lebanese President Elias Sarkis, and thereafter played an active role in securing financial assistance for Lebanon. Within the overall Summit at Tunis he held a mini-summit meeting with the Gulf leaders to decide on the extent of this financial assistance.

The Baghdad Summit thus increased Arab support and respect for Saddam Hussein, who was fulfilling the role he had mapped out for himself after the July 17-30 Revolution of 1968. This support increased further once he had assumed overall responsibility for the Party and the State, particularly in view of developments after the Summit Conference. The most important of these was the fall of the Shah of Iran after the revolution led by Imam Ayatollah Khomeini. This was followed by the Soviet military intervention in Afghanistan, the arrival of American and Soviet fleets in the region, and America's threats to protect its oil interests by intervening militarily, which meant it would occupy the oilfields under the umbrella of security agreements with some of the states in the region. Moreover, the spirit of the Baghdad Summit deteriorated and needed new blood to revive it. President Saddam Hussein was convinced that the superpowers wished to destroy the spirit of the Summit. He noted certain worrying trends at the Non-Aligned Summit which led him to declare at the Arab Summit in Tunis on 20 November 1979, 'The Arab nation has made certain gains at the Baghdad Summit. National interest requires that we do not go back on these gains in any shape or form.'

A few days before he went to Tunis to open the Tenth Summit, he addressed a meeting of the heads of Arab news agencies and called on the Arabs to revive the spirit of action they had unanimously created at the Baghdad Summit in 'new forms'. In his first interview with the press after taking over complete responsibility, which I held with him on 29 September 1979 (after he had taken part in the Havana Summit and before the Tunis Summit), I asked the President if he was planning a new form of action to strengthen the results of the Baghdad Summit. The President replied:

> The Baghdad Summit should have taken, and was meant to have taken, more effective long-range action than it did. Nevertheless, we can say that the Baghdad Summit defeated Sadat and American imperialism with all its might. A change is taking place in Europe, and their major leaders, who used to support Camp David, are now

saying that Camp David will not achieve peace. Therefore the Baghdad Summit has changed people's minds on the international level, and put an end to the deterioration in morale on the Arab level. Indeed, Arab morale has been greatly strengthened, especially after the move for new ties between Iraq and Syria. It achieved a great deal, but has it achieved all it should? There is no framework, given the current Arab condition, for bringing about complete success, because the frameworks that now exist are based on a number of smaller entities that do not correspond or that are sometimes in opposition to one another. This is the state of joint Arab action — there are twenty-two countries, twenty-two regimes, twenty-two policies, twenty-two leaders. How can we draw up the requisite strategy for national action on this basis? But the Arabs will be able to find a framework for national action by co-ordinating their participation and the degree of participation.

There were indications that President Saddam Hussein was planning to take action to counteract the slowness with which some Arab parties were implementing the Baghdad Summit resolutions, and to establish a new framework for Arab action, but no one had expected it would take place so soon. The new framework was announced as a national declaration for the organisation of relations between the Arab countries [5], to serve as a National Charter.

---

5. The text of President Saddam Hussein's National Charter is as follows:

In the name of God, the merciful, the compassionate.

Declaration:

In the light of current international conditions and possible future developments, and the dangerous repercussions these may have on the sovereignty and security of the Arab nation on the one hand, and on peace and security in the world on the other; in response to the call of national responsibility towards the Arab nation, its people, its land, its civilisation, its heritage; and in line with the principles of non-alignment, Iraq feels itself bound to undertake the initiative to issue this Declaration, first, so that it may serve as a Charter to organise national ties between the Arab region and, secondly, so that it may serve as a commitment by the Arab nation towards those of its neighbours which undertake to respect this Charter.

This Declaration is based on the following principles:

First: rejection of the presence of all foreign armies, military forces and bases on Arab soil, or extension of facilities to such foreign forces in any shape or form, or under any guise or cover, or for any reason whatsoever. Any Arab regime which does not abide by this principle will be isolated and boycotted politically and economically, and every means will be used to struggle against its policies.

. . . .

Second: forbidding the use of military force by any Arab state against any other Arab state, and resolving any conflicts that might arise between Arab countries through peaceful means and in the light of joint national action and the higher Arab interest.

Third: the principles outlined in the second article will be applied to the relations of the Arab nation and the countries neighbouring the Arab nation; armed force should not be used to settle conflicts with these states, except in the case of self-defence and the safeguarding of sovereignty against any threats that might affect the security of the Arab regions and their essential interests.

Fourth: the Arab states will co-ordinate in order to repel any attack or any aggression carried out by any foreign party against the regional sovereignty of any Arab country, or should any such country enter into an active state of war. The Arab states must act jointly to repel any such attack or aggression and to foil it using all ways and means, including military force, a political and economic boycott, and any other means called for by the national interest.

Fifth: the Arab states confirm their adherence to all international laws regulating the use of land, air and sea by any country not in a state of war with any Arab country.

Sixth: Arab countries will steer away from all international conflicts and wars, and adopt a policy of complete neutrality towards any of the parties involved in war or conflict, so long as the parties involved do not launch an attack on Arab territorial sovereignty or on the inviolable rights of the Arab states as safeguarded by international law. The Arab armies will not participate, in whole or in part, in the military conflicts and wars within or outside the region on behalf of any other state or foreign party.

Seventh: Arab countries will commit themselves to setting up developed and effective economic links between them, so as to consolidate and develop a joint Arab infrastructure, and Arab unity. The Arab states will steer away from anything that might adversely affect these links and stand in the way of their development, in spite of the differences between the Arab regimes, and in spite of any marginal political conflicts that might occur between them, so long as the parties in question adhere to the principles outlined in this Declaration. The Arab states will accept the principle of national economic integration. Those Arab states endowed with financial and economic resources will undertake, to the best of their ability, to assist those which are less well off, in order to prevent them from turning to foreign powers which will affect their independence and national will.

Eighth: having drawn up the principles of this Declaration, Iraq hereby confirms its willingness to abide by it towards every Arab state and every party that adheres to it. Iraq is ready to discuss it with the Arab brothers and to hear their comments so

We will look at the steps leading to the proposal of the National Charter. On the eve of 8 February 1980 President Saddam Hussein stood in the People's International Stadium in Baghdad to address the large crowds gathered there to celebrate the anniversary of the 8 February 1963 Revolution which brought the Baath to power for only six months and a few days, after which Iraq plunged back into bloody and difficult times. This was the first time that Saddam Hussein had commemorated the anniversary of this Revolution in his capacity as President. The celebrations were to have been held in a closed hall, but just a few hours beforehand it was decided that the President's speech would be delivered in the open air before the masses. The change of plan was not inspired by security reasons but by national need. After all, had there been any pressing security reasons, the reverse would have happened and the celebrations would have been held in a closed hall rather than in Baghdad's large stadium. The national need for addressing the speech to the masses was not immediately apparent when President Saddam began his speech. He began by speaking of the atrocities the Communists had committed in Iraq, how they 'hanged naked virgins from electricity poles until they were

---

that its principles may be strengthened and its contents developed.

Iraq also stresses that this Declaration is not meant to replace the Arab League Charter, or the Joint Defence Pact, or the economic co-operation which already exists between Arab countries. It simply considers that the Declaration provides additional strength and support for the Charter and the Pact in line with new developments on the international level and the dangers threatening the Arab nation, and the national responsibilities it faces in present conditions and in the future.

O great Iraqi people,

O great masses of the Arab nation:

In presenting this Declaration, Iraq bases itself on its sense of national responsibility which is above all personal or regional interests. While we address this Declaration to the Arab Governments, as they are the parties responsible for adopting it and for abiding by it, we remain deeply convinced that the principles of this Declaration can only be implemented through the struggle of the Arab masses and their support. Only then will it become a Charter for Arab relations, because it meets the Arab people's basic interests, their national aspirations for freedom and independence, and paves the way for Arab unity.

Saddam Hussein,
President of the Republic of Iraq,
Baghdad, 8 February 1980.

dead' and how they 'buried comrades alive'. He then went on to reply to those who criticised the regime on the grounds that all those in power in Iraq were from Takrit, and that 'Takrit rules Iraq.' He warned, in his reply, of the repeated attempts to divide both Iraq and the Arab nation. He declared:

> They think that just as they fooled Abdel-Salam Aref and made him a man conscious of sectarianism, they will make of Saddam Hussein a sectarian man. Miserable creatures. They have no understanding of the Arab Socialist Baath Party. To put their minds at rest, we say to them: Saddam Hussein was born in the village of Ouja which lies south of the district of Takrit. The district of Takrit is part of Salaheddin Province. Saddam Hussein is not a Takriti; he is an Iraqi. Saddam was born in Salaheddin Province. But he is not just of Salaheddin Province. He is also of Irbil Province, of Suleimanieh, of Anbar, of Qadissiyah and Thiqar, of the Tigris and the Euphrates, of Barada and the Jordan and the Nile; he is the son of Damascus, Amman, Cairo and Casablanca. He is the son of all Iraqi cities and the son of the Iraqi people, of the land of Iraq, of the very air of Iraq. He is the son of the Arab nation . . .
>
> Saddam Hussein, who is now President of the Republic, is before all else a comrade in the Arab Socialist Baath Party. I think if the President of the Republic had come from Ainkawa, or Kalala, or Rumeithah, or Rarnajiah, or Anbar, they would have said the same thing — the President comes from such and such a village or from such and such a province. The President of the Republic must be an Iraqi — he is bound to have come from a certain village, from a certain district or province.

At this point the national need for the speech became apparent. President Saddam spoke of the attempts to divide the Arab nation. He then announced the eight-point National Declaration for organising relations between Arab countries. The commemoration ceremony turned into a kind of referendum: at every point he asked the masses if they approved, and they would reply as one man that they did. Before the President announced his Declaration the idea had been discussed and approved at meetings of the Party Command and the Revolution Command Council. The discussions had focused on the difficult international conditions faced by the Arab world which required a new framework to organise relations between the Arab regimes in order to prevent attempts to divide the nation.

As soon as President Saddam Hussein had announced his National Declaration, a wave of relief swept over the Arab world — just as it had after the Baghdad Summit had succeeded. The Arab people saw that the Declaration would guarantee security and stability and were inspired by a feeling of national duty. Arab officials and heads of state saw it as a guarantee for the realisation of peace and so hastened to welcome and support it, without being disturbed by the fact that President Saddam Hussein had not consulted them beforehand. (Only that same morning had the Vice-President of the Revolution Command Council Izzat Ibrahim met Arab ambassadors at his office in the National Council and briefed them as to the Declaration that was to be made that evening.) Saddam Hussein had not followed this course in order to embarrass the Arabs — there was nothing in the Declaration that could be a source of embarrassment to anyone. He adopted it to save time, and so as to prevent the Declaration from sinking into the morass of having to seek an Arab consensus. Moreover, the Arab people would hear the Declaration and exert popular pressure on their regimes to accept it.

The proposed Charter was announced at a time when some states were reluctant to take up their national duty, using their involvement in border problems as an excuse, and when it was essential for the Arabs to unify and integrate their forces in the face of the international plot against them. The Charter came at a time when foreign fleets were sailing in Arab waters and radar equipment surveyed Arab lands. The choice of the 8 February 1963 anniversary — the day when the Baath took over power in Iraq — was not fortuitous. From a purely Party point of view, the anniversary should have been an occasion for a call to bring the Baath to power in the rest of the Arab world, not for coexistence between regimes. It came as a choice between Baathist aspirations and the need to face danger on a national level. President Saddam Hussein acted with a flexibility called for by the circumstances — but this did not mean a change in basic Baath principles. He drew up a plan of action for facing danger at a first stage.

The possibility of co-operation between regimes hitherto labelling one another as 'revolutionary' or 'reactionary' was first raised in a speech by President Saddam Hussein on 6 January 1980, the fifty-ninth anniversary of the establishment of the Iraqi Army, about a month before the National Declaration: 'Dividing people into "reactionary" and "revolutionary" groups is not new in the Arab world; indeed it goes back to the time after the launching of the call to Islam, and the differences in its application in the subsequent stages.' It was as though the President was saying that these conditions were the same at the present time, and that this did not preclude a form of coexistence.

The strongest support for the proposed National Charter came from the Kingdom of Saudi Arabia, which overlooked the fact that the person who had announced the Charter was a 'progressive revolutionary'. The Saudi reaction was the first meeting-point between the two positions. The Saudis also overlooked the question of protocol and the tradition of taking time to mull over the proposal. Just five days after President Saddam announced the Charter, King Khalid bin Abdel-Aziz sent a telegram to President Saddam in which he said: 'The declaration of the Charter's principles is greatly welcomed by us, because its principles are in line with the policy of strengthening the Arab and Islamic stand and consolidating security and stability for the Arab world, particularly in the present conditions.' The Saudi King went further; he called on others to support the Charter as well: 'I am confident that the Arab countries will abide by the principles of the Charter and that it will be put into practice in a way that will serve the Arab and Islamic nation.'

One should note at this point that the Kingdom of Saudi Arabia had figured in Saddam Hussein's thoughts when he was still Vice-President, and when he first began to formulate a framework for organising inter-Arab relations. There was a reference to this during the fifth session of the Arab National Popular Conference held at the Mansour Hotel in Baghdad to discuss the Charter. Saddam Hussein said:

> On my return from a visit to India in 1974 I stopped in the United Arab Emirates and met a number of journalists. At that time our relations with Saudi Arabia were at their worst. Our radio stations attacked them, and there were no exchanges between us. A journalist asked about our relations with Saudi Arabia, and I answered, 'The basic reason for the poor relations with Saudi Arabia is the fact that Saudi Arabia did not take a clear-cut stand rejecting the occupation of the three Arab islands by the Shah's Iran, and did not stand alongside Iraq in its attempt to stop this occupation. Whereas if one of these days the Soviet Union, to which we are linked by a treaty of friendship, were to occupy any part of Saudi territory, the Iraqi Army would fight off these forces even before the Saudi Army.' I added: 'These words are still a valid definition of our stand and our view of foreigners and will remain so as long as we live. We will fight the foreigner in defence of the land and the people, irrespective of our opinion of the regime and the ruler and irrespective of our relations with and our opinion of the foreigner.'

The Charter was proposed after the Soviet role in Afghanistan, which President Saddam Hussein regarded as more of an occupation than as assistance to a revolutionary regime. The timing of the Charter led some Arab regimes to see it as aimed primarily at the Soviet Union. The Soviet Union's reaction was particularly sensitive: even those states like Iraq with which it was on friendly terms considered the bases it set up in some countries of the Third World in the same light as American bases. During my extended discussions with President Saddam, he repeated more than once, 'Giving bases to the Soviet Union is just like giving bases to the Americans.'

President Saddam assumed that the superpowers would not encourage the application of a Charter that would strengthen the non-aligned world. Nevertheless, twelve Arab states and the Palestine Liberation Organisation agreed to hold a summit conference to adopt the proposed Charter within three weeks of its announcement. More support was forthcoming after Sudan had declared its support for the proposed Charter, and after the changes in Democratic Yemen. Why did Iraq then cool towards the idea of holding a summit to adopt the Charter? Was it because it found itself involved in a long-term conflict with Iran? Was it because of fears that the superpowers would abort the idea in one way or another? Or had President Saddam, after gaining both official and popular Arab support for the proposed Charter, decided to wait until an ordinary Arab summit for its adoption, during which time Arab support would have been consolidated? Whatever the reason, Iraq cooled somewhat towards the idea of the summit. President Saddam Hussein must have sensed an Achilles' heel in the international restraints on his role, but must have decided to take advantage of this weakness only when full success was ensured. Moreover, the President is working on the adoption of the proposed Charter by the forthcoming Non-Aligned Summit to be held in Baghdad in 1982.

Five points remain to be made about President Saddam's proposed Charter. In the first place, President Saddam remains unconvinced that the United States can defend any country, particularly as this has become a dangerous gamble that America will not now undertake for anyone's sake. Thus the regimes that had depended on American protection would soon find that the proposed Charter would be a better guarantee. President Saddam also knows that the form of Soviet protection is not acceptable, and that it will lead to the downfall of those regimes that accept it — which also means that the proposed Charter is the best guarantee of protection.

In the second place, President Saddam realises that the lack of Arab unity results primarily from mistrust. When he addressed the Arab Ministers of Labour meeting in Baghdad on 9 March 1980, one month after the Charter was announced, he declared,

'It will be impossible to achieve political unity between the Arabs until psychological unity is achieved and until it is based on day-to-day needs and interests.' He was confident that the Charter he proposed would, with time, do away with the feeling of apprehension and mistrust.

In the third place, he made it clear that Iraq was not proposing the Charter in order to safeguard its own interests. He told the Arab Ministers of Labour:

> We call on the Arabs not to use weapons against one another. Whoever believes that this principle was established for Iraq's sake, I say — and I speak as the President of the Republic of Iraq — that any Arab who can use weapons against us, let him do so. To say this is painful, of course, and we do not believe that the Arabs have the right to raise their weapons against us. But let him who suspects that this was done simply for the good of Iraq come to us, and we will tell him that whenever he has the strength to launch a military attack on us then let him do so.

In the fourth place, there were many matters related to the proposed Charter that President Saddam did not raise because of his official position. As President of the Republic, he had to take into account the sensitivities of various Arab and international quarters to matters of which he personally was convinced. The matters President Saddam did not raise were referred to in the document presented by the Baath Party on 25 March 1980 to the National Popular Conference held to discuss the National Declaration under the slogan, 'No military alliances, no foreign bases. All Arab forces for the liberation of Palestine.' The document [6] received his approval, in his

---

6. The following are excerpts from this document:
A number of Arab states, vulnerable because of their strategic position or because of their wealth, do not have sufficient means for self-defence and are thus at the mercy of others. Whatever excuses — whether honest or in recognition of existing realities — these states give for accepting foreign protection and for accommodating foreign quarters, this does not change the basic fact of the matter. There are other Arab countries which are capable of facing up to aggression.
Although a number of states in the non-aligned movement are in effect allies of one side or another, the non-aligned movement is valuable because at least it has prevented the formation of military alliances and the resulting political restrictions . . .
There are those who link the timing of the Declaration with the Soviet Union's intervention in Afghanistan. We have not lessened

capacity as head of the Party, before it was presented for discussion at the conference.

In the fifth place, a charter already exists to organise relations between the Arab states, the Arab League Charter. The flaw in this Charter is that it is not binding on the member states; but the Charter proposed by President Saddam is binding in that it also provides for sanctions such as economic or political boycotts. Moreover, President Saddam's Charter forbids recourse to military force for settlement of inter-Arab conflicts, and it does not permit recourse to military force against countries neighbouring the Arab world except in cases of self-defence. Although the proposed Charter does not include a paragraph excepting Israel from the above condition, it clearly refers only to those states with whom the Arabs have diplomatic relations, such as Iran, Turkey and some of the African countries. The proposed Charter is not restricted to security and political matters, however, and calls on the Arab countries to set up solid economic ties with one another. The Charter was intended to be an overall integrated plan for political and economic security. The economic aspect might be attractive to those Arab countries which prefer to buy security through aid and assistance.

Saddam Hussein explained his views when he told the Arab Ministers of Labour on 9 March 1980:

---

our criticism of this intervention and we will stand against intervention of this kind in any other place it might happen; but the United States' exploitation of this intervention is equally dangerous, as is its search for military bases in the Arab world.

The Soviet intervention in Afghanistan has aggravated this dangerous condition and has led to increased international conflict over resources and strategic positions involving the Arab nation and exposing it to external threats and the dangers of regional conflicts stemming from the conflicting strategies. The Arab world would, in every case, be the loser in these calculations.

The intervention is an assault on Afghanistan's sovereignty and contradicts the definitions and laws regulating international relations between states, the most important being the people's right of self-determination without direct or indirect foreign intervention or pressure. People are perfectly capable of defining their national good in line with their aims and interests. Thus it threatens international peace and security and adds to the instability in the region. It brings the international conflict closer to the Arab world. It creates additional excuses for imperialist forces to threaten, attack, and impose themselves as a dangerous military presence.

> It is not possible for an Arab sidetracked by an Arab brother to liberate Palestine. We cannot imagine that the Jews would fear the hungry, and the culturally, scientifically and technologically backward. Israel does not fear the present Arab armies which are three million strong. But it would fear an Arab army of half a million which was backed by a strong economy and an integrated community that was scientifically and technologically advanced. This is why the Charter calls for the establishment of developed and constructive economic relations between the Arab states. When the enemy sees the disparity in our nation — between he who is so hungry that he will steal a mouthful of bread at knife-point and he who is so wealthy that he can find nowhere to deposit his surplus wealth — he is bound to try to exploit this to set us one against the other.

The proposed Charter was also well received by non-Arab political forces, such as Andreas Papandreou, the head of the Greek socialist movement, who said at a press conference in Baghdad on 9 March 1980, after a meeting with President Saddam, 'The principles of the Charter can extend beyond the Arab world, to the Mediterranean and to the non-aligned nations, and to the progressive and socialist parties and movements around the Mediterranean basin, of which our Party is one.' It was also seen as a major link in the non-aligned chain by the Yugoslavs, whose Prime Minister Veselin Djuranoviç told Revolution Command Council member Tareq Aziz during their meeting in Baghdad on Thursday 22 May 1980, 'The Charter proposed by President Saddam Hussein has done a great deal to prevent further deterioration on the international level.'

What, in the final analysis, is the value of the Charter proposed by President Saddam Hussein on 8 February 1980? Has it had any positive results other than the words of welcome it evoked in the majority of Arab people and governments? The best way to answer this question is by posing two interrelated questions. First, would the Arab position not have been weakened further had the Baghdad Summit not been held? The answer is that the Arab stand would have collapsed. Second, had the Charter not been proposed, would those who had set aside pieces of their territory as bases for American or Soviet forces have been able to go on acting without compunction? If the Charter had not been proposed and met with such acclaim, the foreign bases in the area would certainly have been increased and strengthened. The Charter made those accepting foreign forces feel a little less easy and think several times before doing so. The Charter was proposed to safeguard the results of the Baghdad Summit. At the same time it answered a question which until then had remained unanswered for students of Iraq — the question of the Soviet role outside its borders, which the Iraqis clearly described as intervention and as an assault on sovereignty. Now that this matter has been settled by Iraq, which has a treaty of friendship with the Soviet Union, those who accept American bases on the grounds of the Soviet threat no longer have that excuse. The Soviet international strategy sees such proposals as the 8 February Charter as obstacles in the way of its influence.

In conclusion, President Saddam Hussein was flexible in planning for the Baghdad Summit, even to the extent of accepting discussions with President Sadat's regime to ensure the Summit's success. Similarly, when he drew up the framework for the Charter, he avoided entering into the internal affairs of other Arab states so that it should be welcomed by all regimes. He placed the question of Arab sovereignty above the question of national struggle and the historic conflict between 'revolutionaries' and 'reactionaries'. By so doing, he proved that the revolutionary can be at one and the same time an exceptional statesman.

CHAPTER 3

THE INTERNATIONAL MENTOR

'We have an important political weight in the world and we must act accordingly in everything we do.'
(Saddam Hussein in his opening speech at the Arab Summit in Tunis on 20 November 1979)

President Saddam Hussein announced the National Declaration because circumstances required it. Following the Baghdad Summit, some of the states which had attended it clashed with one another. Each clash lessened the impact of the Summit and was another card in President Sadat's hands. At each clash President Sadat would tell the Egyptian people, 'Look at those who tried to gang up on me; they are fighting and plotting against each other; how much better our situation is than theirs.' These Arab conflicts occurred in spite of President Ahmad Hassan Bakr's warning at the Baghdad Summit when he summed up Saddam Hussein's analysis at the Command Council session on holding the Summit. In his opening address to the Arab kings and presidents, President Bakr said, 'If, God forbid, we do not reach agreement at this meeting, then the Arab world will witness a sharp division the like of which it has never seen before. The matter will not end there, for such conflicts do not stop at regional borders but extend dangerously both regionally and internationally.'

In Iraq's view, an agreement at the Baghdad Summit would have spared the Arabs a division in ranks and the dangers of international intervention. But, in spite of the agreement reached at the Summit, some of the states entered into secondary conflicts which could have invited superpower intervention in one way or another. Even President Sadat was ready to intervene when he proposed sending troops to Morocco so that it might fight Algeria. On the other hand, thanks to the spirit of President Saddam Hussein's proposed Charter, the Arab Foreign Ministers did not have too much trouble improving Libyan-Tunisian relations following the Gafsa incident.

Since taking over full responsibility for the State and Party, President Saddam has worked on three major levels: continuing the struggle against the Camp David agreements, and consolidating the Charter he proposed; preparing for the Non-Aligned Summit to be hosted by Iraq in 1982; and consolidating the role he drew up for himself after taking over full responsibility.

Within three months of Saddam Hussein's becoming head of state, Baghdad became an important centre of Arab and international activity. Scarcely a week went by without an Arab ruler or a Third World leader visiting Baghdad. Most of those visiting Baghdad had just met President Saddam at the Non-Aligned Summit held in Havana. His initiative at that summit had left a favourable impression, especially on the African leaders. When, for example, they proposed visiting him at his residence during the Summit he replied that he would take it upon himself to go and visit them, without making an issue of protocol. The African and Asian leaders who visited Baghdad received an unprecedented welcome, almost as though President Saddam was thanking them for the stand they had taken during the Havana Summit against the Camp David accords. To give just one example, President Samora Machel of Mozambique was accorded the treatment that the head of state of a major power could have expected.

At the Havana Summit, it seemed as though President Saddam had become the leading Arab figure in the non-aligned movement, and Asian, African and Latin American countries behaved towards him on this basis. This role had in the past been filled by Gamal Abdel-Nasser and then by Houari Boumedienne. After the death of President Tito of Yugoslavia, the only figure of international stature within the non-aligned movement was Fidel Castro — and the United States was acting against him. It is appropriate that President Saddam Hussein should have become the major Arab figure in the non-aligned movement. The Arab role required within the movement now is different from that of the 1960s. At that time it was a political role because independence and liberation from imperialism were the burning issues. But now that most African, Asian and Latin American peoples are politically independent, the next step will have to be economic independence.

There are three factors that make President Saddam Hussein the most suitable Arab candidate to play this role within the non-aligned movement. In the first place, he is ensuring internal stability so that the development process can be smooth and efficient. In the second place, he has established once and for all his independence of international influences on the decision-making process. By the same token, he has strengthened his relations with the countries of the Third World without interference in their internal affairs. He has liaised with the rulers of these states and not with opposition groups. It is worth recalling here that his stand on the Soviet intervention in Afghanistan was not an easy one to adopt — it could only have been taken given maximum independence in Iraq's relations with the Soviet Union. President Saddam Hussein saw this as a perfectly natural stand within the framework of the treaty of friendship and co-operation Iraq had with the Soviets. It was, however, in contradiction to the Soviet view. In the third place, the Arab leader within the non-aligned movement must have a powerful economic base. Iraq's strong economy is one of President Saddam's major strengths.

This is why so many Third World leaders visit Iraq: they can have both political support and economic assistance. And Iraq does not extend only economic assistance, it also extends expertise, which it is by now in a good position to supply. Many of the non-aligned leaders who visited Iraq felt that they could benefit from its socialist experience. Some wanted to apply Iraq's literacy campaign on its Popular Army model. They were also interested in the idea of building a socialist society while keeping the possibility of capitalism through a careful balance between the public sector and the private sector. President Samora Machel, for example, was particularly struck by this and felt it could solve a number of problems in his country.

Reference has already been made to the flexible tactics adopted by President Saddam Hussein to ensure the success of both the Baghdad Summit and the National Charter. President Saddam adopted the same flexibile approach at the Non-Aligned Summit in Havana in order to counteract the Camp David accords. The Yugoslav delegation, for example, had not wanted to antagonise President Sadat. But President Saddam was able to change the Yugoslav stand. He was also able to block certain African states in their attempt to prevent the condemnation of Sadat's regime. The results of these efforts were apparent at the meeting between President Saddam and the Mali President Moussa Traoré. President Saddam explained to the African leaders:

> The sanctions are not aimed at Egypt, its history and its people; you know full well that every Arab cherishes Egypt, its people and its struggle. The sanctions are aimed against the actions which harm the Arab nation and the Arab struggle. Sadat is not just committing suicide — he is exposing others to danger as well, the Palestinians, the Syrians, the Jordanians and every Arab in the Arab nation.

President Saddam Hussein acted as though there were no differences between him and President Hafez Assad so as not to affect the results of the conference. The two Presidents met several times and participated in drawing up drafts and resolutions, to the surprise of those attending the conference. Some delegates even asked President Saddam how he managed to act naturally with someone he had accused of involvement in a plot to overthrow him. He replied, 'We are at a foreign conference and we have certain matters to resolve. If we do not co-operate we will not achieve the results we want.'

By the time the forthcoming Non-Aligned Summit is held in Baghdad in 1982, most of the non-aligned leaders will have visited Iraq and it will have opened embassies in most African and Latin American states. It is clear that the 1982 Summit will be concerned with the issue of economic independence for the Third World. President Saddam is directly supervising studies of the economic question. The forthcoming Summit may well finalise the economic principles proposed by President Saddam at the Havana Summit, when he suggested the establishment of a long-term aid fund to protect developing countries from the effects of inflation. According to this proposal, the industrialised developed countries, irrespective of their political and economic systems, would contribute an annual amount equivalent to the inflation they export to the developing nations. The oil-producing developing nations would also contribute to the fund. When he proposed the idea of the fund at the Havana Summit, President Saddam said, 'It would, if applied, solve one of the basic problems in relations between the economies of the developing countries and the economies of the industrialised developed countries, and would be a corner-stone of the new international economic order.'

President Saddam Hussein outlined the bases for discussions at the forthcoming Non-Aligned Summit during a series of meetings he held with the visiting President of the Seychelles, France Albert René. He suggested the following points for discussion:

First: it is essential to develop economic, political, cultural and technological ties between the countries of the non-aligned movement. This will enable them to play an effective role in ensuring world peace and stability and the freedom and dignity of peoples everywhere.

Second: independence is no longer simply a matter of will. One must now ensure independence through economic, scientific and technological factors which are irrevocably linked.

Third: so long as the countries of the non-aligned movement do not set up effective economic, technological, cultural and political ties they will continue to lack a measure of independence. The gap between them and the rich developed countries will remain in the fields of science and technology, and will continue to affect the independence of the countries of the Third World.

President Saddam Hussein is also planning to tackle the question of the cracks in the non-aligned front which have deepened over the past ten years. As he sees it, a number of countries have turned to Marxism or have fallen under the influence of Communist countries in order to protect themselves against increasing American pressure on their progressive systems of government. Far from providing the kind of counter-balance they seek, this weakens their national will and restricts their freedom of choice. Similarly, some non-aligned countries seeking to protect themselves against Communist intervention have turned to the West.

President Saddam's solution to the divisions and weaknesses within the non-aligned movement would take the form of a charter similar to the National Charter he proposed on 8 February 1980. The charter would also convince those Arab states which have become disillusioned with the United States that they can find international guarantees by joining the non-aligned movement. This would have been impossible before the Camp David deal. Afterwards, however, those Arab countries which had rejected all criticism of their relations with the United States began to express reservations about the American stand. This new situation bodes well for the non-aligned movement. President Saddam would be very happy to set up strong links with these states and to extend aid if only they would definitively reject the idea of having foreign bases on their soil. One example is Somalia: President Saddam rejected the arguments of the Somali President Muhammad Siad Barre for granting the United States military facilities because of the dangers faced by Somalia. President Saddam pointed out that Iraq had fought Iran in 1973, although it was one of the strongest members of the CENTO alliance, without giving military facilities to anyone.

At every opportunity, President Saddam reiterates Iraq's stand on the Arabs and on the Palestinian cause. One of his most famous statements in this respect is: 'We in Iraq are willing to place our neck under the feet of the Arabs if it will serve the cause, but we will never allow foreign feet to tread on a single toe.' Anyone following the speeches and statements of President Saddam will have noted that these feelings are being expressed more and more strongly. This was particularly the case when Iraqi-Iranian relations deteriorated (*see* chapter 4).

President Saddam makes every effort to clarify Iraq's stand on the United States during his talks with Arab officials. He does not subscribe to the view that America does not know where its real interests lie and does not realise the serious effect that its unlimited support for Israel is having on its interests. He believes that not only is America fully aware of where its interests lie but Israel is America's weapon to prevent the Arabs' full liberation and eventual unity. This is why America works to strengthen the Zionist entity. The flexible approach adopted by President Saddam in his National Declaration of 8 February 1980 has so far not extended to Iraqi-American relations. The Indian embassy continues to handle American interests in Iraq. Nevertheless, although diplomatic links remain broken, Iraq has adopted an objective approach to economic relations.

A number of attempts have been made to convince Iraq to restore relations with the United States, but the mediators have failed in their quest. How long can diplomatic relations between Iraq and the United States remain broken off? They will remain broken if we base our analysis on the statements made by Saddam Hussein as Vice-President. However, a new situation may arise now that he is President, although there has been no indication of flexibility so far. Indeed, President Saddam Hussein summed up his views on relations with America in his speech to the delegates attending the Arab People's National Conference held in Baghdad to discuss the National Declaration:

> There have been attempts over the past five years to convince us to renew diplomatic ties with the United States but we have rejected these. We refuse, not because we are afraid of anyone, but out of our love for the Arab people and for the principles we have adopted. We have no diplomatic relations with the Americans —we consider them to be enemies of the Arab nation and enemies of Iraq, and we have been acting on this basis for the past twelve years. We will repeat these words at every opportunity.

He went on to outline the basis for resuming relations:

> We will not shed tears and we will not plead with the Americans to send their representatives as others do. So long as the United States is occupying our lands through the Zionist entity we will continue to look upon it as an enemy of the Arabs. Israel occupies Palestine thanks to the strength of the United States.

The American stand on Israel is not the only reason for the strained relations. Iraq is also unhappy with the methods used by the American Administration, and the continuous American attempts to destroy the 'Bakr-Saddam' tandem in order to impose the American line. Iraq finds it difficult to forget the American press campaigns against every Iraqi move, the American involvement in coup attempts, and the massive American armament of the Shah in order to restrict Iraq's role. The Americans also hint from time to time that the regime in Iraq is weak and needs someone to protect it; after Saddam Hussein took over power, American officials even said that there were Cuban soldiers in Iraq.

At the beginning, President Saddam Hussein's replies were cool and calm. For example, in a speech he made while on a visit to Najaf (the main centre of the Shia sect, 150 kilometres from Baghdad) on 17 October 1979, three months after he had taken over power, he declared,

> The sons of Iraq are sovereign over their land. Only they and the sons of the Arab nation have any place here. Iraq will fight tyranny wherever it is following in the path of Imam Ali, God rest his soul, and Sayyed Hussein, and Khalid bin al-Walid, and Salaheddin al-Ayoubi, and all the Muslim leaders who have passed over these Arab lands — and it will be victorious.

But a week later he said, before a massive audience,

> Iraq is a lake of oil: this is the reason for the United States' hatred and for the greed with which the great powers look at Iraq.

There is a possibility of a change in President Saddam's view of the United States and a resumption of diplomatic relations for three reasons. In the first place, the Baghdad Summit and the National Charter both revealed a new flexible approach; it is possible that this same flexibility may lead to a kind of normalisation of relations with the United States. Secondly, the continued break in diplomatic ties between Iraq and the United States will eventually reflect the same sort of situation brought about by the Kingdom of Saudi Arabia's refusal to recognise the Soviet Union or to set up diplomatic ties with it. Thirdly, the philosophy behind President Saddam's planning for the Baghdad Summit and the National Charter can be summed up in his words, 'There may be a break in the clouds over our relationship with some of the rightist and reactionary states, but this should not prevent us from being on the alert for thunderstorms, hail and snow . . .' Although these words were said about Arab states, they indicate a willingness to be flexible. There might well have been some improvement in Iraqi-US relations earlier had not the American secret services been involved in the plot against Saddam Hussein when he became President. President Saddam could well review relations with the United States if he scores a victory over the Americans. This might have happened, for example, if the Baghdad Summit had issued resolutions condemning the United States, as Saddam Hussein had wanted. The conference results were nevertheless a major achievement, given America's concern about its interests and allies.

What strengthens Iraq in this respect is the unusual approach it has adopted to balance its relations with the superpowers. Although it has broken off relations with the United States, it has not fallen within the Soviet sphere. Instead it has opened the way to a number of European countries which had been working for years to strengthen their ties with Iraq. France comes at the top of the list (indeed, French is to be taught as the first foreign language at Iraqi schools as of 1981, whereas it had previously been taught at university level only), followed by Italy and West Germany. Some types of French armaments are being developed to suit Iraq's particular needs; Iraq imports many of its weapons from France. There is also a possibility that France, in co-operation with some European countries, will help Iraq obtain nuclear arms by the end of the 1980s.

Although diplomatic relations exist between Iraq and Great Britain, they are lukewarm at present. The British would like to improve them but President Saddam thinks that this will only be possible when Britain is no longer 'in the American line politically', and when the British stop 'behaving the way they used to in the past, taking stands that do not reflect developments in Iraq since the 17 July 1968 Revolution, and when they finally erase their image of Iraq as one of the jewels in the British crown'.

Just as there are difficulties in Iraqi-American relations, so there are difficulties in keeping Iraqi-Soviet relations on a firm footing. However, Iraqi-Soviet relations can be maintained at their present level because they were established after the 17 July 1968 Revolution and with the present Soviet leadership. Abdel-Nasser, on the other hand, faced many problems because he first set up ties with the Soviets under Khrushchev, only to find himself dealing with the Soviets of Brezhnev; this required a different approach, which led him to revise relations in his turn. Moreover, Saddam Hussein himself has handled relations with the Soviets from the very beginning. He has thus avoided the problems faced by Abdel-Nasser when there were a number of power centres in Egypt and the Soviets dealt with Abdel-Nasser through the power centre favoured by them. Saddam Hussein is personally responsible for relations with the Soviets to this day. Saddam Hussein has always avoided playing off the two superpowers against each other. He has not used a strain in relations with the United States to get his demands met by the Soviet Union, nor has he developed his relations with the Soviet Union to persuade America to review its position. The Soviets, for their part, were not satisfied with this level of relations and tried to intervene in one way or another. They used certain Eastern states in an effort to change conditions in Iraq to suit them. Iraq's response was severe, and no less so because it was unannounced.

Although relations between Iraq and the United States have been broken off, the relations between Iraq and the Soviet Union are still reasonably good and a treaty of friendship and co-operation continues to link the two countries. But Iraq treats both superpowers with equal caution. President Saddam will never forget that the Soviet Union tried to arm the Iraqi Communist Party and to infiltrate the Iraqi Army. When this attempt was discovered and crushed, the Soviets were very upset and used their foreign allies to act against Iraq with equal violence. The Soviets remain unconvinced that a state can adopt an independent approach without this being considered an alignment with one side or another. President Saddam has decided to live with the Soviets' conviction, in the hope that one day they will come to understand the nature of Iraq's independence, and will stop insisting that the Iraqi Communist Party should be allowed a free hand as a condition for better relations between the two countries. At the same time, President Saddam's statements indicate that there is no special warmth in relations with the Soviets. On one occasion, for example, when the President visited the town of Balad, some fifty kilometres north of Baghdad, he told the people about an incident in Iraqi-Soviet relations. In 1969 Iraq was in bad financial straits and a member of the Revolution Command Council was sent to tour foreign states to try to raise a loan to see them through their difficulties; he returned with five million dollars. President Saddam went on:

> In the winter of 1970 we had to repay the friendly country a loan they had made to us. I headed a delegation to this country to request them to postpone repayment of the loan, which was seventeen million dinars, from 1970 to 1971. They refused. In 1975 the ambassador of this friendly country came to me and requested postponement of the repayment of an Iraqi loan of over two hundred million dinars; we accepted out of respect for our friendship.

President Saddam Hussein did not name the country in question, although it was the Soviet Union, possibly because he thought it impolite to do so, or because he did not want his listeners to come to hate the Soviet Union because of its refusal to stand by Iraq at a difficult time. It is worth noting that he used the words 'came to me', which confirms that he personally directs relations with the Soviets, as well as those with Europe and Africa.

On another occasion, he said in the speech he delivered on the fifty-ninth anniversary of the founding of the Iraqi Army,

> The foreign intervention in Afghanistan is a dangerous development, for which no excuses or explanations may be found. It is wrong and inexcusable and a source of worry for all freedom-loving peoples who struggle to ensure their sovereignty and free will. We reiterate these principles and our firm and unshaken belief in them. We warn against exploitation of the foreign inter-

> vention in Afghanistan to excuse other foreign intervention in the region. We will stand with all our power against any attempt to make this region an arena for superpower conflict, whereby they realise their ambitions and their strategic plans at the expense of the independence, sovereignty and security of the countries of this region.

He did not name the Soviet Union in this instance either, saying simply, 'the foreign intervention in Afghanistan'. His description of the intervention as a 'wrong and inexcusable' act was more than the Soviet leadership could accept. The choice of occasion, the fifty-ninth anniversary of the founding of the Iraqi Army, was significant, as most of its weapons are Soviet-made.

The fact that President Saddam did not mention the Soviet Union by name in either instance does not mean that the Iraqi leadership is afraid to call a spade a spade. The document presented by the Party to the Arab People's National Conference underlined its condemnation of the Soviet role in Afghanistan. On another front, the Iraqi newspaper *Al-Thawra* wrote bluntly about the limits of Soviet expertise in its edition of 3 January 1980: 'It is obvious that the Soviet Union is unable and unqualified to meet all the Arabs' development requirements, even the requirements of those prepared to pay in hard currency.' The Soviet Union rejects this analysis, on the basis that it can meet all the needs of development along Marxist lines. President Castro's experience, however, does not appear particularly encouraging.

Before Saddam Hussein became President, the Soviet Union tried to change its relations with Iraq by using Bulgaria as a destabilising base. Bulgaria played this role even though it stood to lose a great deal in the fields of commerce and tourism; hundreds of Iraqi tourists used to visit its shores, especially Varna, bringing in much-needed hard currency with them. Iraqi-Bulgarian relations remained tense until some Iraqi Communists in Bulgaria killed a Baathist student. This happened after Saddam Hussein became President, and he used it as an opportunity to restore normal relations. To begin with, he decided on harsh diplomatic measures in response to the crime. Bulgaria hastened to send its Deputy Prime Minister, then its Foreign Minister, and finally its First Deputy President, but President Saddam decided to end the coolness in relations only when the head of state Theodor Zhivkov visited Baghdad on 28 May 1980. A joint communiqué was then issued in the spirit of the Baghdad Summit and the National Charter. It set such firm foundations for relations that Zhivkov described them as the 'best relations between Bulgaria and an Arab state'.

Saddam Hussein was vice president of the Republic during his first visit to Yugoslavia (1976). The solid relationship which linked him there with the doyen of the historical heads of the non-alignment movement bore fruit, during the non-alignment summit (Havana 1979), which the two heads of state brought to a successful conclusion.

Saddam Hussein's visit to Moscow the following year (30 January to 3 February 1977). Relations between the two countries took into account the particularities of the Iraqi leadership and its ambitions.

These photos show the different stages of the negotiations which do not appear to have always been easy (as is shown by the gestures and expressions of Brezhnev and Saddam Hussein).

The Cuban President Fidel Castro was among those who gave Saddam Hussein (while he was still only vice president) the importance owed to a future head of state. This was clearly apparent during the Iraqi Vice President's first visit to Cuba (14-19 December 1978), then again during the Havana non-alignment summit when Saddam Hussein had become President.

Saddam Hussein (then vice president) with the Syrian president Hafez al Assad.

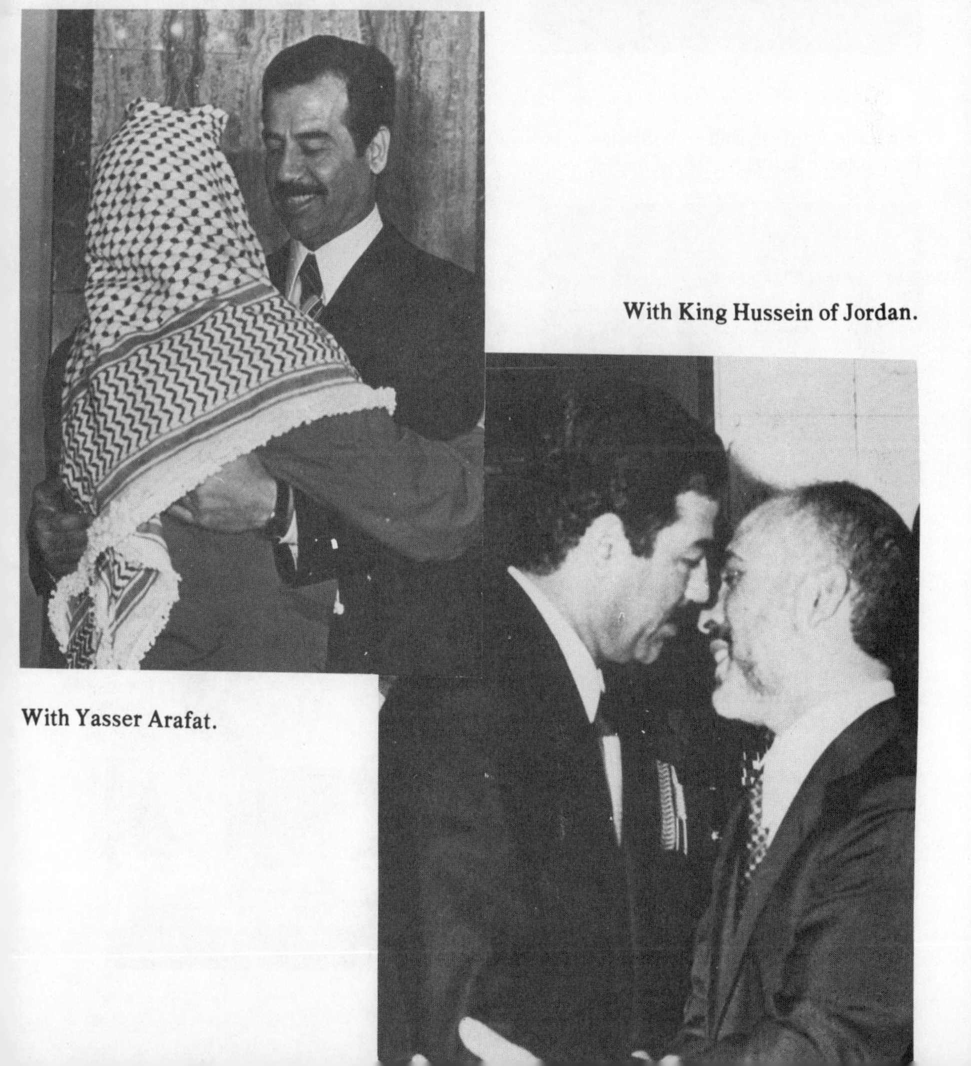

With King Hussein of Jordan.

With Yasser Arafat.

With the late Algerian president Houari Boumedienne.

and with the present Algerian president Chadli Bendjadid

With the emir of Bahrain, Sheikh Issa Ben Salman Al Khalifa.

The only meeting with the Iranian revolution took place when Ibrahim Yazdi, the Iranian Minister of Foreign Affairs, visited him at his residence during the non-aligned summit of 1979.

With the Pakistani President Dia Al Haq

With Suleiman Demirel during a visit to Turkey in 1977.

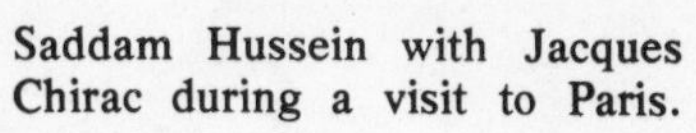

Saddam Hussein with Jacques Chirac during a visit to Paris.

and with Raymond Barre in Baghdad.

President Saddam Hussein praying in the holy places of Najaf.

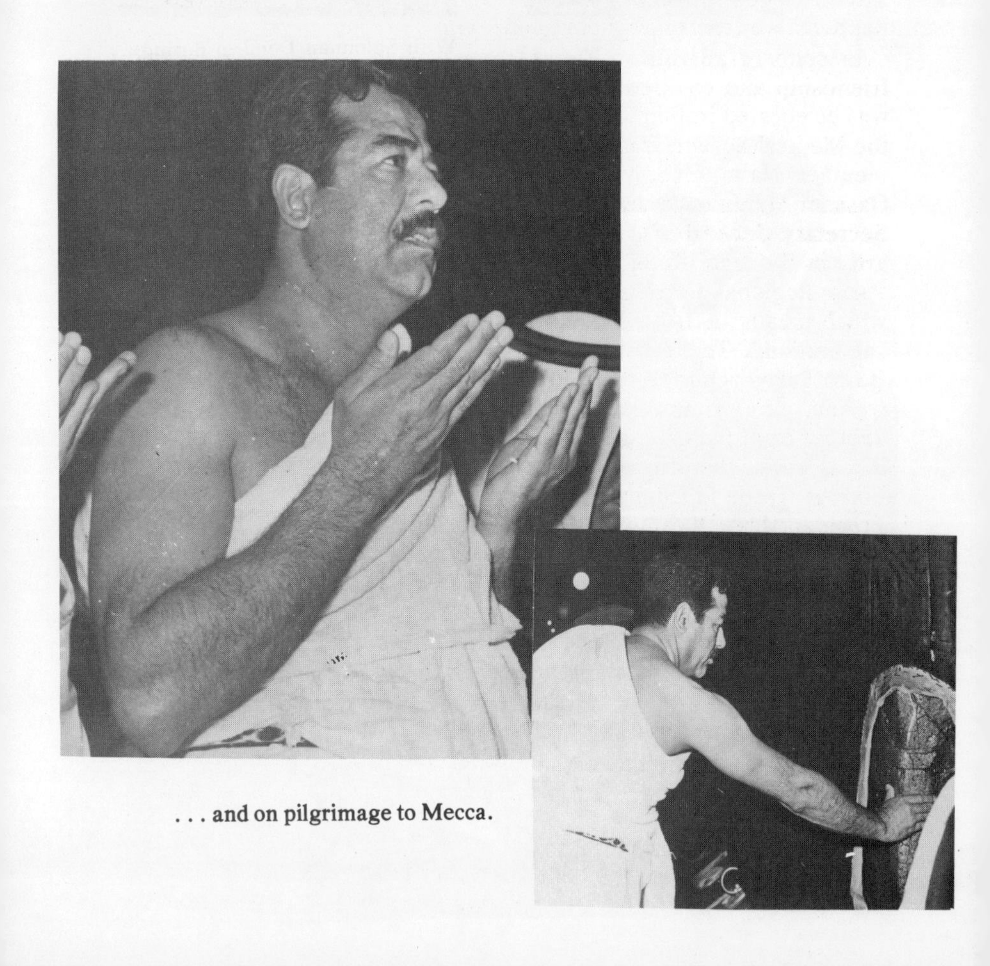

. . . and on pilgrimage to Mecca.

Saddam Hussein's assumption of full responsibility would have been a suitable occasion for the Soviets to send one of the high-ranking officials at the Kremlin to congratulate President Saddam but they did not avail themselves of the opportunity. Nor did President Saddam find it necessary to send any of Iraq's top officials to Moscow for talks, although his deputy Izzat Ibrahim went to Prague in May 1980 and Tareq Aziz visited Yugoslavia. The warm reception given to the Iraqi officials in Prague and Belgrade was an indication of the importance Czechoslovakia and Yugoslavia attach to relations with Iraq, and both countries welcome President Saddam's leadership. Relations between Iraq and the Soviet Union deteriorated following the discovery of Communist cells within the Iraqi Armed Forces. Following the execution of the members of this organisation, Saddam Hussein said in a press conference on 18 July 1978: 'We are not the kind of country that becomes an American satellite when it is angry with the Soviet Union, or a Soviet satellite when it is angry with the United States. Whenever this happens, we remain Iraqi pure and simple.'

In spite of all this, the eighth anniversary of the treaty of friendship and co-operation between Iraq and the Soviet Union was celebrated in Baghdad on 13 April 1980, at the Bakr Hall in the Medical School. Iraq was represented by National Command member Naim Haddad, Regional Command member Jaafar Oassem Hammoudi and Aziz Sharif (a non-Baathist), who is Secretary-General of the National Council for Peace and Solidarity in the Iraqi Republic. The speech was delivered by Baath Party Regional Command member Abdel-Fattah Muhammad, which means that the Baath Party participated officially in the celebrations. The following day *Al-Thawra*, the organ of the Baath Party, reported the celebrations in a small front-page item without any commentary. But perhaps the juxtaposition of another front-page item, equally small, was commentary enough: it was about the official visit paid by the Chinese Minister for Foreign Trade Li Chaing to Revolution Command Council Vice-President Izzat Ibrahim that same morning. Izzat Ibrahim told the visiting Chinese official, 'Relations between Iraq and China are progressing along exemplary lines, and they must be strengthened to cover new fields serving the Arab nation's struggle.' It cannot have been coincidence that the Chinese official was given the appointment on the day of the Iraqi-Soviet treaty anniversary. The celebrations were in no way special, although they were the first after Saddam Hussein had become President. The Kremlin did not send a top-ranking official to represent it at the celebrations, and was simply represented by the Soviet ambassador. The ambassador had, in any case, not once been received by President Saddam since he assumed power.

At that time the new Iraqi ambassador to Moscow, Abdel-Rahman Ahmad al-Dawri, chosen by President Saddam, was preparing to present his credentials. The Iraqi embassy in Moscow had been without an ambassador for nine months — the last ambassador, Mortada Said Abdel-Baqi, had been among those who took part in the plot against the Baathist leadership in 1979. The choice of al-Dawri appears to have been carefully made; he is a trusted Party member and a former military man. On 28 April 1980 he presented his credentials to Vasily Kuznetsov, the First Deputy President of the Higher Soviet Council. He conveyed President Saddam Hussein's greetings to Brezhnev and referred to the 'development of friendly relations between the two countries in line with the bilateral treaty of friendship and co-operation based on mutual interests and mutual respect of sovereignty and non-interference in internal affairs'. The Iraqi ambassador was clearly reminding the Soviets of the first article of the treaty which provided for 'respect of independence and sovereignty and non-interference in internal affairs'. But Kuznetsov overlooked this and spoke instead of the friendly relations the two countries enjoyed and 'the Soviet Union's concern to develop wide-ranging and fruitful relations with Iraq in all fields. It will continue to develop good relations with Iraq.'

Iraq is geographically the closest Arab country to the Soviet Union. The good relations which the Soviet Union has with the Kurds on the one hand, and its support of the Communists in Iraq on the other, have made relations between Iraq and the Soviet Union less cordial than they should be. They will not improve as long as the Soviet Union behaves like a superpower, refusing to accept any comments on its policies by its friends and preferring to shape its relations with Iraq along the lines of its relations with the East European states. Nor will they improve as long as it does not believe in the right of others, such as Saddam Hussein, to try to create an Arab national force that can play a role far removed from the arena of superpower conflicts.

While one can understand the Soviet Union's discomfort at President Saddam's balanced policy towards the two superpowers, it is sad that this should be reflected in Iraq's relations with one of the Palestinian groups, the Popular Front for the Liberation of Palestine (PFLP). The PFLP objected strongly because Iraq did not distinguish between the friend, the Soviet Union, and the enemy, the United States. How, asked the PFLP, could Iraq have stood out against the Soviet Union's intervention in Afghanistan? At the April 1980 meeting of the Steadfastness and Confrontation Front in Tripoli, the PFLP Secretary-General George Habash declared, 'The Popular Front can no longer accept the current line of Iraqi policy.' He was objecting to President Saddam's 8 February 1980 proposal of a National Charter, and Iraq considered this to be tantamount to the announcement of a break in relations. Subsequently relations between the PFLP and Iraq deteriorated, although they had been extremely close and, of all the Palestinian resistance groups, the PFLP had enjoyed the most support from Iraq, in spite of he PFLP's Marxist line. At the same time, the PFLP's relations with Syria blossomed, although Syrian-Iraqi relations were characterised by extreme caution. The PFLP offices in Iraq were closed. At this time, the Algerian President Chadli Ben Jedid, one of the principal members of the Steadfastness and Confrontation Front, met the Iraqi ambassador to Algiers. He said, according to news agency reports of the 24 April 1980 meeting, 'The National Charter proposed by President Saddam Hussein can play a part in unifying the Arabs and in preventing foreigners from interfering in their affairs.'

In breaking with Iraq, the PFLP may well have relied on the support it enjoyed from South Yemen, under the leadership of Abdel-Fattah Ismail, and South Yemen's close ties with the Soviet Union. What happened, however, was that Abdel-Fattah Ismail was overthrown and Ali Nasser Muhammad came to power. President Saddam had certainly not expected South Yemen to send a delegate to him on 21 April 1980 to explain why Abdel-Fattah Ismail had 'resigned'. The Iraqi media reported the visit in an ordinary manner in spite of the strained relations between Iraq and South Yemen. The next day, President Saddam Hussein took the initiative and sent a cable of congratulations to Ali Nasser Muhammad, who had become Secretary-General of the Socialist Party Central Committee and President of the Higher People's Council. The cable read:

> I wish to express, in the name of the people and Government of Iraq, and in my name personally, our congratulations and our good wishes, hoping that brotherly Popular Democratic Yemen will enjoy every success. Our best wishes and hopes for your health and happiness and for the prosperity of the Arab people in Democratic Yemen.

The cable showed that Iraq was not unhappy with the changes in South Yemen and the removal of Abdel-Fattah Ismail. Abdel-Fattah Ismail had strengthened his country's ties with the

Soviet Union at the expense of those with the Arab world and had kept his country's relations with Iraq in a state of conflict. Ali Nasser Muhammad, on the other hand, had never adopted an antagonistic position towards Iraq and he was expected to lessen Soviet hegemony over South Yemen. This Soviet influence was one of the reasons why Iraq had backed the South Yemeni opposition groups, whose leaders had visited Iraq and met President Saddam a few days before the fall of Abdel-Fattah Ismail.

The PFLP could not understand why this basic change had taken place in South Yemen, its 'strategic depth'. The same day that the PFLP offices were closed in Iraq, 24 April 1980, Ali Nasser Muhammad replied to the Iraqi cable of congratulations and expressed his 'wishes for your health and happiness, and all progress and prosperity for the brotherly Iraqi people, and every victory for our Arab nation in its struggle against imperialism and Zionism and their lackeys'. When it loosened its ties with Iraq, the PFLP could not have imagined that Abdel-Fattah Ismail would be swept away so easily by Ali Nasser Muhammad or that Ali Nasser Muhammad would agree with Iraq's stands on the Iranian revolution and the Afghan struggle (both these stands were criticised by the PFLP). Nor could the PFLP have imagined that South Yemen would be persuaded to support Saudi Arabia and the other conservative states which the PFLP considered were 'reactionary' and belonged in the same category as imperialism and Zionism. In brief, the PFLP could not have imagined that Ali Nasser Muhammad's leadership would abide by the spirit of the Baghdad Summit and the National Charter proposed by President Saddam on 8 February 1980. The PFLP had criticised the Charter because it dealt with both the Soviet Union and the United States in the same way, whereas the PFLP supported the Soviets even in their foreign interventions, including that in Afghanistan.

On the whole, however, Iraqi-Palestinian relations are good. It now looks as though President Saddam Hussein is of the opinion that dealings with the various Palestinian organisations must be within the framework of the Palestine Liberation Organisation and the Arab Liberation Front; he has come to this view as a result of his experience in leadership during the years since the Revolution of 17 July 1968. Iraq's share of the financial aid granted by the Arabs to the Palestine Liberation Organisation is paid regularly and on time. Urgent military needs are also met within a clear-cut strategy for Palestinian military resistance. On 21 May 1980 President Saddam Hussein surprised the Palestinians living in Iraq with a Revolution Command

Council decree allocating a sum of one hundred dinars as a housing allowance for every Palestinian working in government offices or the socialist sector. The Council also allocated twenty dinars to those Palestinians who did not hold a university degree. This decision was taken following similar grants made to Iraqi citizens, and is to be followed by further grants. President Saddam took into consideration how the Palestinians would feel were they to see the Iraqis getting all the benefits of the Revolution while they received nothing.

The Palestinian cause is at the core of President Saddam's words and actions. The Party founder Michel Aflaq told Mozambique's President Samora Machel on 12 December 1979, 'The Palestinian cause is the cause of this age, and it is the standard by which we measure the Revolution in our Party . . .' But President Saddam went much further. He told the ninth Iraqi Women's General Association meeting on 12 March 1980, 'Every stone laid in Iraq, every Iraqi training to use weapons, every scientist studying how to lay strong and firm foundations for Iraq — all these have as their central aim the liberation of Palestine. If Palestine is liberated, Arabs everywhere will be free.' During the Baghdad Summit there were worries that the Iraqi-Palestinian stands would clash because of the assassinations in Arab and Western capitals, but Saddam Hussein refused to broach this subject, and the Iraqi and Palestinian delegations acted together to ensure the success of the conference. Those who had hoped for a split, and even encouraged it, were disappointed by the excellent relations between the two delegations. President Saddam focuses on his Arab duty in every speech he makes and at every conference. Among his most quoted statements are: 'The 17 July Revolution is not only for Iraq but for all the Arabs' and 'We in Iraq are willing to place our neck under the feet of the Arabs if it will serve the cause, but we will never allow foreign feet to tread on a single toe.' The President does not promise moral assistance alone: 'All our principles must be directed towards the Arab cause; all our efforts, our blood, our wealth are for the Arabs, and for all humanity whenever it needs us.'

The Baghdad Summit was a milestone in the history of the Arab nation. In view of his success in unifying contradictory Arab stands at this Summit, President Saddam is drawing up similar plans for the Non-Aligned Summit to be held in Baghdad in 1982, so that it may serve as a milestone for the non-aligned world. Iraq has fulfilled its commitments according to the political and economic solutions proposed by President Saddam at the Havana Summit. According to *Al-Thawra* on 22 May 1980, Iraq paid a quarter of a billion dollars during the second half of 1979 to compensate developing countries for the rise in the price of oil. It paid hundreds of millions of dollars in aid to African, Asian and Latin American countries over and above its financial aid commitments to these countries for 1980. *Al-Thawra* described these commitments as the 'burden of duty carried by Iraq'.

Thanks to the visits to Iraq by a number of non-aligned leaders and the talks held during these visits, the Non-Aligned Summit will doubtless be as successful as President Saddam hopes. The success will not be restricted to pumping new blood into the non-aligned organisations. Its importance will be in the birth of an 'international mentor'. Marshal Tito played the role, although not fully because his strength was moral rather than material and derived from his historic rebellion against the Soviet Union. But Saddam Hussein derives strength from a number of sources: his country occupies a strategic position; he is a strong economic power; he adopts an independent line without having to rebel against anyone; and he has clear-cut and long-term views on the energy question. President Saddam sees this last question as having been the basis of international conflict since the early 1970s, and he intends to reach a solution of it through the proposals he made at the Havana Summit. Should the Non-Aligned Summit in Baghdad adopt these proposals, which Iraq is already implementing, then Saddam Hussein will become the 'international mentor'. President Saddam proposed that the energy question be discussed comprehensively within the framework of the North-South dialogue at the United Nations because it is one of many major economic questions, although not the only one. His proposal noted also:

> The question of energy should not be looked at separately as a matter concerning exporting countries. It should be looked at within the framework of how the industrialised consumer countries need to organise their consumption and diversify their sources of energy to meet their needs. They must calculate their needs on the basis of a comprehensive view of humanity's needs, not on the basis of getting what they want irrespective of the world's energy needs and the dangers of uncontrolled consumption.

The increased support of non-aligned nations for these proposals and for the proposed Charter will be an important factor at the forthcoming Non-Aligned Summit and will strengthen Iraq's stand. At the same time it is unacceptable to the superpowers and they will doubtless try to prevent it, since they both have an interest in preventing Iraq from moving outside the sphere they have allotted to it. As already noted, President Saddam is well aware of this and he will wait for an auspicious moment before he attempts to break through this barrier. It is a dangerous situation, and one which calls for caution. Thus every step before the Non-Aligned Summit in 1982 will be characterised by two things: Saddam Hussein's increasing strength, and the superpowers' increasing need to stop him becoming the 'international mentor' after the Summit.

CHAPTER 4

A DIFFICULT COEXISTENCE . . . AND A CERTAIN WAR

'The Arabs, though few in number, are many in Islam and strong in unity. Your role is to polarise the Arabs and to marshal their forces. Send them into battle but do not go yourself. If you leave this land, the Arabs will rise against you from all sides and you will find that the problems you leave behind will be worse than those you would face abroad.

'Should the Persians look at you tomorrow, they would say, "Here is the heart of the Arabs; if we pluck it out we will have nothing more to fear." This will make them redouble their fury and their determination in their attacks against you. As for what you have said about nations marching to wage war on the Muslims, the Almighty would no more want them to do so than you would, and He is more capable of changing what He does not wish to happen. As for what you say about their numbers, we have never in the past relied on numbers but have fought from the conviction of victory and divine assistance.'

(Imam Ali bin Abi Taleb, upon being asked for advice by Omar ibn al-Khattab on whether to go to fight the Persians in person)

On 1 April 1980 thousands of university students and officials were milling about in Mustansiriyah University, which lies on the outskirts of Baghdad. Several Arab and foreign guests were amongst them, having come to participate in the 'World Economic Meeting' organised by the National Union of Iraqi Students in co-operation with the Asian Students Union. The meeting was to be inaugurated by Vice-Premier and Revolution Command Council member Tareq Aziz. The Iraqi student union leader was introducing Tareq Aziz to some guests when a bomb was hurled at the Vice-Premier. The student union leader saw it and cried out a warning. Tareq Aziz threw himself to the ground as far as possible from the bomb, putting into practice what he had learnt during his military service. He escaped with a few minor injuries, but his guard was severely injured and dozens of people were wounded. He was in a state of shock when he was taken to hospital. Ambulances hurried to the university to carry away the wounded, while officials went to collect Tareq Aziz's speech from his office so that Revolution Command Council member Hikmat Ibrahim could deliver it. Security officers caught the youth who had thrown the bomb. He had also thrown a second bomb which injured several more people. On checking his identity papers, it was discovered that his name was Samir Mir Ghulam and that he was a naturalised Iraqi of Iranian origin.

President Saddam was outside Baghdad when the incident occurred. By coincidence he was visiting Soueirah Province, part of the Wasit Governorate. A number of naturalised Iranians live in this province, which is so close to the Iraqi border with Iran that one can see the top of Iranian mountains from it. It is also an area where there is a lot of Communist activity. President Saddam's speech to the people of Soueirah contained, ironically enough, a well-meaning warning:

> We say to the great powers who are enemies of Iraq, and we say to the smaller states who are also enemies of Iraq, and we speak to you all: Iraq does not wish to be anyone's enemy unless that state wants to be the enemy of Iraq. If such states imagine that they can attack the sovereignty and honour of our people or of Iraq, then we will act accordingly. We do not wish to be the enemy of any state in this world, but we are ready for whoever wishes to fight against us. We say to everyone who wants to be Iraq's enemy and the Arab nation's enemy that we will be as pointed spears, ever ready to fight with the aggressor.

The tone of this speech indicated that President Saddam's visit to Soueirah was not as much of a coincidence as it might have seemed, and was not simply one of the routine visits he pays to various parts of Iraq. He intended to say what he said, as close as possible to Iran and in an area inhabited by a number of naturalised Iranians, whom Iran was planning to use against Iraq.

The World Economic Meeting was opened as scheduled at Mustansiriyah University and the bomb attack was reported on the radio. After returning from Soueirah, President Saddam gave instructions for flowers to be sent to all those who had been injured in the attack. Later that day he went to visit them in person. The following day, he went to Mustansiriyah University, to the spot where the attack had taken place. He addressed thousands of students under the pouring rain, and it was clear from his tone that the speech was a pledge to avenge the deaths. He declared,

> Yesterday precious drops of blood were shed by the young men and women of Mustansiriyah — the cause was a contemptible lackey called Samir Mir Ghulam. He and his masters thought they could achieve something great. But we say to them, and to all those foreign imperialist forces who think they can overcome this Revolution — let them try. The Iraqi people is now a large and powerful mountain that they cannot shake with all their bombs. By God, the innocent blood that was shed at Mustansiriyah will not go unavenged.

The second attack took place four days later, on 5 April 1980. During the funeral procession for the victims of the first attack a bomb was hurled from an Iranian school. A number of people were killed or wounded. This was a major affront to President Saddam. He had to act quickly to counteract the people's feeling of terror because both attacks had been launched in broad daylight and the perpetrators had not even bothered to hide. Moreover, the first bomb had been aimed at Tareq Aziz, who may have been chosen not only as a member of the Revolution Command Council but also because he was a Christian. President Saddam took two immediate steps. The first was his visit to Mustansiriyah University and his declaration that innocent blood would not go unavenged. The second was his visit to the wounded in hospital, where he was amazed at the high morale of everyone to whom he spoke. Many cried out, 'We will die so that Saddam may live,' and the young women said they would return to take part in the struggle as soon as they had recovered. The President saw that there were many non-Iraqi Arab youths among the wounded and a young Palestinian, which angered him even more. He had the film of his visit broadcast on television to show the young men and women's bravery to the people. The viewers saw him kneel by a wounded woman's bedside because her mattress was on the floor — there had not been enough empty beds at the hospital to handle the number of wounded. Subsequently any of the wounded who needed special treatment were sent abroad.

The Iraqis' spirit was kindled when they saw the film. In the rest of the Arab world, wherever the news item was broadcast, the people were amazed to see how the Iraqi President had managed to transform a tragedy into an occasion for action and to infuse his people with a willingness to tackle anything. An eight-year-old girl was among the wounded. President Saddam's words to her were so moving that the Iraqis wept when they saw this scene on television. President Saddam himself was close to tears when she told him how her new dress had been covered in blood; he immediately gave instructions for another new dress to be presented to her. The little girl was later invited to visit the Presidential Palace, where she was treated like a heroine. After having dealt with the psychological effects that the bomb attacks had had on his people, President Saddam took the necessary security measures. Over 30,000 Iranians living in Iraq were deported to the border with Iran. The two bomb attacks had come after increased activity by the Al-Da'awa Party and the whole question of naturalisation had to be reviewed.

President Saddam did not want the bomb incidents to lessen the importance of the thirty-third anniversary of the Baath Party, as this was the first anniversary following his assumption of full responsibility. He met the Party leadership at the National Headquarters of the Baath Party on 7 April 1980, and it was clear that he had something in mind. This came to light during the Council of Ministers' meeting the following day. President Saddam chaired the meeting, and decided to raise the question of the three Arab islands occupied by Iran — the islands of Greater and Lesser Tumb and Abu Musa. The Iraqi Foreign Minister Dr Saadoun Hammadi then carried a message to the United Nations Secretary-General Dr Kurt Waldheim calling for Iran's immediate withdrawal from the three islands. Arab and Western embassies in Baghdad wrote reports analysing the situation and speculating that Iraq might, given the bomb incidents and the call for the restoration of the islands through diplomatic channels, make a military move against Iran. At the Council of Ministers' meeting President Saddam declared:

> Our people is ready to enter into any battle in defence of its honour and sovereignty and in defence of Arab honour and sovereignty in any part of the Arab world. This is a regime characterised by struggle and a people characterised by struggle, a people whose

> strength has been forged through trials and tribulations. This role is not new to our people because it stands on the path of development; it enacts its natural role, represents its geographic location and delivers its new message in life. Whoever stretches their hand out to our country, we will cut his hand off without hesitation.

The bomb incidents came at a time when Iraq was enjoying security and stability on the home front, with Saddam Hussein as President; the country's importance was growing on the Arab and international levels following the role it had played at the Baghdad Summit, the Non-Aligned Summit in Havana and the Arab Summit at Tunis, and its initiative in proposing the National Charter.

Prior to the two incidents a number of Al-Da'awa Party underground cells and arms caches had been uncovered and dismantled. This is why the security forces felt the bombings indicated that the Party was on its last legs — otherwise Al-Da'awa would have tried to distinguish between civilians and government officials in its attacks. Al-Da'awa had been thrown into disarray by the arrest of its moving force, Ayatollah Muhammad Bakr Sadr. This is why Party members resorted to desperate and useless actions such as the Mustansiriyah University attack. It had taken some time to uncover the Al-Da'awa Party cells. The security operation had been proceeding slowly and ineffectively until the Karbala incident. This took place five months before the Mustansiriyah attack; one person was killed and sixteen wounded when two men opened fire with machine-guns on a religious procession observing the Shia sect's holy day of Ashoura. Thereafter the security forces redoubled their efforts as such attacks could bring about sectarian strife in Iraq. What made it difficult to crack down on Al-Da'awa, in spite of the Iraqi security forces' expertise in this matter, was the fact that their cell structure was organised on vertical lines and the members of one cell did not know the members of another. Al-Da'awa was set up in Iraq after the 1958 Revolution. It is similar to the Muslim Brotherhood in Egypt and other Arab countries in that it rejects the concept of Arab nationalism. The Shah supported Al-Da'awa activities in Iraq, and after the revolution in Iran the Party enjoyed even more support. It established a cell structure and armed its members. It used religion as a pretext on which to hit at the stability and security President Saddam was consolidating in Iraq, and the feeling of unity inspired by his visits to all parts of the country.

The Karbala incident was not the first time the Al-Da'awa members had hurled bombs at Ashoura marchers, but there had been no casualties on previous attempts. The attack on Mustansiriyah University was the first time they had aimed at government officials. Whether or not one accepts the security forces' assessment that the Party was on its last legs, the bomb incident meant that more than security measures were needed to counteract Al-Da'awa ideas. Whoever threw the bomb at the Mustansiriyah crowds must have known that he would be captured or killed, and his readiness for this kind of sacrifice raised a number of issues. The Iraqi authorities had originally decided not to pass many death sentences on captured members of Al-Da'awa, but after the two bombing incidents they went ahead with the executions. Among those executed was Muhammad Bakr Sadr. Although this was not announced at the time, the news of his execution spread in Iraq. Muhammad Bakr Sadr was the second man in the Party and the second man in the spiritual leadership of the Shia sect in Iraq after Ayatollah Ozma Abul Qassem al-Khouti.

Until 8 April 1980 President Saddam's policy had been to warn those acting against Iraq's interests of the dire consequences of their actions. After that, however, he changed his tone and redirected the media's approach to the conflict with Iran. He began to use unprecedented terms in referring to Imam Khomeini, whom he dubbed 'that mummy Khomeini'. He compared him to Begin and Carter in a speech in Mosul on 5 April 1980; and on 25 April, at the Regional Festival of Popular Arab Poetry organised by the Iraqi Ministry of Information, he declared,

> Khomeini is under the illusion that he can occupy the country that gave him hospitality for fourteen years. He can conquer it if he wishes by doing good and with ties of brotherliness, but he cannot extend his racism over one iota of this country's soil. Khomeini knows that he can only cross the Arab Gulf over the dead bodies of Iraqi martyrs.

This change came after Imam Khomeini had begun to attack President Saddam personally and urged the Iraqi people to revolt against him. Imam Khomeini's campaign reached its peak when he declared, in a speech that lasted twenty minutes, 'The Iraqi regime which is attacking Iran is attacking the Quran and Islam; Iran will occupy Iraq and will reach Baghdad.' On 22 April Imam Khomeini revealed that Ayatollah Muhammad Bakr Sadr and his sister 'Bint al-Huda' had been killed and he accused the Iraqi regime. He called on the Iraqi Army to 'leave your barracks and do not suffer this humiliating regime a minute longer; overthrow Saddam Hussein as we did the Shah'. Radio Iran also broadcast fabricated news about Iraq to create confusion; for example, there was an item saying that Iraq had asked the Egyptian Army to send troops to help it fight Iran.

The Iranian Foreign Minister Sadeq Qotbzadeh had previously sent messages to all the Islamic countries asking them to help Iran free Bakr Sadr, declaring, 'Iran is now convinced that the struggle against the regime in Iraq is an indivisible part of the struggle against imperialism.' The Soviet ambassador to Iran asked his Government to stop supplying Iraq with arms because otherwise Soviet relations with Iran would deteriorate.

In his speech at Mosul on 5 April 1980 President Saddam had for the first time defined the conflict with Iran as one between 'the Arabs and the Persians'. Calling Imam Khomeini a 'Shah in a turban', President Saddam went on to say that President Abul Hassan Bani Sadr was 'full of vengeance against Arabism and against the Islam carried by the Arabs to the furthest parts of the world, including the land where Bani Sadr lives at present'. He said he had asked the leaders of the Palestinian resistance what they had received from the Iranian revolution and they had replied, 'By God, we have not received a penny from them, not a bullet or a rifle; they merely repeat time and time again that they have broken off relations with Israel.' During his speech President Saddam also said, 'The Iranian people will find us ready to assist them [if they rid themselves of Imam Khomeini and President Bani Sadr] because it is not a bad thing for us to avoid unfriendly relations with the peoples of Iran, as long as conflict is not called for by our national duty. When it is, we will struggle with all our means. Poor Bani Sadr — he does not know that half our forefathers died on the battlefield.'

In the same speech President Saddam replied to President Bani Sadr's claim that Iraq had sent intermediaries to mediate with Iran. President Saddam said that the former Iranian Foreign Minister Ibrahim Yazidi had visited him at the Havana Summit to request the normalisation of relations between Iran and Iraq. President Saddam had replied that Iraq too wanted normal relations — on condition that Iran returned the three islands, restored the part of the Shatt al-Arab it had taken under the 1975 agreement (signed by Iraq under duress), and ensured the national rights of the Arab people of Arabistan. According to eyewitness accounts of the meeting, President Saddam told the Iranian Foreign Minister,

> I am speaking to you as a brother and I hope you will accept what I have to say. After the revolution you behaved as though you had done the world a favour, especially the Arab world and Iraq. This

> is not logical. Your revolution should have taken place twenty years ago. You are a quarter of a century behind Egypt and several years behind the other Arab revolutions, although the dictatorship and tyranny you suffered in Iran were terrible. After your revolution you should have visited Iraq and Algeria and other countries with revolutionary experience to explain the aims of your revolution so that they could get to know you and stand by you. Every day you are doing things which harm those who should in fact be your allies. I advise you to mend your bridges with others. This will reveal your real enemies and your real allies. I also advise you to stop acting as though your revolution were unique.

President Saddam did not reveal Yazidi's answer, but subsequent events told their own story: Yazidi was removed from his post, and the attacks on Iraq increased.

Although relations were very tense at that time, neither country broke off diplomatic relations. President Saddam had ruled out the option of war for 'national reasons', so the Iraqi Army was instructed to impose self-control although a warlike climate prevailed on the border with Iran. At the same time, the Iraqi people were mobilised to fulfil their national duty in the confrontation with Iran. President Saddam told the Regional Festival of Popular Arab Poetry on 23 April,

> It is not only the Army that wears khaki. The Army is born every time an Iraqi woman gives birth to a son or a daughter on the banks of these two rivers. I say to our enemies great and small: if they imagine the land of Iraq will be open to them once they have overcome half a million men in khaki, they are wrong. Millions upon millions will be born to defend the soil of Iraq. Bani Sadr deludes himself if he thinks the Iranian army can walk into Iraq. Not even the Army of the Soviet Union or the United States can walk into Iraq.

On 27 April 1980 came a surprising announcement: the Iranian authorities reported that President Saddam Hussein had been killed when in fact he was alive and well. A spokesman at the presidential palace in Tehran quoted sources close to Ayatollah Khomeini as saying that a coup had taken place at half past eleven that morning and that President Saddam had been killed. Agence France Presse was the only news agency to pick up the item and relay it. The spokesman said that the news had been confirmed by a telephone call to the General Commander of the Revolutionary Guards Daoud Waza'i in Qasr Shirin on the border with Iraq. Since the source of the news had been the Iranian presidential palace, the world media treated it seriously and provided their audiences with analyses and details. The news was given more credibility by the Iranian Foreign Minister Sadeq Qotbzadeh, who was on an official visit to Syria. At a press conference in Damascus before he went on to Lebanon, he declared, 'It makes me very happy to be able to announce the news I have just received: there has been a military coup in Iraq; Saddam Hussein and his regime can go to hell.'

In Baghdad, the Iraqi officials were careful not to react to the story in a way that would serve the Iranian purpose. Instead of issuing a statement denying the reports, they simply broadcast a news item that President Saddam Hussein and a number of Iraqi officials had gone to Baghdad airport to greet the President of the Seychelles, France Albert René. The Iranian media continued to insist that there had been a coup in Iraq. They said that President Saddam Hussein had been arrested and that a member of the 'Organisation of Muslim Mujahidin in Iraq' had fired at him during an official visit to an army camp. At this point the Iraq News Agency distributed a statement saying that the coup had never taken place, that President Saddam Hussein enjoyed the best of health and that 'the clique in Tehran and Qom which fabricated this news are so deluded that they must be living in a fantasy world'. In the evening Iraqi viewers saw sadors had been invited. Radio Iran broadcast the news of the Seychelles President to which Arab, Asian and African ambassadors had been invited. Radio Iran broadcast the news of the coup, but by this time no one took any more notice of it. The incident particularly upset the Iraqis because Sadeq Qotbzadeh had been able to use the Syrian capital to broadcast his joy at the 'fall of the Iraqi regime'. The Iraqi daily *Al-Jumhouriya* said in an editorial, 'Every atom in the Golan Heights watered by the blood of the Iraqis who went to defend Damascus from the danger of defeat [during the October 1973 war] will provide stones to hurl at you and your friends who express joy in Qassioun at what your sorcerer told you.' *Al-Thawra* said simply that it was amazed at 'the insanity of people who fabricate stories and distort the truth'.

President Saddam Hussein normally invites visiting officials to accompany him on tours of the country and to the main areas of interest. As a challenge to Iran he invited President René to accompany him on a casual stroll through Baghdad during the rush hour on the day after the news of the coup attempt was broadcast by the Iranians. The third day after the fabricated news was broadcast, the Iraqi President met the President of the Seychelles in closed session. He then headed a meeting of the Council of Ministers, at which he declared,

> The strength of our Revolution is worrying our enemies. Its constant progress consolidates its force and strengthens its ties with the people. The solidity of our Revolution drives us forward in the service of our principles. No one can stop our people's march any longer. We are wholly for the Arabs and for Iraq. Our relations with the world are based on this, and on joint interests in the service of our principles. The defence of truth gives a regime the support of its people, which cannot be secured by any foreign protection.

The fabricated news item came two days after the abortive American attempt to rescue the hostages at the United States embassy in Tehran. The failure of the American desert landing intoxicated the Iranians. Iraq treated the news with contempt. The only editorial to comment on the event appeared in *Al-Iraq*, the organ of the Kurdish organisation in Iraq. The paper said, 'The American landing operation was simply play-acting; the statements issued by the Iranians and the Americans about the operation are very similar in content and wording and are meant to mislead.' By now, the international media were beginning to take news coming out of Tehran with a pinch of salt. In desperation, the Iranian media insisted that President Saddam had indeed been killed and the man who was greeting officials and hearing meetings was his double. They claimed that the Iraqis would only announce President Saddam's death once a successor had been found.

By this time, Iraq had completed the operation to deport over 30,000 Iranians. Those excepted from the deportation measures were Iranians who opposed Imam Khomeini's regime, the people of Arabistan, and Iranian families holding certificates of Iraqi nationality. The sum of between 500 and 1,000 dinars was given to each family, and they were allowed to take their money out of Iraq. The numbers involved were not as great a burden for the Iranian authorities as the time in 1971 when the Shah's regime had to deal with some 40,000 Iranians deported by Iraq when Iranian-Iraqi relations were at their worst.

The attacks and counter-attacks continued. Iran declared that deporting the Iranian families was an inhumane act. Iraq replied by broadcasting the confessions of Abdel-Amir Mansouri (said to be the top man in Al-Da'awa) who revealed that 'Imam Khomeini sent large quantities of money, weapons, explosives and poisons to us in Iraq.' Iran said the Iraqis were non-believers; Iraq retaliated by broadcasting the dozens of telegrams of support President Saddam receives daily from religious leaders. Radio Iran declared that the Kurds in Iraq were neutral in the Iraqi-Iranian conflict; Radio Baghdad broadcast a telegram from the religious men of Ibril with their pledge to President Saddam Hussein that they would 'defend the Iraqi Revolution and their President against the barbaric acts of the agents of the Iranian regime'. That same day, by coincidence, the Iranian Kurdish religious leader Shaikh Izzedin Husseini broadcast an appeal to the Iranian people to 'unite against the regime in Iran and to form a people's government'. The Iranian dailies printed false news items about President Saddam's health; President Saddam instructed the Iraqi dailies to reprint the fabricated items. On one occasion, Radio Tehran announced that Iranian border guards had forced an Iraqi helicopter to land in Iran and placed its eight-man crew under arrest. The Iraqi Foreign Ministry replied that the helicopter belonged to the Ministry for Youth and called for its return. The propaganda campaign was accompanied by border clashes. Iraq's embassies and missions abroad became the target of Iranian attacks. Iraq responded to the attacks, but without claiming responsibility for them.

The Iraqi press now no longer used the word 'Iran' but the expression 'the Persian clique'. A number of editorials said that this was a clash between two nationalities, the Arab and the Persian. Tareq Aziz wrote a series of editorials; this was significant because, as a Christian, he had been the target of the first bomb attack and of the Iranian propaganda campaigns. In his editorials, Tareq Aziz criticised those Arab states which backed Iran (Syria, Libya and some Palestinian resistance groups) and concluded, 'There are many religions, Islamic sects and ethnic groups coexisting in Iraq within the framework of a strong indivisible national unity. Let anyone who thinks they can break this unity try.'

Is there no common ground for coexistence between Saddam Hussein's Iraq and Ayatollah Khomeini's Iran? Can mediation efforts resolve the conflict between the two sides? An attempt will be made to answer this question by reviewing the following sequence of events. Some five weeks before Saddam Hussein took over complete responsibility an editorial in *Al-Thawra* asked, 'Why does the ruling circle in Iran wish to destroy relations with Iraq?' It concluded by cautioning, 'He who issues a warning has done his duty.' The paper revealed that on 13 February 1979 the Iraqi Government had sent a memorandum to the provisional Iranian Government headed by Mehdi Bazargan in the wake of the Iranian revolution. The memorandum spoke of Iraq's 'interest in establishing the firmest of brotherly links and ties of fruitful co-operation with neighbouring peoples and countries, on the basis of mutual respect of sovereignty and non-interference in the internal affairs of others, and respect for the legitimate aspirations of peoples through an expression of free will'. The memorandum also noted that religious and historical links between Iraq and Iran 'should be an element strengthening good relations in the new era between Iraq and Iran and the rest of the Arab world'. The memo expressed Iraq's satisfaction with the 'statements issued by Ayatollah Khomeini, the outstanding religious leader, and by the leaders of the Iranian popular movement, about relations with the Arabs and the stand *vis-à-vis* the colonising Zionist entity'. The memorandum concluded, 'We look forward to the establishment of strong and fruitful ties and co-operation between Iraq and the new Iran to strengthen joint efforts and serve the mutual interests of the two countries, consolidating freedom, peace and stability in the region.' *Al-Thawra* commented:

> In 1969 we warned the Shah's government not to be aggressive towards Iraq but it paid no attention to our warnings, for which it paid a high price: it has disappeared and Iraq remains. Today we caution and remind the rulers in Iran of the foolishness of the aggressive adventure waged by the Shah against Iraq. If they heed this advice, they will find us ready and willing to build relations based on good neighbourliness and fruitful co-operation. If they do not heed it, we are not to blame; it remains to be said that those who play such games will pay dearly for them. The arm of Iraq is stronger and longer than they think and than gamblers and sick people have told them.

Iran never replied to the memorandum. Although the memorandum should have improved Iraqi-Iranian relations, in fact the opposite happened, for a number of reasons. In the first place, Imam Khomeini could not forget that Iraq deported him just a few months before the revolution and that he had to lead the final stage from Neauphle-le-Château in France. Iraq was well aware of this and, in seeking to resolve the question of Iranian-Iraqi relations, it began by explaining the reasons for deporting Khomeini. It pointed out that when the conflict with the Shah was at its most bitter, Iraq served as a platform for all kinds of Iranian opposition groups, including Khomeini's. Iraq assisted the opposition groups in every way it could, and placed its radio stations at their disposal. A number of programmes were broadcast about the lessons of the Iraqi Revolutions of 14 July 1958, 8 February 1963 and 17 July 1968, and about the best forms of underground revolutionary action. Details were given on how to set up revolutionary headquarters, how to publish pamphlets and other means of secret opposition. For six years Iraq supported the opposition groups; Khomeini was allowed to use

Iraq as a centre for his activities and was treated with the utmost respect.

After the Algiers agreement between Iraq and Iran in 1975, Iraq stopped the activities of the Iranian opposition groups on a reciprocal basis. But Khomeini continued his operations and stepped up his activities in 1978, causing the Shah to complain. The Iraqi authorities did not want relations to worsen with Iran, so they sent a member of the Revolution Command Council to ask Khomeini to respect the Iraqi stand. Khomeini refused to be flexible, and told the Iraqi official, 'I will continue the struggle against the Shah's regime, and if the Iraqi authorities object I will leave Iraq.' A few days later, Imam Khomeini left Iraq and headed for Kuwait, but the Kuwaiti authorities refused to allow him in. He contacted the Iraqi authorities from the border and asked to be allowed to return for a few days before finding another base. The Iraqi authorities immediately agreed. At the very moment that Imam Khomeini was in the border area, the Iranian embassy requested in the name of the Shah that Imam Khomeini be allowed to remain in Iraq; the Iraqi authorities refused. Imam Khomeini then left Iraq for France. Iraq learnt that the Imam would have preferred to be in an Arab country such as Algeria, so at the Baghdad Summit Saddam Hussein asked the Algerian Foreign Minister Abdel-Aziz Bouteflika to ask the Algerian President Houari Boumedienne to allow Imam Khomeini to stay in Algiers. The Iraqis stressed that he should be given Arab protection although Iraq, because of its circumstances, could not allow him to continue his political activities openly in Iraq.

Nevertheless, Iraq had already done a great deal for Imam Khomeini. For example, the Algiers agreement had provided for an exchange of visits between Iranian and Iraqi officials. It had been decided that the Shah would visit Iraq, with trips to Najaf and Karbala forming the mainstay of the programme. The Iraqi officials were told that the Shah could not visit Iraq while Khomeini remained there. The Iraqis replied that Imam Khomeini was a religious man and an Iranian political exile who had sought refuge in Iraq, and that Iraq could not turn away a refugee. The Iranian authorities then requested that Imam Khomeini be moved to another city during the Shah's visit. The Iraqis refused, and the visit did not take place.

Clearly, several things have not gone according to Imam Khomeini's plan. He has thus become more rigid in his approach and has let matters run a course that is not in the interests of the Iranian revolution. He had, for instance, thought that once the Shah had been overthrown a number of other regimes would also topple and 'Khomeinism' would spread in the region. He had expected the regime in Iraq to fall because, during the time he spent in Iraq, instability prevailed and the Iraqi Army was weak. The strong Iranian Army built up by the Shah would, he thought, be more than a match for the Iraqi Army. Once the Iraqi regime crumbled, the regimes in Kuwait, the Emirates and Saudi Arabia would follow suit. This scenario was based on dreams rather than reality. Seated on his prayer-rug in Najaf, Imam Khomeini was fed on hearsay and rumours. By contrast, detailed reports of his activities reached the Iraqi authorities. During the six years Khomeini spent in Najaf, the Iraqi authorities were working hard to encourage stability in the country, strengthen the Army, eradicate social injustice and ensure complete solidarity between the people and the regime. By the time the Iranian revolution occurred the Iraqi Army was as strong as the Iranian Army had been in the past.

Imam Khomeini had also based his beliefs on what he saw as the bankruptcy of nationalism in the Arab world. He was convinced that Iraq could not use Arab nationalism to repel an assault in the name of religion. He also thought that the glaring social injustice in parts of the Arab world would provide him with popular support in the Arab and Islamic world. His plans went awry for two reasons. In the first place, he proposed a state based on the concept of the *faqih* (religious leader), which caused more unease than anything else in the Arab world, on both popular and official levels. In the second place, his view of Arabs and Arab nationalism was completely unfounded.

The language barrier also played a major part in destroying Imam Khomeini's scenario. He and most of the other ayatollahs spoke only Persian; those who knew Arabic refused to use it. Most military and civilian officials spoke German, French or English as a second language. The Iranian Foreign Minister Sadeq Qotbzadeh sounded more like a Commonwealth leader than an Iranian when he attacked Iraq in English during his visit to Damascus. President Bani Sadr sounds more like a European leader when he gives statements to the press in French, criticising the Gulf leaders and calling for the export of the Iranian revolution. Can these be the leaders of a Muslim Iran?

It would not be an exaggeration to say that the Arab world's initial reaction of joy when the Iranian revolution succeeded was no more than they would feel at the success of any revolutionary leader such as Che Guevara, Ho Chi Minh or Fidel Castro. Thus Imam Khomeini completely overestimated the support he had in the Arab world. Such support as did exist was similar, say, to that which existed for Abdel-Nasser in Iran, when some Iranians wished they could do for Iran what Abdel-Nasser had done for Egypt.

To sum up, Imam Khomeini would have enjoyed popular Arab support had he not proposed the concept of *vilayet-e-faqih*, (a state headed by a religious leader), and if he had returned the three islands, called the Gulf the 'Islamic Gulf' rather than insist on the 'Persian Gulf', changed the social situation in Iran, solved the question of minorities in Iran and decided to adopt a reasonable approach towards Western technology rather than do without it altogether. Had he not waved sectarianism as a banner for change, Khomeinism might have taken root in the Arab world. And he would not have clashed with the regime in Iraq, because the Iraqis would have seen all these moves as additional support to the social and political revolution being carried out in their own country.

Even Palestinian support of the Iranian revolution is no longer as warm as it was in the days when Iranian revolutionaries trained in Palestinian camps with weapons paid for by the Arab countries. So far, Iranian support of the Palestinian revolution has consisted of turning the Israeli embassy in Tehran into an office for the Palestine Liberation Organisation, and some financial assistance. The Palestinian resistance is not interested in money, however, because it receives funds from a number of Arab and Islamic states. In this respect, it is useful to recall the statement made by Rafiq Natshe, the PLO representative in Saudi Arabia and member of the Fateh Central Council (to which he was elected at the Central Council's meeting in June 1980). At a press conference in Riyadh on 9 June 1980 Natshe declared, 'Fateh appreciates the support it receives from the Kingdom of Saudi Arabia, which is greater than the support of any other part of the Arab and Islamic world.' By using the word 'Islamic', it sounds as though Natshe is saying what his colleague Hani al-Hassan in Tehran cannot say about Iran's assistance to the Palestinian resistance. It is also useful to recall Yasser Arafat's remark to the Steadfastness and Confrontation Front meeting in Tripoli, in April 1980, that the Palestinian resistance had contracted its largest arms deal with Hungary and the arms were paid for in full by Iraq.

Although the Palestinian resistance is not getting the support that Iran is capable of offering and which is morally incumbent upon it, the Iranians behave as though they were the resistance's main backers. During the Arab People's Conference in Iraq held to discuss the National Charter, one of the resistance leaders, Hayel Abdel-Hamid (Abul Hol), declared that the three islands occupied by Iran were Arab islands. The PLO representative

Hani al-Hassan bore the brunt of Iran's rage and had to make strenuous efforts to placate the Iranians, although he could not accept their reasoning. At one point the Palestinian resistance had hoped that Imam Khomeini would help it in the diplomatic initiative it had undertaken. The Iranians could have made US recognition of the PLO a condition for the release of the American hostages, for example, or they could have asked for the release of Palestinian prisoners from Israeli gaols. Iran has taken neither of these steps. Nevertheless, the Palestinian resistance has remained, on the whole, a supporter of the Iranian revolution and has adopted a neutral position in Iran's conflict with Iraq, although Iraq meets its commitments to the Palestinian cause in full. The Palestinians may have tactical reasons for doing this: their supporters may have a score to settle with the Iraqi regime; those who are neutral may find it politic to exert pressure on the Arab regimes by using Iran's support as a lever from time to time.

Imam Khomeini did not accept the proposal that the three islands occupied by Iran should be handed over to the Palestinian resistance, which would in turn have restored them to their rightful owners. If he had accepted this suggestion, he would have found a solution to the question of the islands and strengthened the Palestinian resistance at the same time. It is quite clear that Imam Khomeini does not wish to return the islands to the Arabs, and in this way hopes to underline their powerlessness. It is as though he is saying, 'You let the Shah wrest them from you by force and now you want them back through goodwill.' The Shah occupied the islands in full view of the world on 30 November 1971. At that time the power balance in the Arab world was different. Iraq's forces were much weaker and it had no strength to back its objections. There was a kind of unwritten truce between Iran and the rest of the Arabs, with the exception of Iraq and Libya. Why does Khomeini not use the islands' strategic position against Arab interests since he does not want to return them? The islands are poised at the entrance to the Arab Gulf in the Straits of Hormuz; they were occupied by the Shah in order to control the entrance to the Gulf, through which an oil tanker passed every twelve minutes. This is a card Iran can use against the West if it so wishes — although it has not yet done so.

The three islands, particularly the largest, Abu Musa, were used by SAVAK forces as a base from which to infiltrate the Arab world. The Shah's argument for occupying the islands was that they would otherwise be used by Arab revolutionaries to stage operations against the West. As there is now a revolutionary regime in Iran, one would have assumed that it would use the islands in the same way. Nothing of the sort has happened. Nor does it look as if Iran has any intention of restoring the islands to their rightful owners. After President Saddam had sent a message to the United Nations Secretary-General Waldheim requesting the return of the islands, in the wake of the attack on Mustansiriyah University, President Bani Sadr went to Abu Musa to take part in Iranian military manoeuvres in the Gulf, as though challenging President Saddam to do something about it.

Iran knows that the islands' rightful owners cannot do anything about recovering them. But a security pact between Iraq and the United Arab Emirates might reverse these calculations. It is worth noting that Ras al-Khaimah's ruler, Shaikh Saqr bin Muhammad al-Qassimi, paid a visit to Iraq on 2 June 1980 and declared that 'Iraq's stand on the matter of Iran's occupation of the three islands is worthy of respect and consideration.' It remains to be seen whether this visit is part of Iraq's plans to regain the islands, and whether Shaikh Saqr's visit was backed by the rest of the Emirates or was just a personal initiative. It should be remembered that the Qassimi tribe controlled the three islands during the thirteenth century and during the first two decades of the nineteenth century, as well as parts of the Omani and Iranian coasts. In spite of their long resistance to the British, the Qassimis were eventually forced to sign a protection agreement with Britain in 1820.

The Gulf rulers have not sought a security pact with Iraq although Iranian ayatollahs now claim Bahrain, Kuwait and the Emirates. The Gulf rulers may have their reasons, but Iraq will not necessarily sit idly by without taking appropriate action. During my meetings with President Saddam in November 1979 I asked him whether the visits of Iraqi officials to Bahrain and Kuwait were related to the claims of the Iranian ayatollahs that they were part of Iran. He replied,

> We wanted to tell our brothers in Bahrain and Kuwait that foreign forces will be powerless to attack the sovereignty of any Arab land or people. As long as we are in a position to fight back we shall do so. Iraq's geographical position may not enable it to place its armies to face the Zionist entity, but it is certainly capable of positioning its forces against any threat aimed at Bahraini or Kuwaiti sovereignty, and at the Gulf in general. We will never allow anyone to touch the Arabness of the Gulf, its land or its people. Our officials have relayed this to our brothers, and have told them that we are present and ready to assist them to the extent they want and to the extent that they need.

Iraq's stand has only increased Iran's stubbornness. On a visit to

Kuwait in April 1980, the Foreign Minister Sadeq Qotbzadeh was asked, in Arabic, about Iran's position on Iraq's call for the restoration of the three islands. He replied, in English, that Iraq too was originally part of Persia. This increased the Gulf's wariness of the Iranian revolution and placed those Arab states supporting Iran in an unenviable position. Iraq's position on the Arab islands and on Kuwait and Bahrain stems from its own sensitive, strategic position. It should not be forgotten that Iraq lies at the end of the Arabian Gulf, and that it is the beginning of the land route linking Asia to Europe. Iraq took this into consideration when it stood by the Emirates and broke off diplomatic relations with Iran and Britain in the wake of Iran's occupation of the islands in 1971. This is why Iraq is seeking to develop relations with an independent Gulf. Things would have been much easier had Britain not sown the seeds of dissent between Iraq and the Gulf states during its long imperialist rule, and had it not encouraged so many Iranians to emigrate to the Gulf states, with predictable results.

Some Iraqi fuel has been added to the Iraqi-Iranian conflict. For example, Iraq belittled Khomeini's victory over the Shah's regime. This may have been because of the Iraqi concept of revolutionary action, its pride in its Party and its struggle to bring the Party to power and consolidate its rule. Or it may have been because the Iraqis take pride in the fact that they carried out their revolution against the monarchy some twenty years before the Iranian revolution and that, far from putting their king on a plane to enjoy the fruits of his tyranny in exile, they made him and his family pay for it with their lives.

The Iraqis often refer to Arab victories over the Persians, especially the defeat of the emperor Qasra Anu Sheruan at the hands of the Muslim Arab armies. They are making a film of the battle of Qadissiyah, the great battle that took place between the Arabs and the Persians at the dawn of the Islamic age and in which the Arabs defeated the Persians. In their information campaigns, the Iraqis focus on the fact that the Iranians have twice been liberated from the rule of emperors, and both times thanks to the Arabs. The first time, they say, was when the Arabs defeated Qasra Anu Sheruan, the second was when Imam Khomeini overturned the Shah using the weapon of religion, a weapon that Arabs had spread to other nations. Moreover, the Iraqis picture Imam Khomeini as an ungrateful man who has forgotten all the assistance the Iraqis gave him in the past. They have often broadcast the reasons behind Khomeini's departure from Iraq, and their attempt to persuade Algeria to give him refuge. But the most important factor adding fuel to the flames is Iraq's stand on Arabistan.

Whenever these matters are raised with Iraqi officials, they ask, 'Who started it first?', adding, 'Would you like us to wait until the Persian conquest to do something about it?' When one points out that both Iraq and President Sadat's regime are against the Iranian revolution and that it is strange they should meet on this point, the Iraqi officials reply that Iraq has adopted a stand of principle whereas Sadat's stand does not mean he is a man of principle. When one asks why Baathist ideology should be in conflict with Imam Khomeini's attempts to set up an Islamic system of government, they reply that the Baath Party drew on Islam for its ideology long before Imam Khomeini was heard of. They point out that the Baath Party founder Michel Aflaq wrote a book entitled *The Memory of the Prophet of Islam* in 1943 and that there was no strong Islamic current imposed on him or forcing him, a non-Muslim Baathist, to base himself on Islam. They add that Imam Khomeini's creed can only be imposed by impossible forces and that it will divide the Muslims instead of uniting them. They think it unlikely that Khomeini will accept Fateh's solution for Palestine, based on the coexistence of Arab Muslims, Christians and Jews. As for Arabistan, the Iraqi officials point out that their support of self-determination for the people of Arabistan began long before the revolution in Iran. They also stress that the Iranian revolution's success is partly based on the people of Arabistan's fight against the Shah's regime, a struggle based on nationalist not religious principles. It was the people of Arabistan who went on strike in the oil-fields and installations, thus bringing about the fall of the Shah.

The above analysis shows why war broke out between Iraq and Iran in September 1980. It is worth remembering Imam Khomeini's statements made some twelve years ago (when the Baath took over power in Iraq) that the possibility of war between the two countries had not been ruled out, but simply postponed. The Imam made these statements in the book entitled *Islamic Government*, a series of lectures he delivered before religious scholars in Najaf. In the book, Imam Khomeini asks: 'Is it enough that we are masters over Najaf?' and adds 'But we are not masters of Najaf.'

CHAPTER 5

THE STYLE OF THE ABBASIDS IN AN AGE OF TECHNOLOGY

'Safeguard Muhammad and his message in his nation, then God will protect you and look after your interests.

'Ensure that the outposts are heavily manned, secure the borders and protect the roads and homes of the people; provide the people with the services they need and ward off harm; always have money in store and make sure the treasury is full, for you know not what evils fate holds in store for you each day; recruit as many men and soldiers as you can.

'Never put off today's tasks until tomorrow, otherwise matters will accumulate and be lost; resolve each matter as it comes up, use your judgement and set your mind to it; have men awake at night so you may know what will happen during the day, and during the day so you may know what will happen at night.

'Take the initiative yourself; do not go beyond the bounds of morality. Think the best of people — yet think the worst of your appointed governors and secretaries; be always alert. Be wary of he who seeks your constant company, yet lend an ear to your people. Arbitrate in conflicts and appoint active deputies who will not be distracted.

'My son, do not sleep, beware of sleep. Your father has not slept since he inherited the caliphate; he never shut an eye but his heart was awake.

'This is my testament to you; may God protect you.'

(Excerpts from the will of Caliph Mansour to his son Al-Mahdi, delivered when he fell ill on his way to the Hijaz in 158AH)

In less than nine years Iraq has acquired a powerful and well-equipped Army, which is now a major force in the strategic balance of power in the Middle East. Saddam Hussein has paid as much attention to the development of the Armed Forces as to the development of the Party, so that the strength of one would not outstrip the other. He did not want the Army to fall into the same trap as most armies in Third World countries. Thus, he allowed officers in the Iraqi Army to become involved in politics on condition that they were members of the Baath Party. The rationale was that Baath Party members would work to strengthen the civilian rule of the Party, whereas a member of the Communist Party or a religious extremist would work within the Army to topple the regime in favour of the Communist Party or the Al-Da'awa Party.

When the Communist grouping in the Army was uncovered, Saddam Hussein realised the danger, and the importance of implementing the 'theory of Baathist action in the Armed Forces'. He acted with maximum firmness and the organisation's members were sentenced to death. Those executed included both officers and soldiers. Following the executions, the Soviet Union began an indirect propaganda campaign against Iraq. Saddam Hussein replied in a press conference on 18 July 1978: 'Those who were executed were not executed because of their political beliefs but because of their subversive activities.' One of the journalists asked if the operation could be described as a purge of the Armed Forces, but Saddam Hussein rejected this forcefully. It was, he said, 'bringing to account those who had broken Iraqi laws which forbid any party activity within the Armed Forces other than the Baath Party'. Although he did not refer to the Soviet Union by name, Saddam Hussein went on to say that 'those who try to play with the Iraqi Army are inspired by dishonourable and evil motives'.

The Iraqi Army has a long record of nationalism dating back to its establishment in 1921, which illustrates the 'theory of Baathist action' referred to above. It participated in the national armed revolution of 1941 against British imperialism. It never stood in the way of popular demonstrations or uprisings whenever these were of a nationalist nature, and it stood with the masses during the 14 July 1958 Revolution which toppled the monarchy in Iraq. The principle of 'Baathist action' was crystallised by Saddam Hussein after it had been confirmed in the Eighth Report of the Regional Command in January 1975: 'It is essential to redouble our efforts to build an Army based on the principles and ideas of the Baath Party and on its nationalist and socialist nature.' Thus several young and active Baath Party members have been appointed to leadership positions; those who did not follow Baathist ideology were passed over. Since the 17-30 July 1968 Revolution, non-Baathist officers due for retirement have been replaced by Baathist officers who are both qualified and committed. Military academies in Iraq now accept only Baath Party members, which means that most of the officers of the 1980s will be Baathists. The seeds of Baathist ideology were sown in the Army in the early 1950s, but were not developed until after the 17-30 July 1968 Revolution. Baath Party ideas and principles are now taught in the Army just as they are disseminated in civilian sectors. The group responsible for 'political direction' in the Army disseminates the principles of the Party, and deepens the Army's understanding of the political role that the Iraqi officer must play. Conferences and political discussions are held regularly at barracks and air bases. The general thrust of the discussions is summed up in the two slogans of the Armed Forces, 'The good Baathist is a good soldier' and 'The good soldier is also a Baathist in the service of the nation.'

The military Baathists feel a strong link with Saddam Hussein because he has made the Armed Forces more than a military machine. His most quoted statement in this respect is, 'We reject the idea of a professional army, as propounded by rightists, and we consider non-involvement of the Armed Forces in politics a dangerous slogan.' Saddam Hussein has defined the role of the Armed Forces on both domestic and Arab levels. Of the first, he said, 'The Army must be the crowning glory of the people, and not an instrument of oppression.' Of the second, he said, 'The Iraqi Army is the Army of the Arab nation, and it must respond to the call whenever danger threatens.' In 1980 President Saddam Hussein attended the graduation ceremony of the '7th April Course', which included those members of the Armed Forces who had received the 'membership of honour' given to the active, dedicated Baathist. His presence at the ceremony indicates the importance he attaches to military men becoming Party members at this stage. The ceremony was also an opportunity to reply to Imam Khomeini's charge that 'the Iraqi regime which attacks Iran is attacking the Quran and Islam'. At the ceremony, the first he had attended as President, Saddam Hussein declared,

> You are the principal builders of the house we are constructing together. Do not forget that you are soldiers with a message, and that you must be in the vanguard to carry the banner, like the Islamic armies when they reached China and Spain. This new Arabism is a new breath of Islam in all its aspects and a new breath from heaven . . . Anyone who stands against the new

few days after he succeeded
resident Al Bakr as President of
he Republic (seen together in the
econd photo) President Saddam
Iussein inaugurated the head-
uarters of the National Command
f the Ba'th, in the presence of
resident Bakr, Michael Aflak,
ieneral Secretary of the Party, and
ther leaders of the Party.

Inspecting a division of the Iraqi army

Visiting a nursery school in Baghdad.

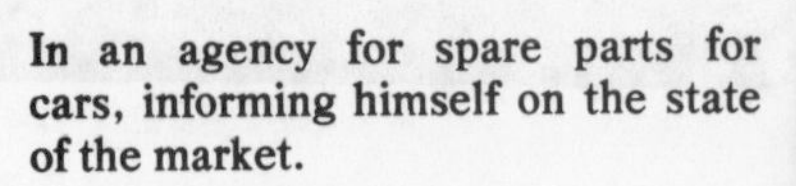

In an agency for spare parts for cars, informing himself on the state of the market.

In front of a tent at Takrit with his youngest daughter.

In the marshes of Zi Kar where the people live on the water.

SEPTEMBER 1980 — IT'S WAR

It's war, and on 5 October 1980 Iraqi 'Migs' attack the Tehran refinery which catches fire.

With the soldiers . . .

. . . and with the masses.

After hard fighting Iraqi soldiers occupy the town of Khoramshar which reverts to its old name of Al Muhammara.

Fifteen kilometres inside Iran Iraqi soldiers raise their flag and show their joy.

President Saddam Hussein accompanied by Prince Fahd, Crown Prince of Saudi Arabia.

President Saddam Hussein with King Hussein of Jordan who continues to support Iraq.

The Iraqi President, in military uniform, during one of his many tours which put him in direct contact with the population.

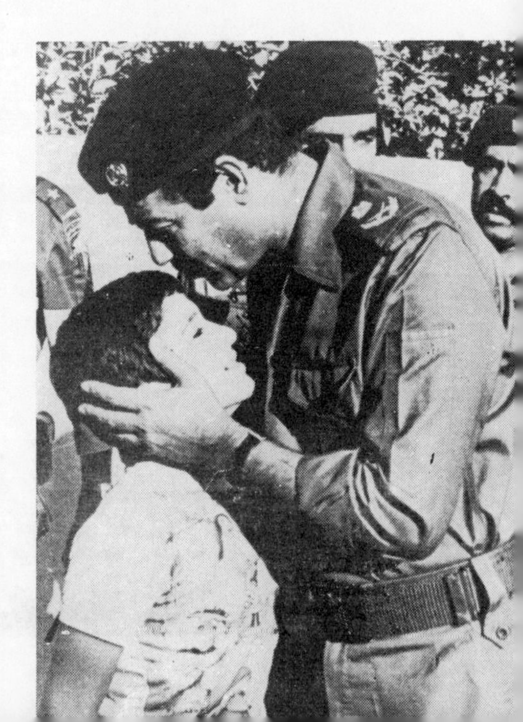

> Arabism is standing against Islam, no matter how he tries to disguise his actions.

The next day the newspapers reported that President Saddam had attended the ceremony in his capacity as Regional Secretary-General and Deputy Secretary-General of the Arab Socialist Baath Party, and not in his capacity as President of the Republic. The papers did not refer to him as the 'leader President' but as 'comrade', which was meant to show that he valued the Party role above that of the state.

Top officials respond with confidence to questions about the strength of the Armed Forces and affirm that the Iraqi Army is now stronger than the Turkish Army or the Iranian Army. In comparing the Iraqi, Iranian and Turkish armies, the Iraqi officials point out that the Turkish Army has not had any experience in battle since the First World War — with the exception of its military intervention in Cyprus, which cannot be considered a war. As for the Iranian Army, the Iraqi officials note that its fighting strength had not been put to the test in battle; for years the Iranian Army had been engaged in internal conflicts. Even the three islands of Abu Musa and Greater and Lesser Tumb wrested from the Arabs were not taken after a battle. The Iraqi Army, on the other hand, has had a good deal of experience in battle. It fought a major battle against the English in 1941. It participated in the 1948 War against the Zionists. It was involved in the difficult battles against the Kurdish rebels in the mountainous regions for ten years. In 1970, 1971 and 1972 it often clashed with the Iranians on the border, which continued until the 1975 agreement brought about a form of wary coexistence. And in 1973, it fought in the Arab-Israeli war on the Golan Heights. As a result, the Iraqi Army has experience not only of traditional warfare, but of guerrilla warfare and various types of terrain.

The diversification of the sources of arms has not caused one section of the Iraqi Army to suffer at the expense of the other. Iraq's diversification was carried out in a completely different way from that of the Egyptian Army, when President Anwar Sadat's publicised attempts to diversify his sources were aimed at discrediting the quality of Soviet weaponry. Iraq's French Mirages were not brought in at the expense of the Soviet MiGs, and the Iraqi Army is almost unique in its co-ordination of Soviet weapons and French weapons. The Iraqi Army is based on Soviet tanks whereas the Air Force depends on French-made fighters, transport planes and helicopters. The Iraqi Navy is also being strengthened and there are plans to make it a major force.

It is no longer a secret that Iraq is seeking to acquire nuclear arms because of President Saddam's intention to make the Iraqi Army the Arab world's defence force. The Army is being prepared both psychologically and materially for the role it is expected to play. President Saddam's repeated references to the Army's national role are indications that the level of armament is now satisfactory. He would not be making these statements if his aim were simply to raise morale. He knows the immense difference between what the Army was in 1968 and what it is today. According to Western studies of military strategy, when Saddam Hussein took over complete responsibility on 17 July 1979, Iraq's Armed Forces stood at 250,000 men, with 2,500 tanks, 2,500 armoured vehicles and over 700 fighter planes and bombers. The balance of arms purchases will tilt in favour of France or the Soviet Union, depending on which is willing to provide the most developed weapons and the nuclear facilities Iraq requires.

Iraq's economic power enables it to build the strongest army in the Middle East. Clear instructions have been given to remove any obstacles facing the Iraqi soldier, on both the military and the personal level. At the same time, President Saddam is careful on two counts: first, the Baathist officer should not begin to feel that he is part of an élite because of the special treatment he receives; secondly, there is no room for bureaucracy in a strong army. At a meeting with the military two weeks after he took over complete responsibility Saddam Hussein said,

> Frankness and mutual openness must characterise relations between you, since you are comrades with the same faith and comrades-in-arms in the service of that faith. The Muslim Arab leader of the Islamic armies at the time of the conquest was not separated from his men by any bureaucratic institutions, either in life, or in understanding or in carrying out his duties; the banner and the sword were equal before all.

The existence of a 'back-up force' in the form of the Popular Army relieves the regular Army of responsibility on the domestic front. The Popular Army was set up by the Baath Party to ward off the dangers facing the nation, and to counteract Israel's ability to mobilise thousands of civilians when it launches a surprise attack. President Saddam has paid a great deal of attention to the Popular Army from the time it was set up in 1970. Both Party members and non-Party members receive rigorous training so that if the regular Army is sent on a mission outside the country's borders the Popular Army will be able to defend the country. It holds itself in readiness in case it should be called on for assistance. The Popular Army trains its members in the use of rifles, machine-guns, armour, tanks and anti-aircraft weapons.

The Popular Army Commander is Taha Yassin Ramadan, a long-standing Baathist who was appointed First Deputy Prime Minister when President Saddam took over. Just four days before President Saddam announced the 8 February 1980 Charter, the tenth anniversary of the Popular Army was held, at which Taha Yassin Ramadan told a press conference that the number of trained fighters totalled a quarter of a million and the number of commandos was in tens of thousands. He said that the commandos could reach a set target within half an hour.

Popular Army training is conducted after office hours so as not to harm national production. The first women members of the Popular Army were trained in 1977. Seven months after President Saddam Hussein's assumption of power, the Military Air Academy in Takrit also opened its doors to women. Speed is one of the main aims of the Popular Army. The smallest fighting unit is the patrol, which is made up of fifteen fighters, a leader and an assistant. Each four to six patrols form a fighting base, in which the number of fighters can reach up to ninety; each base also has a leader and an assistant. The sector is the next stage of the pyramidal structure adopted for the Popular Army, and it is made up of six bases. The region comes next, and the regions together form the General Command. Just before the tenth anniversary of the Popular Army, a successful test mobilisation was carried out and the patrols took over towns, villages and main roads. The Popular Army has also taken part in the defence of South Lebanon during Israeli raids on Lebanon. It should be noted that, together, the Iraqi Army and the Popular Army can field half a million fighters. The proportion of fighters to the population, which now stands at thirteen million, shows that President Saddam is basing himself on facts when he mentions the role of the Iraqi Army within the Arab nation.

Although President Saddam is not a military man, he has the ability to make both officers and soldiers feel he is one of them. Now that he is President of the Republic, he pays regular and surprise visits to the Armed Forces. He had previously left these visits to President Bakr, as he had not been assigned an official military role. Among his responsibilities now is the post of Commander-in-Chief of the Armed Forces. To strengthen the ties between the Commander and his men, President Saddam often visits military bases and units. He usually carries out these visits in the early morning and breakfasts with the men, asking them what problems they have in the Army or on a personal level, and suggesting solutions. At the same time, he reminds them of their national duty. On one of these visits, he defined this duty as follows:

> We are all the sons of one large province called Iraq, and when we are on duty we must accept whatever responsibility is assigned to us, wherever we may be. We are also the sons of a province larger than Iraq, the Arab nation. When national duty calls we must respond in any part of this nation.

Although it is not possible to give many examples of President Saddam's links with the soldiers, because of the secret nature of the Armed Forces, a few incidents will serve to illustrate his links with the ordinary people, since he believes that firm ties are essential between the leader and the citizens, civilian and military alike.

Mosul, which overlooks Ninevah and Ashour, has a monastery similar to Saint Catherine's in the Sinai desert. Near the monastery lies a Christian village with thirty Christian families. The monks at Mata monastery often receive visits from Christians on pilgrimage to this holy site, which was built in the fourth century AD. On 18 April 1980 they received a visitor who was not a Christian and whose visit was unexpected — President Saddam Hussein. They were amazed when they saw him alight from his helicopter. President Saddam toured the monastery, asking about the health of the older monks. He decided to send two of them abroad for eye treatment at state expense. He then visited the village, which had suffered a great deal during the Kurdish rebellion, and gave instructions that 1,000 dinars be given to each family to make up for what they had endured. President Saddam often visits towns and villages in Iraq, but the visit to the monastery was symbolic as it had been looted and damaged during the Persian occupation of the country. President Saddam discussed this role with the head monk, Ishak Sas, and also referred to the important part the Arab Christians played in the struggle against the Persians.

On another occasion, some shepherds in a field suddenly saw a tall man wearing the traditional headdress (yashmak) among them. 'Who are you?', they asked. 'Saddam Hussein,' he replied. 'I have come to see if all is well with you.' 'So you are President Saddam; welcome, welcome,' they cried. The President sat with them and chatted about everyday matters. He shared their bread and goats' milk, and asked if they had everything they needed. They complained that they had no rifles to defend themselves and their flocks, so he gave instructions that they be given rifles immediately. One of the shepherds told the President that his son was ill and he could not afford medical treatment for him. The President took the boy to Baghdad with him, and had him placed in a hospital there. The President's aides were asked to make notes on how best to improve the shepherds' lives so that they could contribute to the development of the country's livestock, and to pass these notes on to the departments concerned. Earlier that day, President Saddam had received the top students and teachers from Al-Sharqiya Preparatory School for Boys at the Presidential Palace. He talked to them about their education and asked if they had any problems; small gifts were then presented to the students. The President told them, 'If young people of thirteen, fourteen and fifteen are thinking of the future of the Arab nation, then everything is for the best.'

The Iraqis often see President Saddam playing two different roles: he appears to them both in the character of a simple villager who is one of them, and in the character of the statesman who must operate within the rules of protocol. On 16 April 1980, for example, he addressed the people in Qada' Khadr in Ninevah Province, wearing the yashmak and tunic; in the evening, wearing a suit and tie, he headed the Iraqi delegation at the official talks with the visiting President of the Maldives, Mamoun Abdel-Quyum.

In the early morning of 8 October 1979, just a few months after he had taken over complete responsibility, President Saddam was driving along a Baghdad street when he saw a young boy the same age as his second son Qussei standing on the pavement. He asked the boy where he was going, and when he said that he was on his way to school, told him he would give him a lift. The boy had no idea of the President's identity. When President Saddam asked him, 'Are you a Baathist?', he replied, 'Yes, sir, we are all Baathists.' Just before they reached the Atifiyeh Secondary School for Boys, the boy asked, 'Who are you, sir?' 'Saddam Hussein, and I will visit your school with you.' The boy was thrilled at the thought of his schoolmates and teachers seeing him appear in the company of the President. President Saddam asked the teachers and students a number of questions, and listened to all they had to say.

Another morning the President knocked on the door of a house and asked the young boy who opened, 'Where is your father?' The boy replied, 'He's asleep.' President Saddam said, 'Go and tell him that President Saddam would like to share your breakfast.' After the man had recovered from his amazement, he asked the President to excuse him for a few minutes. President Saddam knew that the man probably wanted to prepare a special breakfast, so he told him, 'I only want what you have every day. I want to know if you have everything you need.' The man was somewhat confused and found himself saying, 'We haven't had eggs for a few days because they are in short supply at the moment. You'll find we can only give you bread and butter, jam and tea.' The President made a note of this, and within days the market was well stocked up with eggs.

President Saddam used to go on such fact-finding missions before he became President, and the number of such visits increased after he assumed complete responsibility. One of the first of such visits after he became President was to the fruit and vegetable markets of Karrada and Shawaka. Wearing the yashmak and national dress, he asked about prices in the market. He found they were much higher than he had expected. He asked one of the shopkeepers why his prices were higher than the official prices given on television; the shopkeeper replied sarcastically that the official price was irrelevant. At this point the President tore off his yashmak and revealed his true identity. The shopkeeper fled in fright. He was asked to return by President Saddam and, on being assured that he was in no danger, promised that he would in future always go by the official price.

President Saddam prefers to pay his surprise visits in the early morning to find out for himself how things really are. Most of his visits are to working-class neighbourhoods, where he asks about the elderly, chats with the children and examines the kitchen to find out what the people lack. The visits enable him to take appropriate decisions on the social level. Not only does he discover the truth about the people's needs and break down the barriers between the people and their President, he also makes heads of departments think twice before they submit reports on social conditions in the country. He has encouraged a television programme called 'Discussion of the Month', during which people put questions by telephone to officials, who then have to give clear and convincing answers. President Saddam's visits are now widely reported on radio and television. When I asked him why he went on such visits he replied, 'So I can see for myself what the people's problems are; I learn a lot through my meetings with the people.'

Not only does President Saddam pay surprise visits to the people; the people are often invited to visit the Presidential Palace. There is a special direct telephone in the President's office which he uses to speak to the people; he receives letters from citizens; and there is the weekly meeting at the Palace, which is usually attended by some two hundred citizens who come bearing their problems and complaints. President Saddam installed a special telephone for hearing citizens' complaints when he was still Vice-President, and many people telephoned once they discovered they could speak to the Vice-President himself. Saddam Hussein instructed his aides not to put through anyone who threatened to 'leave Iraq' if his demands were not met, but to put through all other calls.

President Saddam sometimes invites visiting heads of state to accompany him on his tours. After holding talks with the Algerian President Chadli Ben Jedid on his one-day visit to Iraq, he took him to visit the home of one of the citizens. The visit was reported on television that evening. However, President Saddam's most regular visits are to Iraq's kindergartens and schools. This may be partly because he grew up without a father, and was later deprived of seeing his own children grow up because he was so involved in bringing the Baath Party to power. But the main reason is certainly that he has faith in the future generations of Iraq, and wants to ensure that they are receiving the best education possible. He is the author of such statements as, 'Our national human resources begin with the child'; 'We want to make the small child the centre of his family, to spread enlightenment and to develop in the best possible way'; 'The child is to his teacher as a piece of raw marble is to the sculptor; the teacher has the opportunity to turn this into beautiful shapes, more perfect than nature or time can produce.'

Whenever the President receives a group of children at the Presidential Palace, the newspapers are instructed to cover the event as though it were a major official happening. Indeed, on the day that the fabricated news about a coup attempt in Iraq was being broadcast in Iran, the major news item on the front page of the Iraqi papers was of President Saddam meeting children from the two kindergartens of Bara'em and Rayahin. He heard them sing their favourite songs, distributed gifts and met the teachers. As a result of the President's initiatives in this respect, other top officials, and even the founder of the Party Michel Aflaq, are now meeting the youth of Iraq on official occasions. Michel Aflaq has gone so far as to expand his Party theory and add to what Saddam Hussein said on the 'Baath theory on the child'. When Michel Aflaq met the children of the Yarmouk and Jumhouriya kindergartens on the occasion of the thirty-third anniversary of the Party, he declared,

> There is a strong link between the Baath and children, because the Party is working for the future, and its stands and principles are drawn up to guarantee the future of the Arab nation. This does not mean that the Arab Socialist Baath Party does not work for the present, but that it wants to build the future for the children of

> today, for the coming generations which are the support of the nation and its future. The Arab Socialist Baath Party is the school of the Arab generations.

President Saddam commemorated the eighth anniversary of the nationalisation of oil in Iraq, on 1 June 1980, in an unexpected way. (He considers the nationalisation to be his greatest achievement, and this was the first anniversary he had celebrated since his assumption of full responsibility.) He invited a group of young boys and girls from the Party Vanguard to the Presidential Palace. Then, much as a father tells his children a bedtime story, he told the children how the nationalisation had taken place, and what life had been like in Iraq beforehand. He wanted to show them that this great step had been taken for them, the generation of the future.

President Saddam also told the children about the importance of discipline in the Party, and how the revolutionary must be convinced of the truth of his mission. These children, who had also been chosen because they excelled at school, would one day occupy top positions in the state; they would always be inspired by the President's story. President Saddam told them how the oil companies used to trick Iraq in the days before nationalisation, telling the authorities that there was no demand for oil on the market in order to keep the prices down and company profits up. He explained that Iraq's treasury had been empty before nationalisation, whereas afterwards its revenues were in billions of dinars and enabled the state to build schools and factories and hospitals. 'This money,' he said, 'bought those nice uniforms you are wearing, which cost the state twelve million dollars.' Before nationalisation, the Iraqis used to see the flares from the oilfields from far away, because only the English and a few chosen Iraqis were allowed into the installations. President Saddam recalled how some poor Iraqis would go near the installations to try to find left-overs to eat and would be 'chased away by the English as if they were little better than dogs'. He told the children how the oil companies had the power to change governments they did not like, and to replace governors and officials, because they formed a kind of state within a state. He told them that the Iraqi farmers and workers had not known what a five dinar piece looked like, whereas farmers now earned thousands of dinars, and the minimum weekly wage was forty dinars with the possibility of earning more through working overtime.

President Saddam then told the children that he had had supper with a farmer a few days earlier. This man had told him, as he praised God, that his crops brought in an annual income of around 8,000 dinars, and sometimes more. 'Nationalisation,' he said, 'has made the ground firm under our feet. Previously it was like a swamp; wherever you stepped you might sink in.' Using the simplest terms, the President explained that children in those days could not afford 'the nice clothes you have on now' although the oil was Iraqi oil. They used to look wistfully at the children of the British and the Dutch, who were well-dressed because their oil companies controlled Iraq's oil. In the past, children did not have the toys they have today. There was no heating, 'and when we went to school our hands were so cold we couldn't hold our pencils. The teacher would take pity on us and send one of the boys to his house to fetch some wood so that we might light a fire in the classroom.' President Saddam recalled that in those days an important official or the President would never visit their towns and homes. A visit by the Motassarif (Governor) would take place once every few years, and the people would wash the streets and decorate the city just to watch him arrive, have a meal with a local dignitary and then leave. 'We could not even talk to a policeman,' he said, 'but now you are talking to your comrade Saddam Hussein.' The President also wanted the children to pass on some messages to their elders, such as how his special telephone for the citizens was being misused by people who wanted cars, medical treatment abroad or higher salaries. He asked them to help him in this matter and to stop people from rushing at his car to present petitions for unjustified needs. He said, 'I want you and your fathers, brothers and relatives to teach and enlighten people. Tell them that Saddam Hussein respects you and loves you, but you must be disciplined. I want to tell people that personal gain is wrong and is against the democracy we wish to preserve in our relations with the people'. The President's visits to schools and kindergartens have been good for the children — and now every mother dresses her child with special care before sending him to school, in case the President should pay a surprise visit.

At this rate, President Saddam will have become personally known to most of the Iraqi people within the next few years, and they will have seen his face and shaken him by the hand. The President carries out these visits in spite of the protests of his security officials, who complain that they cannot ensure his safety when he visits an area which cannot be reached by car, or when he goes to the market in disguise or drops in on an Iraqi family. But President Saddam realises that these visits will lose their impact if they are hedged about by security measures. Saadoun Shaker, a member of the Revolution Command Council and Minister of the Interior, told me during an interview in April 1980 that he had tackled this issue with the President, pointing out that in other countries the necessary measures are taken before the head of state meets the people. Saadoun Shaker thought that by explaining to the President how the security forces of East European states investigate an area two weeks before the head of state is scheduled to visit it, and examine the minutest details down to the very food that is to be served, he would be able to convince President Saddam to change his mind. But the President remained adamant that excessive security would ruin the informal nature of the visits. What Saadoun Shaker had not taken into consideration was that President Saddam has inherited the style of the early Muslim Arab rulers and is acting within a tradition he is convinced is the best to run the state, a tradition which is in direct contrast to the demands of technology and the vexed question of security.

President Saddam's visits have also been very useful in crystallising the social and economic resolutions adopted in the Command Council and in directives to officials. For example, on 31 July 1979, barely two weeks after he had taken over complete responsibility, he told a Council of Ministers' meeting:

> We are still getting complaints from people who want to deposit or withdraw money; from those who want to pay their electricity or water bills; from those who want to pay their taxes; and from those who need a building permit. This is a shameful state of affairs, considering that the Revolution is eleven years old, and there is no excuse for it. This is not what we are here for, or what the Arab Socialist Baath Party represents.

On 5 January 1980 the Revolution Command Council decided to waive income tax for people with low incomes, which means that the President must have become aware of real difficulties among the people during his tours and visits. On 29 December 1979 he told the Council of Ministers: 'We do not want the people to see socialism as an imposed burden, but as a means for happiness and as a weapon with which to fight our enemies.' He added, 'We must understand that socialism is one of the ways to increase production to meet the people's needs, without ignoring developments in the world.'

On 28 April 1980 the President issued a memorandum to all ministries, saying that any draft laws involving social changes had to be discussed with the people and with trade union representatives before being presented to the Presidency. He said he would not look into any draft law that did not meet this condition 'as one of the revolutionary ways to build comprehensive democratic ties with the Iraqi people, to strengthen and enrich them through discussion and to enrich the organs of the state through the comments of the people'. On 23 April 1980 the Revolution Command Council issued two decrees for the protection of children, one banning the use of child labour to shine shoes or sell cigarettes, and the second imposing penalties on any bartender who served anyone under the age of eighteen. In all these instances President Saddam must have taken note of what people said when he met them during his visits. He saw for himself the things that did not accord with the image of a revolutionary state with a vast income, extending aid to other developing countries. He wanted his surprise visits to eradicate the kind of bureaucracy that stood in the way of development, and to spur those responsible into action. When the bureaucracy becomes as dynamic as the President, he will have accomplished what he set out to do.

The problem of bureaucracy has been occupying Saddam Hussein for some ten years. In all his meetings with the citizens, he has put into practice what he used to request of ministers and administrators, and he has issued a number of directives. The most important meeting in this respect was the conference held in September 1976 to study the working paper on the fall in production. At the conference Saddam Hussein reaffirmed the importance of the human element in administration, and the need for programmed development. He also stressed the importance of involving the people in administration and seeking their opinion before drawing up plans. Following the precedent of the President's meetings with the man in the street, Iraqi officials have begun to adopt new methods of behaviour towards the citizens and to act in a non-bureaucratic way in matters affecting people's everyday lives. Replying to accusations that his meetings with the people were simply a way of seeking support, President Saddam said during a visit to Ba'aqouba on 6 November 1979,

> It is not a sign of weakness to ask for renewed commitment and confidence from the people because they are the basic source of strength. The real weakness and distance from the people comes when the revolutionary becomes a ruler who rules from behind a desk, and who acts in a traditional way rather than remaining a revolutionary who believes in the constant reaffirmation of principles.

The other fundamental aspect of President Saddam's rule is his theory of reward and punishment, which he has outlined on two occasions. Before he assumed complete responsibility for the State and the Party, he held a meeting with members of the

Party Command on the measures to be adopted in the autonomous region (the Kurdish region). He said,

> Be sure, my comrades, that our hearts quake at the thought of unnecessary violence, no matter how slight. At the same time, we have the strength of character to behead those who betray their nation and conspire against their people, no matter how many. We must act in accordance with needs and principles and not in isolation from them.

The other occasion was on 4 November 1979, some weeks after he had become President, when he met those responsible for security in the capital. He said, 'We give both rights and responsibilities with the sharpness of the sword. Rights must be guaranteed and responsibilities must be carried out.'

These principles are put into practice. On 16 January 1980, for example, four Iraqis were executed after being sentenced to death by a Revolutionary Court for their part in accepting bribes from foreign companies in exchange for state secrets. The news was given front-page coverage in the press the next day. Of those executed, one had been the Under-Secretary, and another the Director of Engineers, at the Ministry of Irrigation; the other two had been businessmen. The Court also sentenced two men, a lawyer and the head of the Legal Affairs Department at the Central Statistics Bureau, to life imprisonment. Although in other countries of the Third World bribery is an accepted fact of life, President Saddam decided on such drastic measures because he felt that the Under-Secretary of a ministry was already receiving enough from the State, as was every employee. There is no excuse for bribery, as long as the Revolution guarantees its citizens a comfortable and dignified life. I asked an Iraqi official if the sentence was so harsh because of the identity of the foreign state with whom the four men had had dealings. He replied,

> I do not think that had anything to do with the sentence. The fact is that honesty among State employees is of first importance for President Saddam and the Party. We see no reason for anyone to accept bribes. We live in a revolutionary age now, not in the days of the monarchy when there were excuses for accepting bribes because an employee's salary was not enough to live on. He had no job security, indeed he never knew from one minute to the next how long he would remain in his job. Now the citizen's needs are assured, and generously so. If a citizen needs a house, the State provides it. If he falls ill, the State provides medical treatment and, if necessary, sends him abroad. The State does this for the most junior employee. If all the causes of bribery are removed and it still exists, it becomes high treason. Moreover, ministers and

> heads of institutes handle millions every day. Although they may be honest, it becomes increasingly easy to corrupt them, and this kind of corruption is no longer a question of morals but of high treason.

Such a decision had never been taken before; President Saddam probably considered that firmness was necessary in order to nip bribery in the bud because the development process in Iraq is of such vast proportions.

Another example of President Saddam's system of reward and punishment was the case of the civil servant who claimed that a doctor had been responsible for her father's death. President Saddam ordered an investigation committee to be set up. When it was proved that the doctor was indeed guilty of malpractice, his licence was withdrawn, he was put in gaol for six months, his travel documents were withdrawn and his certificates invalidated. At the same time, a colleague of his was rewarded for his excellent work, and the next day the newspapers printed both items so as to show that the man who carries out his duties will be treated differently from the one who is careless.

President Saddam has for many years paid particular attention to the nation's heritage and culture. This is why he has encouraged the production of an epic film about the battle of Qadissiyah and its hero Al-Qa'aqa. On 29 January 1980, the Revolution Command Council decided to introduce a number of prizes and gold medals for excellence in culture and science. They are named after famous Arab scientists and historians: the Hassan bin al-Haitham medal for science and technology, the Ibn Khaldoun medal for social sciences and economy, the Ibn Rushd medal for philosophy and logic, the Jahez medal for language and literature, the Wassiti medal for fine arts and the Khalid bin al-Walid medal for military science. Once these prizes become well established, the Arab complex about international medals will disappear. There is also scope for an 'Arab' Nobel prize or a Third World prize, and President Saddam will probably be the one to set up such a prize.

The President cares deeply about the nation's cultural heritage, and when he says the names of Ali bin Abi Taleb, Hussein bin Ali, Abu Bakr al-Seddiq, Omar ibn al-Khattab and Khalid bin al-Walid, it is as though he is reciting a prayer. He always carries in his mind the image of the great Arab and Islamic leaders who ate and slept with their people. He never forgets the image of those who constructed a nation, who encouraged literature by paying authors their books' weight in gold, who carried the sword and the pen and excelled both on the battlefield and in the field of knowledge. Tareq Hamad al-Abdallah, the Revolution Command Council Secretary and Director of the President's Office, wrote an article in *Al-Jumhouriya* on 4 April 1980 entitled, 'Our leader and the justice of Omar, the principles of Ali and the courage of Khalid'. He is one of the people closest to Saddam Hussein and his opinions must be considered authoritative.

A number of poems have been written about President Saddam, taking their inspiration from Baathist writers and political analysts. The President has, in his turn, encouraged poetry by attending the five-day Regional Festival of Popular Arab Poetry in April 1980. His opponents may attack him with writings on the walls abroad, but the poets sing his praises at home. He spoke to them in their own language when he declared on the last day of the festival, 'The people of Iraq confirm to all those filled with hatred and greed that we are a sword, a palm-tree and an olive branch.'

Whenever any harm befalls an Iraqi citizen, President Saddam will stand by his side so that he feels at one with the President in the service of his country. For example, during the crisis between Iraq and Bulgaria after Iraqi Communist students in Sofia had killed an Iraqi Baathist student, the Bulgarian authorities wanted to settle the matter as quickly as possible so it would not weaken their economic ties with Iraq. The Bulgarian President Theodor Zhivkov thus undertook an official visit to Iraq on 28 May 1980. President Saddam took his Bulgarian visitor to Babel, not to visit the historic ruins and the Nebuchadnezzar Museum, but because the student's family lived in that province. Together, they went to pay their condolences to the dead student's family. The Bulgarian President must have respected a President who showed such concern for his people's feelings, particularly since it was a low-key visit not covered on radio and television.

Another example was the visit the Iraqi Foreign Minister Dr Saadoun Hammadi was scheduled to pay to Britain on 6 June 1980. Preparations for the visit had been going on for months, and the British attached a good deal of importance to it: this was the first official Iraqi visit at this level for a quarter of a century, and it came at a time when Britain's relations with Iraq were still strained, which was affecting Britain's economic interests. Before the visit, however, the British press began a propaganda campaign against Iraq, and tried to link the occupation of the Iranian embassy in London with Iraq, although there was no proof of such a link. Iraq noted the escalation of the campaign and then, since Iraq does not differentiate between a country and its media, called off the visit twenty-four hours before it was due to take place. Outright cancellation of an official visit, as opposed to postponement, is meant to register a strong objection in the language of diplomacy. The cancellation of the visit reminded the Iraqis of the days when they used to stand in long queues, waiting for British left-overs. Ironically enough, the cancellation of the visit coincided with the eighth anniversary of the nationalisation of oil which swept away the remaining British presence in Iraq. The visit to which Britain had attached such importance did not take place.

Five days after cancelling his visit to Britain, the Iraqi Foreign Minister went on an official visit to Paris. There he met the French President Valéry Giscard d'Estaing, who accepted an invitation to visit Iraq. Another French gesture took place earlier, in April 1980, when President Giscard d'Estaing received the Revolution Command Council member and Oil Minister Tayeh Abdel-Karim, although he was not in Paris representing President Saddam Hussein, but as head of the Iraqi delegation to the Fourth Franco-Iraqi Joint Co-operation Session on education, oil and minerals, industry and agriculture, and irrigation. The Iraqi Oil Minister's meeting with the French President was particularly appreciated as it came at the time of Iran's fabricated news about a coup attempt against President Saddam. The French President also wanted to make some return for the special reception President Saddam Hussein had accorded the new French ambassador to Baghdad after President Saddam had assumed complete responsibility. When the ambassador, Pierre Rocalve, presented his credentials to President Saddam on 23 April 1980, the Iraqi media treated the event as a special occasion, and splashed the picture on the front page of the newspapers as well as reporting President Saddam's statement in the banner headline. President Saddam had declared,

> We are confident your mission will not be difficult because you are in a country which is very happy with the way relations with France are developing, on the basis of qualifications and in the service of the two peoples and humanity at large. We want you to work honourably in the service of your country, but we would wish you to remember that the Iraqis too will be working in the service of their country. Anything to be done for the good of France will involve another party, Iraq, and you must see Iraq's interests side by side with those of France. Iraq, for its part, will act according to these principles. This is the meaning it gives to friendship with the world's nations, including France.

A month later President Saddam received the credentials of the

West German and North Korean ambassadors, but these occasions were not played up by the media as in the case of the French ambassador. It is symbolic that the two ambassadors were given the same day on which to present their credentials, because they had something in common in that their countries were divided into a Western and a Communist state; a divided nation is in a tragic situation, no matter how prosperous the country. Perhaps President Saddam was expressing his hidden feelings towards the two countries when he told the West German ambassador, 'We must remember that we are part of humanity and that our happiness is part of the general happiness.'

President Saddam outlined his approach to government and to relations with the outside world in a speech delivered in Mosul on 15 April 1980, in which he declared,

> If you read the history of Iraq you will find that it was either a shining light leading the way, or that it was trampled under the feet of invading armies. Throughout its history it has either been in the forefront of civilisation, of leadership and history, and of the Arab nation, or it has been overwhelmed by tyranny. This is because Iraq's people have special characteristics; its people are the people of the mountains and the peaks, not of the plains and valleys.

It is clear that Saddam Hussein sees it as his role to make Iraq a 'shining light' once more, to endow it with a message of its own. To this end, he has carefully studied Iraq's political and social situation from the moment the 1968 Revolution took place, pinpointing the areas of possible social and political conflict so as to defuse them before they exploded, ruining the plans for the future. The achievement of these objectives needs a leader with the qualities of strength, determination and courage.

Iraq's economy at the time of the 1968 Revolution was certainly not the right basis for a great nation. It was obvious that it would be impossible to start on the necessary social reforms without control of the country's resources and oil wealth — hence the decision to nationalise oil. The oil companies, clearly unhappy with the new revolutionary regime, were trying to weaken it by saying there was no demand for Iraq's oil on the market. President Saddam Hussein recounted the conditions surrounding the nationalisation of oil during the long discussions we held together (*see* chapter 8). He pointed out that Iraq's experts had been against nationalisation. On the eighth anniversary of nationalisation he recalled that some Iraqi politicians had advised nationalising only half the shares, and that the experts had come to the Presidential Palace with facts and figures to prove that Iraq's revenues would drop even further if oil were nationalised.

But Saddam Hussein was unconvinced. He took the decision, 'All shares for the Iraqis; no shares for the foreigners.'

The President's success was probably what made him issue the following little-known directive to the Party leadership:

> You should not act in economic and technical matters before consulting the experts. But you must never leave the direction of the national economy up to the experts. Do not give them the opportunity to assume leadership roles; they must always follow the instructions of the revolutionary leadership, whose abilities are not just defined by technical expertise. Many experts, Baathists included, treat the problems set before them from the technical angle alone, forgetting to link this with the Revolution's concept of a new society and with the other parts of society and the Revolution.

It should also be noted that Saddam Hussein decided on nationalisation for ideological reasons. The picture of the Finance Minister waiting to receive Iraq's share of the oil revenues from the foreign companies so that he could pay the employees' salaries did not accord with the Revolution. A combination of revolutionary thought, nationalism and need led Saddam Hussein to go beyond the expert's figures and to nationalise the country's oil wealth.

There were certain risks involved at the start. The country's budget consisted of 320 million dinars at the time, and monetary reserves were low. The deficit in the balance of payments totalled some 75 million dinars and the overall economic situation was extremely poor. The British, American, French and Dutch companies took a hard line during negotiations, confident that Iraq's poor economy would make the regime back down. But in the thirteen days before nationalisation, Saddam Hussein managed to instil the right spirit in the Party leadership, which was particularly important since some of the members had been convinced by the experts' analysis.

Since the oil companies were not particularly concerned about Iraq's economic or industrial development, they had maximised production at minimal cost. Iraq developed no oil-based industries, and several oilfields remained unexplored and unexploited. Thus, prior to nationalisation, the regime had prepared plans which were to be implemented as soon as the announcement was made. They provided for oil-based industries which would, in time, ensure the revenue needed to finance the country's development projects. It is worth pointing out that the Petroleum Projects General Corporation spent only 8 million dinars on new oil installations between 1964 and 1969. Between 1969 and 1978, however, 500 million dinars were spent on oil projects. By June 1979 the value of oil projects in Iraq totalled 1,000 million dinars. The programme for the development of Iraq's oil and gas resources is proceeding apace. By 1982 the two North and South gas projects will have been completed, as well as the 7.5 million ton refinery in the North.

Oil was nationalised on 1 June 1972. Until President Ahmad Hassan Bakr announced Iraq's complete victory over the oil companies at 1.25 a.m. on 1 March 1973, Iraq had lived through difficult times. It survived only because of popular awareness that this had to be endured to achieve the final results. The announcement brought a widespread feeling of relief, particularly as the government was able to announce that the oil companies had paid out 141 million pounds sterling in back payments, that the Basra Petroleum Company had raised production levels and that the companies had ceded their share in Mosul Petroleum Company without compensation.

The programme Saddam Hussein drew up for Iraq's oil development after nationalisation provided for complete Iraqi control of all oil operations, from the well to the point of export. Iraq later purchased its first tankers to control its marketing operations. The President also insisted that Iraq deal with a variety of countries and companies, and that oil should be sold to friendly countries first, to neutral countries second and to others third. Iraq now deals with fifty-five countries and companies. It sells oil to the receiving party directly without middlemen. Iraq's oil programme is also based on investing oil revenues in other fields so as to provide for the day when the world turns to alternative energy sources or when the oil runs out. One of the major sectors of investment in Iraq is agriculture; 100 million square metres of agricultural land are under cultivation for summer and winter crops.

A brief glance at investment plans and at the contribution of oil revenues to development proves that Iraq would not have been able to develop on such a scale without the nationalisation of oil. The 1970 investment plan totalled only 116 million dinars, of which oil sector revenues accounted for 97 million. In 1971 the plan totalled 202 million dinars, with oil revenues accounting for 171 million. In 1972, the year oil was nationalised, the plan totalled 135 million dinars, of which oil accounted for 109 million. In 1973, by which time the nationalisation process was complete, the development plan provided for allocations totalling 310 million dinars and oil revenues totalled 412 million dinars — in other words, more than had been allocated in the plan. Thereafter, allocations doubled and trebled because oil revenues increased. The 1974 plan totalled 1,169 million dinars, of which oil revenues accounted for 601 million; the 1975 plan totalled 1,067 million, of which oil revenues accounted for 1,001 million; the 1976 plan totalled 1,493 million, of which oil revenues accounted for 1,258 million. By 1980 the plan provided for allocations of 5,240 million dinars and oil revenues rose correspondingly.

Had Iraq not nationalised its oil, it would have been unable to offer the hundreds of millions of dinars in aid and loans it annually extends to the Third World. Nor would it have been able to meet its commitments to the Arab countries. At the Baghdad Summit, when Iraq declared itself ready to extend annual aid worth 5 billion dollars to Egypt for ten years on condition that President Sadat did not pursue his peace treaty with Israel, Saddam Hussein knew his country's income was 30 billion dollars a year, of which oil revenues accounted for the major part. In order to help Egypt, he was willing to sacrifice some of Iraq's development projects and to postpone his plans to make Iraq a modern state within fifteen years. If Iraq had not been in complete control of its oil resources, exploitation and marketing, it could not have played such an important part in the world economy. President Saddam could not, for example, have proposed setting up a world fund in which the oil-producing countries and the industrialised countries would compensate developing countries for the rise in the price of oil and protect them from inflation exported by the industrialised countries. On the domestic level, Iraq would not have been able to repay its loans, and to become a lender in its turn. Nor would it have been able to draw up the economic policy outlined by President Saddam in 1978: 'Our economic policy is not simply based on the needs and requirements of the Iraqi region alone; it is based on the needs and future requirements of the Arab people and the Arab nation.'

One of the achievements in which President Saddam Hussein takes most pride — and which could not have been accomplished had the nationalisation of oil not ensured the necessary revenue — is Iraq's successful literacy campaign. The President can never forget that, but for his determination to overcome his circumstances, he would not have been able to receive his education and would still be a simple peasant rather than the leader of the State and the Party. It is worth examining how the literacy campaign has been able to overcome Iraqi traditions and conventions in a way that has brought it to the attention of the international community. Iraq's society is conservative by nature; it resists change even though this change would be for the better. Both men and women were prisoners of tradition, but women paid the greater price. About a hundred years ago, an attempt was made to break through these barriers and some fathers tried to give their daughters an education. But these attempts failed because of the dominant force of tradition. An excerpt from a book written in 1897 by a well-known Baghdadi religious scholar, Shaikh Naaman bin Abi al-Thana' al-Aloussi, entitled *Why it is Right not to teach Women to Write*, will best illustrate the prevalent beliefs:

> As for teaching women how to read and write, heaven forbid, I can see nothing that would do them more harm. They are predisposed to treachery and deceit, so their mastery of this skill would make it the worst implement of evil and corruption. The minute a woman learns how to write, she will send a letter to Zaid, a note to Amr, a verse or two to Azab — and other lines to other men. Teaching a woman how to read and write is like presenting a base criminal with a sword, or giving a drunkard a bottle of wine. The best of men are those who leave their women in ignorance; it is best for them and bliss.

There were attempts to eradicate illiteracy before the 1968 Revolution. Evening classes were set up at schools in Baghdad and in the provinces, but they were gradually shut down because the students could not afford the fees. There was no planning in the literacy campaigns and even an institute set up for the purpose shut its doors. After the Revolution, literacy was made a development priority. The Constitution included an article on literacy; education was made compulsory, like military service; a budget was allocated for literacy campaigns; Arab and foreign experts were consulted; and conferences were held to decide on the best programmes.

Saddam Hussein followed up these steps from his offices at the National Council; he urged his aides to give priority to literacy campaigns and to reduce the number of illiterates as quickly as possible. The conferences held for this purpose suggested three possible programmes for eradicating illiteracy, one within three years, one within five years, and one within five years for men and seven years for women. Saddam Hussein opted for the first proposal because it was the quickest. A Higher Council for Literacy was set up, and a survey was carried out to assess the number of illiterates and the levels of illiteracy in Iraq. An illiterate was defined as a man or woman between fourteen and forty-five years of age who did not know how to read, write or do simple sums. The literacy campaign was launched on 1 December 1978: 62,000 teachers and several volunteers for remote regions participated. The number of those registered for the regular and intensive courses totalled one and a quarter million, although the programmes had only been drawn up to accommodate 750,000 people. Some parts of the programme had to be reorganised to accommodate the increase. The enthusiasm with which people participated in the campaign was both an indication of the people's desire to learn and of the campaign's success. Moreover, the law on literacy was strict: 'Illiterates will not be appointed to any job; they will not be entitled to any rises, promotions or increases; they will not be allowed to apply for bank loans and will not be given facilities in agriculture, industry or real estate; they will not be given licences for professions, handicrafts or to act as agents for institutes and public utilities, and these licences will not be renewed where they have been issued.'

Over and above this, the law provided for 'imprisonment of one week or a fine of ten dinars or both, for any illiterate not registered at a literacy class although he was notified of the classes and encouraged to register. In case of repeated infractions, the punishment will be imprisonment for a period not to exceed a week.' Another article stipulated 'imprisonment for two days or a fine of two dinars for every person registered in literacy classes who is absent for more than three times a month without legitimate cause. In case of repeated infractions, punishment will be imprisonment for two days'. To give the campaign additional weight and to boost the enthusiasm of those illiterates who were trying to learn, the opening day of the campaign was officially declared the 'Day of Knowledge' and is celebrated like any other official occasion. Arab and foreign delegates are invited to take part in the celebrations. Within two years twelve provinces had been completely cleared of illiteracy. It was estimated that another year was needed to wipe out illiteracy from the six remaining provinces. It is worth repeating that, had it not been for the nationalisation of oil, the country could not have afforded a literacy campaign costing millions of dinars.

UNESCO awarded a prize to the Iraqi literacy campaign during its September 1979 celebrations of the International Day for Eradicating Illiteracy. The award read,

> Iraq has clearly used all the country's resources to consolidate its wide-ranging campaign to fight illiteracy at all levels; it has established dynamic bases; it has used those educational methods appropriate for individual classes of people; it has facilitated the links between regular schooling and non-regular schooling; it has given the international community an example of determined political will in the field of education.

Saddam Hussein viewed the literacy campaign as a campaign against an enemy, indeed, the most dangerous enemy a nation can have. A true social revolution occurred and hundreds of women hastened to join the literacy classes, even if they had to take their infants along, in order to make up for the deprivations of their past. Workers, farmers and those who had been too poor to go to school signed up for the classes and the fruits of education spread.

Saddam Hussein also turned his attention to another major issue after the nationalisation of oil: the Kurdish question. He wanted to prevent anyone exploiting this issue to weaken the State. The Kurdish question is one of those problems that can last for decades if the ruler is traditional and conservative, unwilling or unable to take the necessary steps, having fallen into the trap set by foreign agents. Alternatively, the problem can be ended quickly if the ruler is realistic, and if his ideological outlook permits responsible action. Had the Kurdish question dragged on, it would have meant living with a time-bomb that could explode at any minute. It would have meant exhausting the Army in a local war rather than preparing it for its national duty. It would have meant fewer resources for national development. The war would have dragged on until the rebel party had thrown down its arms and the Army dealt the death blow. But that victory would have been hollow because it would have been the victory of one part of the nation over another, of one part of the people over another. If the Baath could not resolve the question of one of Iraq's minorities, how could it hope to unite near and distant lands? In this light, Saddam Hussein decided to solve the Kurdish question. The Baath theory on minorities was beginning to take shape in his mind. On 11 March 1970 a communiqué was issued which was to lead to a peaceful solution of the Kurdish question: it provided for Kurdish autonomy within one nation. Autonomy would be granted within four years from the date of the agreement.

It is necessary to clarify the Baath Party theory on minorities before we examine its application by Saddam Hussein in the Kurdish question. In its Constitution, the Baath Party defines an Arab as follows: 'The Arab speaks Arabic, lives on Arab soil or hopes to do so, and believes that he is part of the Arab nation.' The definition was phrased in this manner to allow minorities to merge in the Arab world. The Kurds are a special case because of their number; the only part of the definition that can be applied to them is that they live on Arab territory. Moreover, the Kurds are particularly attached to their national customs, language and culture. It was thus necessary to amend the definition to allow for the peculiarities of this group without harbouring a foreign body in the Arab nation. These minorities could not be considered foreign in the sense that a Persian or an Indian is foreign. Nor should their desire for cultural and social development clash with the Arab drive for unity, freedom and socialism.

The problem could have been solved in a different way had Saddam Hussein accepted what the late Kurdish leader Mullah Mustafa Barzani proposed after the communiqué was issued on 11 March. Barzani proposed that the Baath Party should be the unchallenged leader of the Arabs in Iraq and he, Barzani, would be the unchallenged leader of the Kurds in Iraq. In return, he would fight against all other political activists, including the Communist Party. Saddam Hussein rejected this proposal, although the Baath Party could have used such an alliance to consolidate its revolutionary authority. He also rejected a similar offer by the Communist Party, which was allied to Barzani, whereby the Baath would be responsible for the Arabs and the Communist Party for the Kurds. The Baath Party could also have resolved this issue had it succeeded in penetrating Kurdish ranks. Kurdish Baathists remained few; those who reached leadership positions in the Party included Ali Saleh al-Saadi, Karim Shaikhli and Saad Adib, who was Vice-President of the Executive Council. By contrast, the Communists won over a number of Kurds, and they pictured the Arab character of the Baath Party as inimical to the Kurds. It should be noted that, although the Communists had penetrated Kurdish ranks, they did not enjoy mass popularity, probably because of the Kurds' strong adherence to Islam.

Saddam Hussein continued to act according to his plan. Barzani continued his insurrection, in spite of strong Kurdish opposition; the majority felt that the 11 March communiqué satisfied their aspirations and would bring security and stability to the Northern Region. In 1974 a draft proposal was set before the Kurds; it was accepted by all the Kurdish forces other than Barzani's, which meant that the fighting would continue. Many of the Kurds who lived and worked in Baghdad, some in government offices, began to leave for the Northern Region. The security forces submitted reports to Saddam Hussein about the Kurds leaving their homes and jobs to join the rebellion in the North, but the State ordered no counter-measures. Even when Barzani's son Idris came to Baghdad to meet Saddam Hussein, the confrontation did not begin. Idris announced the Kurds' rejection of the proposal in his father's name. Saddam Hussein's reply was that the proposal was to be implemented on a specific date — 11 March 1974 — and that it would be implemented as scheduled. He added, 'I know you will leave now and go to declare a rebellion, but you will regret this because your calculations are wrong.' In the meantime Kurdish ministers began to leave in their government cars to join the rebellion in the North. At this point; the security forces felt sure they would receive instructions to put the ministers under arrest and bring them back to the capital, but Saddam Hussein's instructions were as follows: 'Notify all stations on the way to salute them in the official manner until they reach the North.'

Saddam Hussein's aim was to prove to the Kurds that the State's position was firm and to instil confidence that it had met all its commitments. On 11 March 1974 the autonomy draft proposal became law, and as a result a Legislative Assembly (parliament) and an Executive Council (government) came into being. The rejectionists were given two weeks to accept or refuse. The very minute the deadline passed, orders were given to liquidate the remaining pockets of resistance. Before implementing the autonomy proposal, Saddam Hussein had used psychological as well as physical means to resolve the conflict. He had attempted to win the confidence of the Kurds and to remove the barriers between the Baath Party and the Kurds which had been erected by Barzani and the Communists. This, together with the fact that he supervised the Higher Council for Northern Affairs, went a long way towards bringing down the psychological barriers, and Saddam Hussein enjoyed considerable personal popularity before becoming President. Moreover, some links between Saddam Hussein and the Kurds were completely natural and inspired confidence in those who came to know him and had not been involved in Barzani's rebellion. For instance, Saddam Hussein's brother has a Kurdish name, Barzan, and he occupies an important security post. Saddam Hussein's personal bodyguard, Sabah Mirza, is Kurdish, which implies a mutual trust.

As President, Saddam Hussein continues to act in a way that will inspire mutual confidence between Iraq's Arabs and its Kurds. He also bears in mind that foreign agents would dearly like to upset this situation. He thus gave the following instructions to Party leaders before he became President:

> Do not imagine that the counter-revolution which has been put down could not arise again. You must not indulge in false plans and close your eyes to reality. The international forces that raised this weapon against us could do so again. The only way to prevent this from happening is through action on our part. The Baathists' actions towards, and assessment of, the problems of this sensitive area must be fully thought out. Zionism and enemy powers will continue to exploit the Kurdish question to counter our Revolution

> . . . choosing a time when local conditions are suitable for their strategic aims.

In order to further boost Arab-Kurdish confidence, President Saddam pays visits to the Northern Region and presents certain families with personal gifts. He also encourages those Kurds who have left the country to return. Indeed, the Revolution Command Council issued a decree on 24 December 1979, some five months after Saddam Hussein had become President, providing special incentives for those Kurds wishing to return to Iraq, and Iraqi embassies and airline offices abroad were instructed to facilitate matters. Every Kurd who wanted to return was allowed to bring in a car without paying tax or duty, and to bring in furniture up to the value of five thousand pounds sterling without paying duty. President Saddam also gave instructions that the Northern Region should be given the same weight as the rest of the country in social schemes.

The Baath Party has defined its position on minorities, basing itself on the philosophy Saddam Hussein drew up for the Kurdish question. The Baathist definition of its stand on national minorities in the Arab world was announced at its National Conference — that is, over thirty years after the Party was founded, because it could not tackle all political, economic, social and cultural questions at one and the same time. Moreover, until the Kurdish question had assumed the proportions of an explosive conflict, the question of minorities in the Arab world had not been a major issue. It should be noted at this point that Saddam Hussein's ability to propose a solution to the Kurdish question within two years of the Revolution's coming to power means that he had not spent the period before the Revolution planning ways and means of bringing the Party to power, but had also studied definitive and long-term solutions to outstanding problems. There was also the question of the Chaldean, Assyrian and Syriac minorities, who had been stirred up by the Communist Party to destroy the national and Arab aims of the Baath Party. After the Revolution, however, the Communist influence weakened, and the Baath worked actively to win over these minorities. The Baathist view of Arab history helped in this matter, in that it saw the Chaldeans, Assyrians and Syriacs as people of the Arabian peninsula who belonged to Arab civilisation.

In spite of this view of history, these groups remain a minority within the Party, just as they are in the country. This too may change with time, and with new ideas and social developments. There are elements inimical to the Baath within these minorities, but this enmity can also be overcome, depending on how

President Saddam Hussein decides to unify the forces of non-Baathists. Such antagonism is in any case natural between the sons of the same nation, and is not a difference in essence but a political difference. The question of minorities in Iraq would certainly have remained a problem had the Eleventh Baath Party Conference not adopted the stand it did. Iraq was able to offer its advice on another minority conflict which exploded in the Arab world, when the Berbers in Algeria suddenly demanded cultural autonomy. The 30 April 1980 issue of *Al-Thawra* condemned the way the attempt was made by the Berbers, but noted that the Baath theory on minorities could solve the problem.

The decisions to nationalise oil and to solve the Kurdish problem in an unprecedented way are the kinds of decision a leader takes to make his country a 'shining light to lead the way'. So too was another decision — that concerning Iraq's role in the October 1973 war, especially as Iraq's circumstances were particularly difficult when war was declared on 6 October. The Kurdish insurrection in the North, where some 70,000 armed men were waiting for Barzani's signal to move against key oil installations, was a major threat. The Shah was waiting for a suitable opportunity to give orders to elements he had armed within Iraq to topple the regime, and the Iraqi and Iranian forces clashed several times on the border. Meanwhile, relations with Syria were at a low ebb, both on the political and the Party level. Iraq was thus taken by surprise when Syria and Egypt declared war on Israel, since it had not been consulted beforehand. The front was a thousand kilometres away and the Iraqi forces had few troop- and tank-carriers at the time.

Nevertheless, the leadership did not take long to decide on participation in the October war. Saddam Hussein said there could be no discussion about the matter because Iraq's national role required it to take part, whatever the circumstances. He used words to this effect:

> This is a historic opportunity to develop the war. We know this is just an attempt to break the deadlock and not all-out war, but we will only be able to develop this attempt into all-out war if we take part in it. Moreover, we will not be able to speak out against the attempts at settlement unless we have fought and unless Iraqi blood has been shed on the battlefield.

Some six months earlier he had written a series of articles in *Al-Thawra* entitled 'Where the region is heading', saying that Iraq should not take part in a war which was designed just to break a stalemate and impose a settlement. When war was declared, however, he saw this as an opportunity to change the course of the war from one of limited action to one of liberation. Although this was not achieved, he was subsequently successful in using the Baghdad Summit to foil the attempt to impose a settlement.

Once Saddam Hussein had stated that there was no question about Iraq's participation in the war, the plan of action took shape in his mind. He prepared a communiqué broadcast on Radio Baghdad announcing Iraq's readiness to settle its differences with Iran and to resume diplomatic ties. President Hafez Assad of Syria was contacted that night and told that Iraqi planes were on their way to the Syrian front. Iraqi military units began to move to the Syrian front the next day. Things were different on the Egyptian front. An agreement had been reached with President Sadat under which Iraq offered seventeen million dollars in military aid, and a number of Iraqi Hawker Hunters were stationed at Egyptian bases. Hawker Hunters can circle at low altitudes, escape detection by radar and hit targets with great accuracy. Iraqi pilots thus played an important part on the Egyptian-Israeli front.

The limited-action war, which Iraq had hoped to turn into a war of liberation, came to a sudden end when President Anwar Sadat announced his acceptance of Security Council Resolution 338. Iraq announced in a communiqué that it was ready to continue the battle. A delegate was sent to Damascus to communicate this to President Hafez Assad and to express Iraq's willingness to send the entire Iraqi Army to Syria if Syria continued the war. If Syria decided to accept Resolution 338, then the Iraqi units and planes would return to Iraq. This is what happened when Syria called an end to the war a little later.

From the moment that Egypt, followed by Syria, ended the war with Israel, Saddam Hussein planned a form of Arab action designed to complicate matters for the parties who had entered into a settlement. One of the results of this line of action was the Baghdad Summit, in itself a departure from the traditional Baath Party line which had rejected Arab conferences as a way of settling major questions. This change of policy perplexed some members of the Party Command, but once Saddam Hussein had explained the reasoning behind it they redoubled their efforts to ensure the success of the Baghdad Summit and the National Charter of 8 February 1980. Both the Summit and the Charter come within President Saddam's long-range vision of restoring the role of Iraq as a 'shining light'. This has meant constant developments on the questions of non-Baathists participating in the decision-making process and on the application of socialism.

The first indication of a new approach to the participation of non-Baathists came in a press conference held on 19 August 1979 by the Vice-Premier Tareq Aziz. He announced a series of measures for political liberalisation and said the Party Command was studying the question of general elections. He also said that all political prisoners in Iraq were to be released. There were 725 political prisoners in Iraq at the time; of these 400 were in prison because of incidents in the Northern Region, and 300 were members of various political movements, including 24 Communists. One of the measures was a call to the Iraqi Communist Party abroad to enter into a dialogue with the National Progressive Front, in which the Baath was a major force. Tareq Aziz pointed out that the Front had not 'taken a decision to expel the Communist Party'. The announcement came just one month after Saddam Hussein had assumed complete responsibility, as though he were trying to cancel the effects of the plot in which some Baathist leaders had taken part. Tareq Aziz noted that these resolutions aimed at 'political liberalisation on the internal level' but stressed that 'the decision is not the result of new directives, but a natural extension of the previous stage'.

Almost all political prisoners were immediately set free, the only ones to remain in gaol being those Baathists who had taken part in the plot. Work began on a draft law for a parliament, the last parliament having been dissolved after the July 1958 Revolution. It was to be called the National Assembly, instead of a 'parliament' or 'people's assembly'. At the same time preparations were underway on the draft law for the Kurdish parliament, called the 'Legislative Assembly for the Autonomous Region of Kurdistan'. On 1 December 1979 the two draft laws were released for discussion at all levels. The Iraqis participated in the discussions through the press and on television, in an unusual display of freedom of speech and expression. Although some Baathists expressed fears about a return to parliamentary life, President Saddam insisted that the discussion be as comprehensive as possible. Those who had expressed reservations feared that the reintroduction of parliament would also mean reintroducing the evils of tribalism which had marked the parliament of the 1950s.

The National Assembly as envisaged in the draft law was not to be run on traditional lines, nor was it to be merely a façade. It would participate in decisions and laws which had previously been the province of the Revolution Command Council and the Baath Party. The Assembly would propose draft laws, pass laws in accordance with the Constitution, approve the state budget and the national development plan, and approve treaties and international agreements in accordance with the Constitution. The Assembly would also have the right to call any minister before it for questioning, in accordance with its internal statutes. This unprecedented step meant that a minister, who would also be a member of the Revolution Command Council, could be called on to explain his actions.

The draft law also provided for immunity for the members of the National Assembly: no one had the right to question a member 'about any opinions he might express or issues he might raise while carrying out his duties at the Assembly; no member of the Assembly [could] be placed under arrest during the Assembly's sessions without permission from the Assembly except in the case of a capital offence'. The draft law guarded against misuse and infiltration of the Assembly by setting out the following conditions for candidature. A candidate must: believe in the principles and aims of the 1968 Revolution; have done his military service or have been excused from such service; not have been affected by nationalisation or agricultural reform measures; and not have been 'sentenced for any crime against internal or external state security after the 17-30 July Revolution, crimes betraying public confidence, crimes against the national economy and state finances or state moneys, or crimes against public morals'. The prospective candidate also had to know how to read and write. Some members in the pre-1958 parliament had not known how to read and write and used to sign draft laws and projects by thumb-print.

From the minute it was announced, the draft law sparked an atmosphere of excitement and anticipation, and many people were keen to play a political role. The Baathists noted that the proposed National Assembly allowed for political action by non-Baathists and that Baathists no longer had a monopoly over the political field. It was now up to them to strengthen their links with the people, as though President Saddam was telling his one million Iraqi comrades that the National Assembly was an expression of their ties with the people.

Friday 20 June 1980 was the day fixed for the elections. To avoid any exploitation of the election campaign, the State itself published pictures of the candidates with a small résumé about each one. It was also responsible for taking the voters to and from the polling stations. Two days before the elections, President Saddam had delivered a speech in the town of Ramadi in Anbar Province. Its message was mainly aimed at the Baathists: 'We consider all the candidates for the National Assembly to be sons of the Revolution and sons of the Party, whether they are Baathists or not.' When news reached the President that certain

Baathists had broken the Command directive which provided for non-differentiation between Baathist and non-Baathist candidates, he ordered those Baathists to be punished through the Party, no matter how prominent they were. Some were expelled and others demoted, and their names were published in the papers. On the day of the elections, President Saddam continued his tour of Anbar Province, and visited the polling stations. He asked the voters which candidates they had chosen and why, and what they expected from a member of the Assembly. When the elections were over, he issued a statement praising the citizens' sense of responsibility and discipline during the first elections Iraq had held for twenty years, and the first elections ever at which women were given the right to vote and to stand for election.

On 21 June 1980 a new legislative body came into being, with 250 Iraqi men and women as its members. At present it is led by Naim Haddad, a high-ranking Party member, whose election enables President Saddam to be relieved of the burden of following Assembly affairs in detail. The candidates in the election had numbered 840, with over 56 voting districts and polling stations. The Assembly is not a Baathist parliament as such, but is a parliament of the Baath in the sense defined by President Saddam during the discussions I had with him: 'I believe that the vast majority of Iraqis are now Baathists, whether they are members of the Party or not . . .' When inaugurating the first session of parliament on 30 July 1980, President Saddam told the members of the National Assembly: 'Some say that we will now enter the "democratic stage". This is a big mistake, because the framework too will develop and we will find ourselves in ten years' time before yet another framework for the expression of democracy.' These words indicate that he considers the National Assembly only one of many steps, and that it will develop, together with the Legislative Assembly, rather than remain static. The President went on to say,

> The Party has used different means to express democracy, such as the free elections held by workers, peasants, students and women. There have also been elections in all the unions and professions. These are all expressions of true democracy. The daily interaction between the leadership and the people at conferences and at other forums are also forms of democracy. With the new National Assembly, we will practise democracy in a new framework, expressing the principles of the Revolution.

President Saddam also raised an important point: the elections had not been imposed by the extraordinary pressure of circumstances. 'Had the National Assembly law come at a time when there were difficult conditions in the Party or in the State,' he said, 'people would have said this was an attempt to distract the masses or to provide a safety valve.' The law came when the Party was strong and sound, to act as 'a primary expression of the Party's understanding of life'.

The first part of the 'political liberalisation' has been achieved, and Iraq now has a parliament free from the evils that characterised that of pre-1958 days. The other part of political liberalisation has, however, not been completed: the Iraqi Communist Party in exile did not respond to Tareq Aziz's call for a dialogue, although he had hoped to facilitate its return by pointing out that it had not been expelled from the National Progressive Front. When I met President Saddam on 29 August 1979 I asked him whether the decision to set up a parliament and to invite the Communists to return to Iraq was brought about because of the plot in which some Baathists had been involved. He replied,

> It is true that revolutionaries must not overlook the significance of each event. A revolutionary becomes an anti-revolutionary, however, when his stand is based on reacting to events as they occur: this means he does not have a strategy or any basic principles. The plot took place; the plotters were in a state of reaction. But the framework we are talking about is a revolutionary framework, thus no one should think that it was set up because of the plot. The National Assembly has been under discussion for a long time; some of the plotters were among those entrusted with setting up a National Assembly and worked to prevent it.

As for the Communists, he said,

> The Regional Command sent them a message some time ago, inviting them to a dialogue to restore relations in a way acceptable to both parties. They sent back a message which the Command considers does not represent the necessary stand; it did not respond frankly, openly and courageously to the Command's initiative. This is an old situation; for the present we have nothing new. Any time they are willing to return to the Revolution's fold and to operate within it, we are willing to enter into a dialogue with them; otherwise we are not. The Revolution is progressing; it was not created by the Communist Party and it will not collapse if the Communist Party does not join it. The Revolution is progressing, and any time the Iraqi Communist Party wishes to join it, the Command will study this request and act accordingly.

The fact that President Saddam does not attach great importance to whether the Communists return or not means they are no longer an important or effective political force. In any case, as a result of their continued opposition, some Communists have set up a Marxist organisation called the 'National Organisation' which co-operates with the Baath. The President has left the door open for their return because he wants to consolidate stability and not to leave any opportunity for political or social disturbance.

If President Saddam is successful, the 1980s will be the period of greatest stability Iraq has enjoyed in modern times, as a brief review of its history will show. Since Iraqis took over the reins of government, and before the Baath came to power, no government had lasted for more than two or three years. Even under the monarchy, the governments used to change constantly, sometimes every three months, although the politicians all belonged to the same class and were convinced that the regime should be maintained. Even the governments formed by Nouri al-Said, the strongest leader of that time, did not live long. Prior to that, Iraq carried out a revolution against British imperialism which forced the British to set up a 'national government' to replace the British military governor. The British were forced to establish an Arab monarchy in Iraq, and to grant the country independence. Prior to the British, the Ottomans had ruled in Iraq.

In the 1930s Iraq lived through troubled times. A military coup led by Bakr Sidqi preceded Husni Zaim's military coup in Syria by some thirteen years. A courageous nationalist leadership in the 1940s could have overthrown the monarchy and declared a republic, but this did not happen, in spite of the disturbances at that time which reached a peak in 1948, when Iraq was effectively without a leadership. During the 1952 Uprising, the monarchy had to resort to appointing the Army Chief of Staff, General Noureddin Mahmoud, as Prime Minister, whereas it had previously been careful to give the regime a civilian stamp.

In 1956 the Baath Party organised massive demonstrations against the tripartite aggression on Egypt. The 1958 Revolution followed, but in its second year it was marked by bloody clashes between the nationalists, the Communists and the Baathists. After the Ramadan Revolution of 1963, Iraq suffered increased turbulence and bloody conflicts, and the gaols were full of political prisoners. It went through cyclical changes of government. Abdel-Salam Aref died in mysterious circumstances and was replaced by his brother Abdel-Rahman Aref, whose rule brought further disturbances. The July 17 Revolution came next. At the beginning it was marked by conflict: the exile of Abdel-Razzaq Nayef and the expulsion of certain Baathist leaders such as Hardan Takriti and Saleh Mahdi Ammash. Then the Iraqi Army had to confront the Kurdish rebellion led by Mullah

Mustafa Barzani, in which some 60,000 people were killed or wounded. There were also conflicts, occasionally bloody, between Baathists and other political forces, and amongst the Baathists themselves.

In 1975 Iraq entered a period of stability after fifty years of bloody conflict. The Kurdish insurrection ended in the best possible way for the Northern Region. The Baath Party's authority was consolidated. Traditionally opposed forces chose to co-operate with the Party, and the only people who remained outside this framework were the Communists who moved to certain East European capitals. Had it not been for the plot carried out by certain Baathist leaders and for a few isolated explosions, stability in Iraq would have continued to grow without a hitch and people would no longer have identified Iraq with bloody conflicts. President Saddam's tours of the various regions, his surprise visits to the citizens and the process of political liberalisation he has begun since assuming full responsibility are erasing the effects of half a century of instability. It is not an easy task, and there are those who would like to abort it.

On 18 June 1980, during his tour of Anbar Province, President Saddam said, 'We cannot promise that there won't be a single bomb explosion or rifle shot in Iraq' [because of the anger Iraq's stability was causing in certain quarters]. He also referred to this in another statement on 20 July 1980, during his visit to a military base:

> We wanted to give thirteen and a half million [the population of Iraq] the weight of over forty million. We have now achieved this and we are confident that the balance is weighted in our favour because of our strength, ability and effectiveness. Our hope is to continue and develop this so we may wrest the opportunity to play a historic role, as played by our ancestors in the service of the Arab nation and humanity.

This role is that of a 'shining light'. The only thing that will prevent this is a return to the cycle of instability and violence. I spoke to a number of leading Iraqis about this matter. Their reply can be summed up as follows:

> Iraq has a number of special particularities within the Arab world which must be kept in mind in any study of its current situation. Throughout its long history of over 2,000 years, Iraq has enjoyed strength and prosperity. Strong empires and nations were born on this land, but it has also suffered great defeats at the hands of its enemies and of nature. If we go back to Iraq's history in Babylonian, Assyrian and Chaldean times, and throughout the Islamic

age, we can see that Iraq never lived an ordinary life. It was either a major empire with great responsibilities, having to face serious political, military and cultural assaults, or it was in a state of defeat, occupation and tyranny. This history has formed the Iraqi character, which responds forcefully to any challenge. The Iraqi may submit and suffer for long periods but when he replies he strikes with strength and directness. Others see this as a violent reaction.

We Baathists have grown up on this soil and our character has been formed by it. We faced difficult challenges in the modern age and in setting up the Party. We never had a chance to operate freely and openly, to hold conferences and publish a newspaper without being placed under arrest or tortured. The Baathists in Iraq never had the opportunity enjoyed by the Baathists in Lebanon. The monarchy was a harsh terrorist. Any cultural or political activity was forbidden. The Party members used to meet secretly in their hide-outs. Whoever was arrested would suffer the most hideous torture. Nothing changed after the fall of the monarchy in 1958. The Party spent four and a half years confronting Abdel-Karim Qassem and the Communists, and this is why it had to resort to violence.

When the Baath Party took over power on 8 February 1963 it was confronted by the Communists and by reactionary forces, as well as by Barzani's insurrection in the mountains. On 18 October 1963 the Baathists were overthrown with great violence and hatred. Throughout the rule of Abdel-Salam Aref and then Abdel-Rahman Aref, the Baath was the butt of ugly slander. These were the conditions under which the Baath lived before the 1968 Revolution: prison, deprivation, executions, torture, defamation and harassment.

In spite of the occasional disturbances in Iraq between the 1968 Revolution and the time when Saddam Hussein assumed complete responsibility in July 1979, this stage has been one of the most tolerant, democratic and rational. You should not forget that Iraq lies on the Eastern part of the Arab nation and that it faces greater challenges than other Arab countries. The question of nationalism remains a burning issue in Iraq because of its proximity to the Persians and the Turks, and to other peoples in the East. These conditions are not the same as in Egypt or in other Arab countries which border non-Arab peoples, because those groups are not major political, military or cultural forces, as are the ones bordering Iraq. Thus Iraq lives in a state of constant alert to safeguard its independence and its Arabhood.

Although President Saddam had an extremely difficult life before he took over complete responsibility on 30 July 1979, he has shown extraordinary patience and forbearance. Thanks to this ability the Baath Party has managed to develop and this maturity has led to increased political stability. This will in turn lead to a revision of the current image of Iraq and its revolutionary experience.

Nevertheless, those leaders with whom I discussed the 'bloody' image acquired by Iraq always travel with their guns at their sides. They feel threatened. I accompanied the Minister of Information and Culture Latif Nassif Jassim, one of the men who had fought alongside Saddam Hussein before the Party came to power, to the house of the Minister of the Interior Saadoun Shaker, where both men told me about the time Saddam Hussein waged the underground struggle and how he treated his comrades when they were all in prison. As we got into the car, I noticed that Latif Nassif Jassim took his revolver from its holster and set it beside him before we drove off to Saadoun Shaker's house. I said, 'You're now Minister of Information, you are not in a security post; why do you carry a revolver wherever you go?' He replied in peasant dialect (he had been responsible for the farmers in the Party, and they were among its major supporters), 'There is a common saying among the people of the Iraqi countryside: keep your revolver handy, you may need it one day.'

I was to remember this saying when I heard the news agency report of an attempt to assassinate Latif Nassif Jassim outside the Ministry of Information. The Minister escaped unscathed and then pursued the young man who had fired at him with his revolver in his hand. It later transpired that the man belonged to the Al-Da'awa Party, which had previously organised the attempt on Tareq Aziz's life at Mustansiriyah University. Ironically enough, just a few days earlier I had asked Tareq Aziz why the leadership in Iraq carried guns wherever they went, to which he replied, 'We have become used to this. The leaders in Iraq are revolutionaries who were engaged in revolutionary action for years. This meant that we had to carry weapons. We became used to it and have continued to do so until today.'

The final aspect of Saddam Hussein's efforts to make Iraq a 'shining light' is his development of the theory and practice of socialism. Its basic principle is that prosperity is conducive to political stability. The Deputy Premier Tareq Aziz has been given a free hand in the tourism sector, for instance, and a number of first-class hotels, restaurants, cinemas and theatres are being built. Also in this respect, President Saddam has decided on import facilities for the private sector and for those areas of commerce where the socialist sector cannot operate. The sum of nearly four billion dinars was allocated for imports during 1980. On 17 June 1980 President Saddam went on a tour of private sector factories and plants, which is an example of how the socialist state works to encourage the private sector. He also provided encouragement for the tourist sector by visiting a number of tourist centres and speaking to the workers. All these developments are in line with Iraq's policy of complete independence. It does not need foreign investment in its projects, and its relations with other states and companies are strictly on a contract basis. If all goes as planned, the private sector will continue to flourish and Iraq will be one of the few countries where the public and private sectors coexist without either interfering with the other.

President Saddam's interest in making Iraq a 'shining light' operates on all levels, even the simplest. For example, he heads a campaign to encourage the planting of palm-trees. Each citizen was asked to plant a tree outside his house so that Iraq's date palms will flourish by the year 2000 (they were on the verge of extinction in the 1970s because of the construction boom). A great deal of attention is also being paid to the restoration and preservation of historic sites, such as Babylon, and the protection of other sites from flooding because of newly-built dams. Moreover, President Saddam is making every effort to have Iraq's stolen heritage returned. Ashur Banipal ruled Iraq 2,500 years ago: how can the Iraqis accept that his library should remain in the British Museum, where it was taken at the end of the last century? Nor can they accept that Ashtar's door in King Nebuchadnezzar's palace in Babylon is now in East Berlin, whereas Iraq only has a copy of the original. King Hammurabi's stone tablet is in the Louvre in Paris. Hundreds of other pieces of Iraq's heritage are scattered around the world in museums and palaces, whereas their rightful place is in Iraq. Most of these pieces were taken out of Iraq under the Ottomans and the British. President Saddam's repeated references to this subject indicate that he is planning to take action. If Iraq's heritage is returned willingly, in response to the UN General Assembly's call in 1975 to restore pieces taken from countries to their owners, then well and good. Otherwise, other methods will have to be adopted. President Saddam is as proud of the Arab nation's great heroes as he is of Iraq's ancient past. He respects the memory of Imam Hussein, and projects are under way to beautify Karbala; he also admires figures of Iraq's ancient past such as Nebuchadnezzar. Iraq has 10,000 historic sites under preservation and a Ministry of Archaeology may well be set up soon.

Had it not been for Iraq's financial commitments to developing countries and the Arab world, and the constant drain on Arab strength by agreements like the Egyptian-Israeli treaty, the road towards making Iraq a 'shining light' would not have been so long and hard. President Saddam's method of handling problems as they arise, such as his efforts at the Baghdad Summit and over the National Charter, is in itself the crystallisation of Iraq's role as a 'shining light'.

CHAPTER 6

THE PLEDGE OF ALLEGIANCE

'The qualities with which God has endowed you and which have made you a brave leader and an inspired comrade, the qualities which have enabled you to bring the Party's ideology and principles to fruition, making them a tangible part of life, these are the qualities the Revolution needs as the nation goes through this critical phase, the phase of rebirth of identity and of civilisation . . .'
(Michel Aflaq in the telegram he sent to Saddam Hussein on 17 July 1979)

In his first speech upon assuming complete responsibility on 17 July 1979, Saddam Hussein made it clear that he had not been the second-in-command during the eleven years since the Party had come to power, but that he had been one of two leaders: 'It has never happened before, either in ancient history (including that of our nation since its dawn) or in modern times, that two leaders have been in power for eleven years within one command, without this resulting in a dangerous moral or practical imbalance in leadership . . .'

With Saddam Hussein's assumption of complete responsibility, there was no longer any need for a command with two leaders, one military and one civilian. There is now one leader and many other people in positions of responsibility according to their Party positions. The overall leader is Saddam Hussein, who occupies the following positions: President of the Revolution Command Council, Secretary of the Regional Command, Deputy Secretary-General of the National Command, President of the Republic, Commander-in-Chief of the Armed Forces and Prime Minister. Although there is a Vice-President of the Republic, Taha Muhieddin Maarouf, he does not deputise for President Saddam because the highest authority is that of the Revolution Command Council. The Vice-President of the Revolution Command Council is Izzat Ibrahim, who is also the Deputy Secretary of the Regional Command. Taha Muhieddin Maarouf was appointed Vice-President in accordance with the 1974 Autonomy Law for the Northern Region, which provides for a Kurdish Vice-President.

In 1970 two military Baathists, Hardan Takriti and Saleh Mahdi Ammash, were appointed Vice-Presidents of the Republic. However, the Constitution included an article which said that the Vice-President of the Revolution Command Council (Saddam Hussein) was to assume the responsibilities of the President of the Council and the President of the Republic in case of their absence. First Takriti and then Ammash were relieved of their posts, and the post of Vice-President of the Republic remained vacant until Taha Muhieddin Maarouf was appointed, as part of the measures to resolve the Kurdish question.

It should be pointed out that Saddam Hussein's appointment as Vice-President of the Revolution Command Council was announced in November 1969, over a year after the Revolution. He had not wanted to assume a position in the State and felt it was sufficient that the Party had carried out the Revolution. He remained of this mind until 1974, when he finally decided he would take full responsibility. He had previously carried the responsibility but without being convinced that this was the role he was called on to play. He probably took the final decision because of his success in solving the Kurdish question. Because it had taken over a year to announce Saddam Hussein's appointment as Vice-President of the Revolution Command Council, and because Hardan Takriti and Saleh Ammash had been appointed Vice-Presidents of the Republic after 30 July 1968, some people thought that they were senior to Saddam Hussein. Matters were clarified when he was officially confirmed as Vice-President of the Revolution Command Council, and it was announced that the members of the Regional Command were also members of the Council, which made it a Party institution.

Reference has already been made to President Saddam's adoption of a new form of State structure. It is now time to examine the whys and wherefores of this form. Under this structure, Izzat Ibrahim became Vice-President of the Revolution Command Council, and then Deputy Secretary of the Regional Command. On the executive level, Taha Yassin Ramadan was appointed First Deputy Premier, and Naim Haddad, Tareq Aziz, Saadoun Ghaidan and Adnan Khairallah were appointed Deputy Premiers. Saadoun Ghaidan and Adnan Khairallah also held ministerial posts: Saadoun Ghaidan was appointed Minister of Transport and Communications, and Adnan Khairallah Minister of Defence and Deputy Commander-in-Chief of the Armed Forces. The other Deputy Prime Ministers were responsible for certain State sectors. President Saddam distributed responsibilities in this fashion because he wanted to broaden participation in leadership. It would also free him from having to deal in detail with certain fields.

Three of the Deputy Premiers are also members of the Regional Command and of the National (pan-Arab) Command: Taha Yassin Ramadan, Naim Haddad and Tareq Aziz. Izzat Ibrahim is also a member of the National Command, which includes eleven members now that President Bakr has retired. The other members of the National Command are: Michel Aflaq (Secretary-General), Saddam Hussein (Deputy Secretary-General), Shibli Aissami (Syrian; Assistant Secretary-General), Ali Ghanem (Saudi), Abdel-Majid Rafei (Lebanese), Qassem Salameh (Yemeni) and Badreddin Madthar (Sudanese). According to protocol, the members of the National (pan-Arab) Command are higher than the members of the Revolution Command Council, which is the highest authority in Iraq. At the Eleventh Party Conference in autumn 1979, for example, President Ahmad Hassan Bakr was, according to protocol, third in rank (although he was head of state) because he was preceded by Michel Aflaq, the Secretary-General of the Party, and Shibli

Aissami, the Assistant Secretary-General.

Naturally, the members of the Command do not keep office hours because their posts are not ordinary jobs. Nor is it necessary for every Arab state to be represented in the Command, because the elections are carried out on the basis of the people not the countries. It is thus possible to have more than one member from the same country, and none from another. The major Party organisations are represented, however. Members of the National Command are not considered as representatives of the Party in a given country but are responsible for the Party in the Arab world.

The Party hierarchy and Party protocol are reflected in television and press coverage of events. If Michel Aflaq receives a delegation or an official visitor, he will be given first place on television because he is Secretary-General of the Party. Saddam Hussein, the Deputy Secretary-General, comes next, without this affecting his positions as head of the Command Council and President of the Republic. The newspapers will carry a picture of Michel Aflaq and his visitors on the right-hand side of the front page, and of Saddam Hussein on the left. For example, *Al-Thawra*'s front-page headline on 13 December 1979 read, 'Comrade Michel Aflaq: Palestine is the cause of the century.' This statement was made during the Secretary-General's meeting with President Samora Machel of Mozambique in his offices at the National Command. On the left-hand side, the paper printed a picture of Saddam Hussein greeting the Mozambique President, without playing it up. As a further example, on 29 April 1980 the paper printed a picture of the Secretary-General Michel Aflaq greeting the children of the Jumhouriya and Yarmouk kindergartens on the right-hand side of the page, and on the left carried a picture of President Saddam and members of the Iraqi delegation greeting the Seychelles Republic President France Albert René, who was on a visit to Iraq.

It is necessary at this point to examine the Party structure within Iraq and the Party institutions that have developed, as well as Saddam Hussein's way of dealing with his Party comrades. The Regional Command is the highest authority of the Party in Iraq. It now has fifteen members, after the abortive coup against the leadership. The Command Branch comes under the Regional Command, and acts as the provincial authority — an example would be the Baghdad Command Branch. Each Branch is divided into Divisions, representing major areas. Each Division is divided into Units, representing areas within a city, and each Unit is divided into Cells. There are, moreover, Back-up Groups and Supporters. The Party structure within Iraq is not necessarily the same as the structure outside Iraq, because each region of the Arab nation is entitled to act according to its circumstances once it has received permission from the National Command.

The Regional Command is an elected body. Party members vote for the Unit Command, which in turn votes for the Division Command. The Division Command leaders vote at the Branch Leadership Conference. The Regional Conference is made up of Branch leaders and representatives of the people, and votes for the Regional Command. The Regional Command has a good deal of authority; it can, if it sees fit, dissolve Branch or Division Commands and change the organisation structure between one election and the next. Promotion from one grade to the next progresses in an orderly fashion. Obviously a person cannot join the Party one day and become a member of the Regional Command the next. At the Eleventh Party Conference the internal organisational structure was amended so that those who had not previously voted at Unit and Division levels were not entitled to vote for the Regional Command. To participate in the elections of the Regional Command, a person must have been an active Party member for ten years. These amendments were made because those who were not accepted at the lower levels were obviously not fit to become members at higher levels.

The Party Preparatory School was set up to develop Party cadres and to broaden Party experience. At this 'training centre' students are divided into two levels and given lectures on ideology, economics and politics. The lecturers, who are for the most part senior Party members, also speak about the Party's experience. There are also special one-month sessions for the members of the Division and Branch leaderships. Regular sessions last four months and take about 150 to 200 Party members. The school began on a small scale, but has since developed. There are plans to set up branches in the provinces and to appoint full-time teachers, now that there are over a million Party members, including Back-up Groups and Supporters.

There are also a number of special Party bureaux: the Military Bureau, the Labour Bureau, the Farmers' Bureau, the Students Bureau, the Professions Bureau, and so on. The Labour Bureau is responsible for organising the workers and encouraging them to join the Party, and for training them politically and ideologically so that they may play an effective role. It is indirectly in command of the General Federation of Labour Unions and its organisations. The most important bureau is the Culture and Information Bureau. It supervises the Party Preparatory School and handles the Party's internal publications, a magazine called *Al-Thawra al-Arabiyya* and a political, analytic news bulletin. Even after becoming President, Saddam Hussein still heads this Bureau. It supervises the official and cultural sectors of the State as well as information, and includes representatives from the various fields of information. The Party Command appoints the officials to the Bureau, who are generally high-ranking Party members.

The Party structure and organisation have been Saddam Hussein's main concerns throughout. Had this not been so, according to Party leaders in Iraq, the Party would have been rent by divisions a long time ago and would not have remained as strong as it is. Saddam Hussein appears to have been impressed by a statement in an internal Party memorandum in Damascus in October 1952 and he has always been careful to implement it: 'The organisational aspect is as important as the ideological one, and is indivisible from it.'

Constructive criticism and self-criticism are two of the bases of Party action, and herein lies the secret of its success. One of the reasons for the failure of the Communist Party is the absence of self-criticism. Because of the application of the principle of self-criticism, for example, the Baath Party has changed and developed its leadership, whereas the Communist Party has had the same leadership for thirty years. In Baathist thinking, criticism is a confession of wrongdoing and brings relief to the Party members. Self-criticism is engaged in at weekly Party meetings where members stand up and say that they have acted in an unsuitable way and will never do so again. At other times, a comrade may criticise one of his fellow comrades, and it is up to the rest of the members to decide whether or not to send a report to higher authorities; this has eliminated the possibility of discrimination.

Since the Party came to power, Saddam Hussein has emphasised the importance of the relationship between Baathists. His most quoted statements in this respect are: 'Your greatest treasure is the revolutionary comradeship between you; you must protect it just as you did during the phase of struggle against the State, but now with respect for the State. This must not be an artificial kind of respect that reflects badly on the Party'; 'Let not history say of you that only the exigencies of underground revolutionary action led to love and comradeship between you, and that when the secret struggle ended so did love and companionship'; 'The ties of comradeship must be maintained at all levels and at all stages. Although you seem strong now, this is the best way to keep strong; this is the way to progress. Should you forget this when you are strong you will become weak'; 'We want you, dear comrades, to follow Party principles at every turn when you are in authority, and to apply them in your everyday work so that these may be the principles of a progressive and developed nation'; 'There is a difference in substance between the State and the political structure and organisation, although the State is the Party's State. If the difference between . . . State authority and Party authority disappears, then the Party will become the State's Party, instead of the State being the Party's State, and our role as revolutionaries bringing progressive change will be over. This role will become so weak that the Party will become one of the traditional institutions of the State and the State will no longer be guided and activated by a Party conscience and intellect.'

Saddam Hussein supports his advice with analysis at all Party meetings, and reports are transmitted to the lower echelons. He has said, for example: 'Comrades. Fight with bravery and honour. When you make a promise, fulfil this promise with honour. When you serve your people, do so with humility'; 'Remember that a revolutionary without morals cannot win the allegiance of the people, no matter what his other achievements'; 'The good Baathist runs quickly and well through a minefield; your weapon against the mines is your education; you will be able to defuse the bombs if you are equipped with the principles of your Party and with education. Education is not simply reading books, but mixing with the people and finding out about their problems . . .'

Saddam Hussein has simplified the ideological theories of the Baath so that they can be understood at all levels. One can see this in his writings and through the slogans he has coined: 'Do not become afflicted with pride or you will become dizzy'; 'The pen and the sword have the same tip'; 'The revolutionary who carries a rifle of one kind and ammunition of another will doubtless be defeated. We have a peasant saying which goes, "The rifle will eat only its own bullets"'; 'Education destroys all weapons'; 'There can be no prosperity for a nation which eats more than it produces, and which reaps more than it sows'; 'If you cannot exploit an opportune moment, you must ensure that your enemy does not.' Such slogans are essential if a Party wants to have mass appeal. It is important to reach all levels of the population, the educated and the less educated.

Saddam Hussein is also responsible for the 'dictionary' of Baathist political terms. For example, he has coined the word 'keys' to mean general rules, the words 'decision-making mind' for the Party Command, and the words 'foreign fence' for the borders of the Revolution; the 'inner door' means the heart of the Revolution. He has also coined expressions like 'cultivation ground', 'vertical classification' and 'spiritual negation'. When one meets Saddam Hussein one can expect to hear unusual turns of phrase and extraordinary metaphors. During a discussion I had with him about the Arab condition, he said,

> When we prepare ourselves to run the course, we gird our loins to run at the necessary speed and exert ourselves to reach the furthest point. But then we find an obstacle in our path and everyone is reduced to the same level. This is like putting a thoroughbred with a plough-horse in the same narrow compound: the thoroughbred will only run as fast as the plough-horse. It might even seem that the plough-horse is the faster of the two.

Saddam Hussein has expounded on the Baath theory of socialism:

> Socialism as we see it does not only mean balancing circumstances and material factors. It must also balance the basic factor, the level of production and education which our people have reached, their level of understanding of joint socialist action and running the socialist sector. If the steps we take to implement socialism are not equal in time and length to this factor, then we will be committing a major error and will be exposed to a dangerous reaction in the guise of 'moderation' by the extreme left.

The President also defined the Baathist view of mankind long before he assumed full responsibility for the Party and the State:

> Man is the central aim and one of the major values. The human being must be respected and should never be belittled. Generally speaking, those in the lower echelons who have had less education and experience will tend to belittle one another. Loyalty must be one of the characteristics of the Baathist. Thus the Baathist should not compete with the people on the question of loyalty, because at a point we will reach in about five years' time, there will no longer be many enemies of the Revolution or many reactionaries. Political enemies will shrink and weaken, and all the people will be equal to the Baathists in loyalty. The only difference will be that the Baathist is better able to express this loyalty.

He was thus trying to nip in the bud the feeling that the Baathist was better than others and therefore deserved more. This is why he warned of the dangers of using Baathism, rather than qualifications, as a means of getting ahead. The following statements show this yet more clearly:

> We must strive, and our comrades must strive, to develop our abilities so that we may compete in society and compete with the citizen who is also the legitimate son of the Revolution. We must do away with all illegitimate competition which is due to the lack of equal opportunities. The Baathist might get an opportunity simply

> because he is a member of the Party, whereas that opportunity may be withheld from the ordinary citizen. However, the Baathist must take his opportunity because of his exceptional ability and qualifications . . . not at the expense of the people. When there are two roads, one straight and clear and the other full of obstacles, and when the Baathist is given the first road whereas the son of the people gets the other, the Baathist will obviously move more quickly. This means a Baathist will advance simply because he is a Baathist and not because he has shown ability, revolutionary technique or any expression of loyalty towards the Revolution and the Party.

Saddam Hussein went on to explain the results as follows:

> This situation will result in a gap between the people and the Party, the Revolution and its leadership. If a citizen knows that he has been loyal to the Revolution, the Party and its leadership, that he has abided by the Revolution's programme and that he is more able than the Baathist who has been promoted just because he is a Baathist, then the citizen will be upset and a gap will grow between the people and the Party. We will lose in another way, too, if this situation continues. The citizen, finding this state of affairs hard to bear, will be driven to stand against the Revolution and will go over to the other side, where the enemies of the Revolution lie in waiting. The citizen would not have been against the Revolution originally, but he will rebel against the unjust expression of the Revolution through those people who have not set a better example.

Saddam Hussein underlines this because he wants the Baathist experience in Iraq to be an example 'not only in the Arab world, but to make an impact on the human race in the farthest corners of the world'. This will naturally not be possible if the Baathist uses his position for personal advancement.

Saddam Hussein has also warned the Baathists against forming a 'Baathist class'. He said at a meeting of the leadership,

> Is it right that a man should only feel he is high when others around him are low, or should we become used to the feeling that we are on a peak when the rest of our comrades are also on peaks? . . . True height comes when there is equality at all levels.

At one point, the Baath Party thought that the only way to change the Arab world was through the Baath. But Saddam Hussein has developed this philosophy so that the Baath in Iraq now appreciates any revolutionary experience in the Arab world which is national and progressive and which stands against foreign intervention.

The Secretary-General of the Party Michel Aflaq sent his telegram to Saddam Hussein on 17 July 1979, when the latter took over full responsibility for the State and the Party, because he had mobilised and enlightened the masses to safeguard the Revolution, because he had crystallised the theory of 'revolutionary flexibility' and because he had drawn up the Baath theory on minorities. These and other things are what led Michel Aflaq to say:

> The qualities with which God has endowed you and which have made you a brave leader and an inspired comrade, the qualities which have enabled you to bring the Party's ideology and principles to fruition, making them a tangible part of life, these are the qualities the Revolution needs as the nation goes through this critical phase, the phase of rebirth of identity and of civilisation. I congratulate you on the confidence of the Party and the people in you, and I congratulate the nation on having you as its leader. I wish you every success in your service of the nation and its message.

The telegram sent by Michel Aflaq was not the kind that so often accompanies change in the Third World. Nor was it necessary to consolidate Saddam Hussein's position in the Party or to settle an argument about his leadership — he was strong and he had already settled the dispute among those Baathists who had plotted against him. Rather, the telegram came as a kind of intellectual pledge of allegiance, as expressed by Michel Aflaq's saying that Saddam Hussein had 'brought the Party's ideology and principles to fruition, making them a tangible part of life'.

Prior to this vote of confidence Michel Aflaq had concentrated his attention on the Party in Iraq rather than on any one individual. After his first visit to Iraq in 1969, he said, 'Our Party in Iraq has gone deep into this land and this people, and no force can uproot it now.' He added, 'In our youth we used to look to Iraq and our generation called it the Russia of the Arabs.' On 21 June 1974 he said in a speech in Baghdad,

> Our Party in Iraq has always been characterised by its perseverance, strong will and understanding of its national responsibilities. In spite of the dark phases the Party has passed through in this region, they have been setbacks, not complete breakdowns. There was always someone to carry the responsibility. The Party might have lost some members but it always regained its popular weight because it has always had a sense of responsibility.

In the same speech Aflaq said,

> It is difficult for me not to be sympathetic towards the Baath Party in Iraq because I have loved this Party from its first steps. It

> contains the characteristics of revolutionary action and morals that I have rarely found in other branches and other regions. Although I am tied to my comrades in Syria through the links of revolutionary action, I say my Party is in Iraq. The Party's first place is in Iraq. This is why my joy is so great: at this age I can see and touch the progress made by the Party here. The Party in Iraq makes up for all the troubles and pain the comrades of this Party have endured . . . I have not found the seriousness of the Iraqi Baathists in any other branch of the Party. There are the good qualities of the Arab man in the Baath of Iraq, qualities which, if well directed, will achieve great things and glorious ones too . . . The Party must be equal to the Iraqi citizens in all their number.

On 24 June 1974 Aflaq said, 'The experience of the Baath Party in Iraq is unmatched by any other.' He recalled that he had told Saddam Hussein, 'The Party requires a high level of revolutionary commitment.'

These examples of Michel Aflaq's statements about the Party in Iraq explain why Syria is totally opposed to reunifying the Party under him. He has said that he considers the Party's first place is in Iraq — it is difficult to unify a Party on two levels. Moreover, Michel Aflaq's enthusiasm for the Party has grown since Saddam Hussein assumed full responsibility. On 8 October 1979 Aflaq issued a memorandum to all Party bureaux in the Arab world and abroad, after a meeting of the National Command had unanimously elected Saddam Hussein Deputy Secretary-General. It looked as though the historic leader of the Party was laying the ground for the future leadership. Such a step, taken while Aflaq is alive and carrying out his duties, is extremely significant. This was even more clear in his personal message on 6 April 1980, on the thirty-third anniversary of the founding of the Baath Party:

> You Baathists in this land of revolutionary experience have learned the lessons of your national test and have progressed with awareness, avoiding destructive mistakes and reaching the level of a historic undertaking. Your actions were not those of traditional politics, nor were they pure theory, and your treatment of national issues was not selfish. You did not sink in the swamps of dreams and fantasy. You were faithful to the trust, and you have been loyal to your heritage and to your Party's long struggle. You have translated principles, morals, seriousness and strength — the true marks of the Baath — into a programme for action and life, of a unique heroic character. You have cared for ideas, you have made education a weapon in the battle, and you have translated adversity into revolutionary success. You are the ones who have made Iraq the leader of the nation's renaissance, and have prepared it for a historic role in Arab life. You are the Baath's gift to itself, and the nation's gift to itself.

The tone and choice of words made it sound as though Michel Aflaq was addressing this message to Saddam Hussein personally. He, more than any other, knew that if it had not been for Saddam Hussein the Party would not have enjoyed such strength. There would have been nothing for Michel Aflaq, its historic leader, to praise, and no possibility of transferring its ideals from one generation to the next.

I had several meetings with Michel Aflaq in the days before he issued the above memorandum. During these meetings I asked him three major questions. First I asked him to describe Saddam Hussein, from his personal knowledge of him, from the time he became a Baathist until the time that Aflaq felt Saddam Hussein had brought the Party's ideology to fruition. Had Michel Aflaq ceded his position as the Party's ideological leader to Saddam Hussein and, if so, on what basis? Secondly, how did he feel about the way in which a youthful leader like Saddam Hussein was directing political and ideological affairs? Thirdly, Michel Aflaq had spoken of the Baathist experience in Iraq with unprecedented enthusiasm, going as far as to say, 'I consider that my Party is in Iraq. The Party's first place is in Iraq.' Did this mean that the Party, and the personal qualities he wanted to see in the Baath, were to be found in Iraq and that others should consider the Iraqi experience as an example to be followed? Michel Aflaq replied:

> I first met Comrade Saddam after the Ramadan Revolution of 1963. I heard him speak for the first time at a regional conference in Baghdad, and I was surprised to hear such well-developed opinions in the criticism of the actions of the Regional Command at the time. He also gave a clear picture of what proper Party leadership should be. My first and lasting impression was of equilibrium, calmness, rationality and clarity of thought. This is rare in revolutionary action, at least in our Arab milieu, because hasty emotionalism had been one of the negative characteristics of our revolutionaries.
>
> Within one or two months of this meeting, the Party in Iraq suffered the 18 October setback, which led to the fall of the regime and to many difficulties. Naturally, our thoughts turned to the man who had foreseen these dangers, and equally naturally we entrusted him with a leadership role in the stage of secret action which followed. He preferred, for sound reasons, to excuse himself for a while. Then he became the leader who made the Party strong and steadfast, and rebuilt it on new foundations with reason, courage and initiative, in co-operation with the elder Comrade Ahmad Hassan Bakr, whom I came to know very well.
>
> **Saddam Hussein is the son of the Party.** He entered the Party at a very early age and has known no other surroundings than those of the Party. His education was first and foremost the Party's

philosophy. But these circumstances afford only a partial explanation, because a leader has other qualities which are more difficult to analyse; they are the result of a number of interconnected factors such as heredity, upbringing, social milieu and circumstances. Throughout my time with the Party, I felt happy whenever the Party youth showed signs of genius in some field or other. I can say that, having come to know Comrade Saddam very well after the 17 July Revolution, I became convinced that the Party had, for the first time, bred a leader who possessed all the qualities it had lacked. On a personal level, I feel great affection and love for Comrade Saddam because I always felt he would become a great leader, and I discovered the strength of his moral principles through working with him. This is very important for me; the revolutionary must be honest and of a high moral calibre. This is why I am confident about the future of the Party and the future of the nation, since these basic conditions have been met by the Party in Iraq, a major region in the Arab world. This is a golden opportunity for the Arab revolution.

I am confident that the seriousness which characterises the Iraqi Baath cannot be found in other branches. This does not mean that the Iraqi experience is final and free from errors . . . But my first judgement remains correct and my initial conviction will not change: the real launching pad of the Baath Party is Iraq. I do not reject the idea of Iraq setting an example to the rest of the Arab world, but I do not accept it in the strict, narrow sense, because there is some good to be had from the multiplicity of Arab revolutionary experience; it will enrich the Arab revolution and bring about maturity and balance for the Arab future. A pattern should not mean imposition, or a monopoly. It means that the particular conditions and circumstances were ripe for an experiment, so it took place and produced positive results which may inspire Arab revolutionaries in all fields of battle, and even on the international level.

This is my understanding of a pattern, and I always warn against cutting oneself off in self-satisfaction. I always call for interaction with every philosophy and revolutionary struggle in the Arab arena. We must balance two factors: self-confidence in what we are building as a basic experience in the Arab revolutionary movement for an overall and intrinsic change in modern Arab life, and the practical view that we are working in a backward society and a divided nation, against dangerous enemies who occupy part of our land and threaten our existence and development. We have no choice but to be frank and open about our backwardness, to treat it critically and to learn from our experiences and those of others. We must solve the divisions through being open to our Arab masses and to our national revolutionary classes, which are different from us yet with which we meet on basic national grounds. This kind of flexibility is, in my opinion, always necessary.

Certain factors and certain individuals create history. I consider the Party in Iraq my true original party, not just because of a personal leaning or a sudden choice. This is a basic truth which I realised before others, thanks to my life in the Party from the beginning. Iraq's circumstances, the circumstances of the Party in Iraq, and the circumstances of the Arab world as a whole and the Arab East in particular, all brought this about. It is the Baath Party in Iraq that has grown and developed; it is a Party with a history. It has in-built laws for development, the laws of an organic body. Belonging to the Baath means interaction with the ideas of the Baath from its birth. I do not deny that many of Iraq's own circumstances are reflected in the Party. This is natural and all revolutions in the world carry the marks of the place where they were born. Arab unity is the cure for all the negative aspects of the revolution because, when it is achieved, it will give the true picture of the Arab nation. The renaissance will transform the negative aspects of regionalism into positive factors. The Arab revolution must realise that one part of it, no matter how hard it tries, cannot embody the truth of the whole.

Because of its serious commitment and firm will, together with the price it has paid in blood and spirit for this commitment, and its constancy for over a quarter of a century, the Party in Iraq has excelled and progressed beyond the other branches to become, itself, the origin, the root which puts out branches in its turn, the centre and base. This is a fact we cannot ignore. The Arab citizen sees the results from afar. The important thing is to see the results from within, and to observe the manner in which one of the branches of the Party has grown.

This should have happened in Syria, where the Party was born, but circumstances were opposed to what one had hoped for. Iraq and the Baath Party in Iraq are capable of recovering Syria. When I say that my Party is here in Iraq, this is not a passing whim. I have considered that my Party is here since the 1960s. Iraq is the base, the launching pad. Syria is very important but its proximity to the enemy battlefield, as well as some other circumstances which are well known, have made it too weak to build a strong and stable base. The Zionist and imperialist conspiracy against Syria dates back a long time, and the conspirators found their opportunity in the break [with Egypt]. After that separation Syria was unable to control its own leadership and its own fate. It is unsteady on its feet.

The Party in Iraq has used its relative distance from the battlefield to build a strong and solid base and to prepare for the battle. It first built its society and then its Armed Forces to express this strength. In spite of everything, and in spite of the obstacles created by conspiracies, Iraqi society is tolerant and giving, eager for progress: it radiates well-being.

These pages and chapter 1 have examined Saddam Hussein's

services to the Baath before he assumed full responsibility for the State and the Party, and before the Party's historic leader Michel Aflaq decided he was his natural successor. The final part of this chapter will explain what Saddam Hussein intends to do for the Baath in the next stage, which will be intrinsically different from the previous stages. Some idea of his plans is revealed from his words to a closed meeting of Party leaders after he assumed complete responsibility:

> Since our enemies now exist on three or four fronts, we do not expect these to become two. But what we do hope is that our masses will grow. Now that the membership of the Party in the Arab nation is half a million, we must make this twenty million and then forty million. I do not think there is a party anywhere which has faced the pressures and conflicts faced by the Arab Socialist Baath Party. If we compare the state of the Soviet Communist Party (before and after the October Revolution) with the situation of our Party, if we look at the liberal parties in Europe and their role during the growth of the bourgeoisie on the ruins of the feudal aristocracy, and if we examine political parties in the Third World, we will find that their darkest moment was the division of the nation into two or three parts: Korea, Vietnam, Germany, and so on. But never before has a nation been divided into twenty-two parts. They have divided our [Arab] nation into twenty-two parts and they still find it necessary to divide it further. This is an indication of the importance of our nation, and should be taken into account in examining its development.
>
> How tragic is the situation of a party which calls for revolution without a revolutionary base. A state cannot build a party on a revolutionary base. A state lacks revolutionary party understanding and cannot create a revolutionary base. If a state has not been created by the will of a revolutionary party and on its principles, then it cannot draw up the guidelines for revolutionary action. We must learn from revolutionary action. Thus we must see the difficulties of any political structure which has not been created by a revolutionary party. A structure built in this way does not purify the soul and cannot ensure the minimum level of a correct framework in any other way than the one we have noted.

President Saddam's ideas and principles are given at length in the final part of this book (*see* chapter 8). The President did not neglect the Party when he assumed a leadership role with President Ahmad Hassan Bakr after the 1968 Revolution, and it is clear that he will not neglect the Party now that he has assumed complete responsibility and has been selected by the historic leader to assume the future leadership of the Arab Baath. Because he does not neglect it, both the Party and President Saddam Hussein have remained strong.

CHAPTER 7

ABU ADI

'I will endeavour to be one flame among many, no matter how bright I shine, and one sword among many, not the only sword.'
(Saddam Hussein during a meeting with the Party leadership)

When President Saddam has to work at his office in the Presidential Palace until late at night, a child of five sometimes comes to visit him. He leaves his desk and greets this unexpected visitor warmly. He tries to keep the conversation short so that he can go back to his desk and his papers, but the child often asks him to tell her a story or to draw her a car or a plane. He promises he will tell her a story if she waits half an hour until he finishes his work. The child waits patiently while he reads through the files and dossiers on his desk, signing the papers that need his signature. Every few minutes she asks him if he has finished; she wants her story. Sometimes the President is so engrossed in his work that the child falls asleep; she is carried to a couch and covered with a blanket. Once he finishes his work, he carries her back to her room in the house next door. Sometimes he carries her back on his shoulders and tells her a story while she is tucked into bed. This little girl is Hala, the youngest of President Saddam's daughters.

Sometimes the phone will ring while the President is hard at work on affairs of state, and the thirteen-year-old voice on the other end of the line asks her father if he can spare her an hour in the evening. When the President asks his eldest daughter Raghad what she needs him for, she replies simply that she needs him. He promises he will give her an hour and goes home to find her waiting. It turns out that she wants her father to choose a new dress with her. He drives her to the shops but when they arrive the people gather around their President. Raghad gets her dress, but she does not get the second part of her wish, to go window-shopping with her father. When they get back home, Rana, the eight-year-old, is a little unhappy that her father has bought a dress for her sister but not for her. He tells her to run and fetch a parcel from the car; she finds a beautiful dress he bought her while shopping with her sister. The President's eldest son Adi lives in a different world. A slim young man of sixteen, he is almost as tall as his father and has begun his military training. Qussei, the President's second son, is nearly fifteen.

I asked President Saddam whether he would allow me to visit his home because, as an author, I would like to meet his children in order to give a living picture of his family. (On the whole, he prefers to keep his family life as far from the limelight as possible.) I spent two hours at the President's home with his children. The eldest told me that he was good at physics and chemistry and wanted to go to university to specialise in nuclear physics. He said that Iraq would need scientists in this field once it had entered the nuclear club. He also spoke of his military training and said it was relatively tough: 'Every Iraqi must be trained and prepared.' He has been a Baathist since he was twelve, and is a member of the leadership at school. He reads about the Baath and asks his father for clarification whenever he comes across a difficult point. He said his father had never treated them differently from other children; he brought them up to tell the truth and be honest. Nor did he and his brothers and sisters receive any special treatment at school. His father signed their school gradebooks and kept up on their progress — he could not bear any of them to fail. The President's second son wants to be an officer in the Armed Forces. Both boys are at the Baghdad College, where they study English as well as Arabic. French has now been added as a third language.

The President's two elder daughters are studying at the Karkh co-educational school and both would like to read medicine when they go to university. The President's wife is the headmistress of a school, so every morning at seven she and the four eldest children are ready to be on their way; the youngest remains at home with her nurse. The President has already left the house for the office or has gone on one of his tours of the country to meet the people, which he likes to do in the early morning. On Thursday afternoon and Friday (the weekly holiday), the President and his family spend time in the countryside. When it is hot, he goes swimming with his sons, or hunting. Hunting is one of his favourite sports, although he does not have much time to engage in it now.

A few months after the 1968 Revolution, Saddam Hussein asked Saadoun Shaker to build the Hunting Club, which is known in Baghdad as the meeting-place of most Baathist leaders. Saddam Hussein wanted the club built (he is the honorary president to this day) so that Baathists could have a place to meet socially. In the days of underground struggle before 1968, they had not known this kind of life. To encourage them to come to the club with their families, he would often spend a few hours there with his wife, and they soon followed suit. This broke through the barriers of tradition — Iraqi society used to be very conservative, and previously men were not seen with their wives in public places. The club was more than just a meeting-place or a place to eat and drink. President Saddam wanted it to encourage sports as well, particularly equestrian ones. He also went to other clubs in Baghdad, such as the Mansour Club, the Alwiyah Club and the Hindiyah Club, so as to avoid giving the impression that the Hunting Club was a club for the élite.

From time to time President Saddam wears the Iraqi yashmak and the national dress; he misses this, and often dons the Iraqi *aba* over his suit. The President is always neatly dressed and encourages others to be neat too — he stresses that the days of underground action are now over. He is also very strict about punctuality, both in himself and others. President Saddam wants to be well thought of 'in a hundred years', and this makes him a particularly serious man who does not often relax. When he frowns, or his face is serious, he appears very strict, but when he smiles his whole face lights up. The President started smoking at an early age, then gave it up. Now, after a visit to Algiers when the late President Boumedienne offered him a Cuban cigar, he smokes the occasional cigar. He does not drink much tea, unlike many Iraqis, because tea was forbidden in prison and he did not want to demean himself by asking his gaolers for special favours. He likes bitter black Arabic coffee, however, and cold milk.

Although the President's office is not far from his home, a bed is always made up for him at the office for the nights he works late. A house was built for Saddam Hussein within the Presidential Palace, but he thought the builders had made it too grand. He refused to move and continues to live in his own small house. The hours he enjoys most are those he spends in the countryside. His wife tries to encourage him to work in the garden so he can take a break from the affairs of state. He is a devoted family man and proud of it. Once he and his family were at a tourist centre. His youngest child was asleep in his wife's arms when the button on her sleeve came off. Without waking the child he picked up the button and, taking a needle and thread, sewed it back in full view of his aides and guards.

President Saddam believes that parents should only have the number of children they can bring up properly. Nevertheless, he wants to increase Iraq's population. During one of his meetings with the Party leadership, he pointed out that Iraq's present population increase of 3.2 per cent per annum was reasonable, and explained:

> We think that the population increase in Iraq should be balanced not only in view of what the region needs but also in view of what the Arab nation needs . . . for the short and long term. The Iraqi region has great economic resources and lies on the Eastern part of the Arab nation. It is bounded by two foreign countries [Turkey and Iran] whose populations are larger than Iraq's, and it should thus have a population large enough for self-defence and for the defence of the Arab nation. [1]

---

1. Iraq's population is currently 13.5 million, of whom 3 million live in Baghdad alone; its total area is 438,466 sq km. Iran's population is about 34 million, in an area of 1,645,000 sq km. Turkey's population is 42 million, in an area of 780,576 sq km.

There are now more than a million non-Iraqi Arabs in Iraq, including over half a million Egyptians who have their own streets and cafés. The standard of living and the stability they enjoy are attracting hundreds of other Egyptians. They are not in the least affected by the fact that President Sadat's regime has entered into a treaty with Israel, and efforts are made to make them as comfortable as possible. The experiment to transplant Egyptian families into the mainstream of Iraqi agricultural life has been so successful that efforts are now being made to bring families from the Maghreb.

Until July 1978 the Iraqis knew nothing about Saddam Hussein's home life — how many children he had, how he brought them up, and so on. Saddam Hussein preferred not to transform his private life into a public affair. The only people who knew him as a family man were a few of his Party comrades. But then the magazine *Al-Mar'a*, published by the General Federation of Iraqi Women, ran a cover feature on Saddam Hussein and his family life, and carried a number of pictures of him with his family. They also quoted his views on family life: 'Everything is based on understanding between the members of the family and their understanding of their duty'; 'The most important thing about marriage is that the man must not let the woman feel downtrodden simply because she is a woman and he is a man; if she feels this, then family life is over'; 'I do not differentiate between my children — indeed, when they were children, I loved my daughters most, beginning with Raghad — and I brought them all up in the same way. Some families think the girl brings shame; we do not look on her thus, and I do not differentiate between a son and a daughter'; 'The family relationship must be built on respect; the old must respect the young. Giving up certain privileges is not a loss; it is necessary for the general happiness.' By reflecting on these important aspects of Iraqi society and family life, it was as though the President were saying, 'This is how I behave with my family and my children and how I would like you to behave with yours.'

The *Al-Mar'a* article also carried the story of President Saddam's marriage:

> Our story was like that of many others. Usually a boy or girl's thoughts turn to those nearest them. When I was four or five years old, my mother told me that my uncle's daughter had been betrothed to me by my grandfather. I had not yet seen her, but the thought took hold in my mind. When I ran away from Iraq, after I was sentenced to death for the attempt on Abdel-Karim Qassem's life, I expressed my desire to become engaged to her. As soon as my family knew of my wish, they sent their consent. The engagement was announced while I was in Cairo and she in Baghdad.

> We were married only after the 14 Ramadan Revolution and my return to Baghdad.

Saddam Hussein was born on 28 April 1937. The name Saddam is not a usual one in Iraq, but has since become widespread; it means 'the fighter who stands steadfast'. Saddam Hussein is the type of man to respond to a challenge, but his response is measured. He is, within himself, a religious man. I could sense this during our discussions. He plans, for example, to have copies of the Quran printed for distribution to non-Arab Muslims and to build mosques in African, Asian and Latin American states. I asked him if this was the beginning of a turn towards religion or if it came because he felt the need for religion. He replied,

> The beginning? No . . . it is a confirmation of the Baathist direction. We have never felt a gap between the spirit of religion and the spirit of the Baath. Our Party, thanks to those who drew up its programme, has always seen the Baath as an inspiration to the nation's spirit for its renaissance and the renewal of its aspirations. Is not the Holy Quran sacred throughout the entire Arab nation, and was it not carried to the farthest corners of the earth by the nation's heroes, who shed pure blood as an expression of its every letter? It is only natural that we should care for the Quran.

During his tours and visits, President Saddam can see that injustice still exists. Just days before the first anniversary of his assumption of full responsibility for the State and the Party, the Revolution Command Council promulgated the Social Welfare Law to ensure social security for the aged. The law also provides for 'state homes' for children, young people and orphans.

President Saddam often meets Baathists at all levels and discusses many topics with them, to broaden his understanding. He sees the Baathist whose struggle dates back to the 1968 Revolution and before as the 'hard currency' of the Party — it was these comrades who carried out the Revolutions of February 1963 and July 1968. His comrades of these harsh days are often surprised by his visits to their homes. He asks about their problems and tries to solve them. In his discussions with his comrades, he listens calmly to all views before giving his own, which he supports with examples and analysis. He is sincere in his dealings with others, and respects those older than him in the Party.

Saddam Hussein is not the type of man to let someone else take responsibility for his own actions. Saadoun Shaker told me a story about the time they were in gaol. He and his comrades had cut through the iron bars of their cell, using a file brought by Saddam Hussein's wife during one of her visits to the gaol. They had left the iron bars in place so as not to attract the gaolers' attention. More than a month after they had cut through the bars, Saddam Hussein told his comrades that the Party no longer approved of the plans for an escape. At one point, the Baathists were taken to another cell and several Communists were placed in their original cell. One of the Communists stood at the bars, as prisoners do, and shook them: the bars fell out. The prison guards assumed that the Communists had cut through the bars and began to torture them. Saddam Hussein found out and asked to meet the prison governor. He told him that the Communists were not responsible for cutting through the iron bars; he had done so himself because they had had a plan to escape but it had been postponed by the Party Command. The governor called a stop to the torture of the Communists. He let Saddam Hussein go back to his comrades since he had no punishment severe enough for one who was already condemned to death.

Saadoun Shaker told me that Saddam Hussein was very careful to boost the morale of the Baathists inside the gaol so that they did not submit to the guards and behaved as political prisoners with an ideology and a cause. During the investigation he was asked about the nature of his employment and replied, 'I am a revolutionary in the Arab Socialist Baath Party.' Thereafter all the others gave the same reply. To this day, Saddam Hussein is the last to serve himself at official banquets or dinners. Saadoun Shaker told me this custom had developed during their days in the prison cell when he would eat only after his comrades had eaten. He also told me that, before his arrest, Saddam Hussein had prepared a study for Baathists on how to behave under interrogation. The study, in Saddam Hussein's own handwriting, still exists. Saadoun Shaker recalled that Saddam Hussein was able to establish good personal relations with the guards; they treated him with respect and were willing to help him escape if he wanted.

Saadoun Shaker still remembers the days when Saddam Hussein operated out of a single room, with a mattress and a reed mat on the floor, after they had escaped from gaol. He sat and wrote on the mat as there was no desk in the room, and his writings were then copied and passed on to the Party members. Saddam Hussein only revealed the full story of his escape from prison in 1971. Saadoun Shaker's ties with Saddam Hussein have been close since that time. When some Baathists complained that Saadoun Shaker had been appointed a member of the Baghdad Branch Command in 1971, Saddam Hussein told them, 'Comrade Shaker is the one who helped me escape from prison.' This bore no discussion — had Saddam Hussein not escaped from prison, the Party would not have been organised and would not have become as strong as it is.

Saddam Hussein is impatient when matters are drawn out in endless discussion. At the beginning of the Revolution, for example, some of the leaders suggested that Iraq's official name be the 'Arab Republic of Iraq', others suggested the word 'Democratic' as well, and yet others proposed the word 'Popular'. Saddam Hussein settled the matter when he pointed out that there were no doubts about Iraq's Arabness, and that the Baath did not need to stress its popular democratic nature. Iraq became simply the Republic of Iraq.

President Saddam feels a great deal of sympathy for the poorer parts of the Arab world and admires the dignity of, for example, the Sudanese and the Mauritanians. He respected the former Mauritanian President Mokhtar Ould Daddah after an incident at the Arab Summit in Rabat in 1974. When the Arab kings and presidents were discussing the question of aid, President Ould Daddah said that his country had suffered a great deal in the past few years because of drought and that it had needed aid very badly. At present, he added, it no longer needed as much aid because 'the rains [had] come, the Lord be praised'. Ould Daddah's dignity and pride so impressed Saddam Hussein that he led a drive to collect aid for Mauritania and it received some fifteen million dollars in aid. When the new President, Colonel Muhammad Khouna Ould Haydallah, paid an official visit to Iraq in May 1980, President Saddam's sympathy ensured the visit's success, and the Mauritanian President was given a warm welcome. In expressing his appreciation of the welcome he had received, he declared, 'In line with the principles of the National Charter proposed by President Saddam Hussein on 8 February 1980, and in order to preserve its independence, Mauritania has taken the necessary measures to expel the remaining foreign military elements on its national soil.' It meant a great deal to President Saddam that Mauritania, although poor and in need of aid, was able to take such a stand.

President Saddam is upset by unacceptable behaviour, no matter how close the person is to him. He has said, 'The closest person to me is the furthest from me when he does wrong.' He is still the first to reach the office and the last to leave it. He never calls his aides by their first names, always adding the Party title 'comrade' or any other title the person may have, such as 'Dr'. He has always stressed the question of equal opportunity, saying, 'We want the citizens to feel that they are living in a country where justice reigns, not connections.' He is strict when necessary, but he has also said, 'Do not bind the people's hands and feet, stopping all possibility of movement, and then expect them not to complain or rebel.' The President rejects blind sectarianism, and is against class discrimination. Long before becoming President, he surprised a committee of engineers in charge of a housing project by saying, 'You involved yourselves in politics and adopted discrimination as your basis when you planned two kinds of houses based on the people's social status, not on the size of the family.' The project was changed according to his instructions.

President Saddam does not feel that he rules, but rather that he plays a role in the service of his country. Abu Jaafar al-Mansour played a similar role many centuries ago, and said, 'Temper prosperity with gratefulness, power with mercy, obedience with love, victory with humility; thus will things live long. Never forget your share of the world comes with your share of God's mercy.' Abu Jaafar was the architect of the Abbasid state, and he was succeeded by thirty-five caliphs. Abu Adi is the architect of the Baathist state, and he has travelled a long way along this road. History is repeating itself in Iraq.

CHAPTER 8

AN INTERVIEW WITH SADDAM HUSSEIN

The following interview with President Saddam Hussein was conducted over several meetings that lasted for seventeen hours. The first session was held a few weeks after the President took over full responsibility for the Party and the State on 17 July 1979.

Fuad Matar: How did you become a Baathist? One would have expected your childhood and youth, filled with social hardship, to lead you towards Marxism. If you had read about Marxism before discovering the Baath ideas and principles, would you not have chosen Marxism?

President Saddam Hussein: Traditionally Marxism attracts the oppressed. This, however is not the case in the Arab nation. I had a meeting with President Julius Nyerere of Tanzania only yesterday, during which we discussed world problems including economic ones. These are problems which had already been raised during the Non-Aligned Summit in Havana. I repeated my point of view on the matter. I told President Nyerere that we cannot solve the problems of Tanzania or those of the Third World, and yet we would like to awaken the world's conscience and change its thinking about the relationship between the oppressed and the oppressors. The Tanzanian President remarked that it was unique to find such an opinion coming from a people which was not poor, and to find a country that wanted only to help not to exploit. I replied that, though this might seem strange, if we went back in Arab history, we would find that most of the calls for socialism were made by people who did not come from the oppressed classes. The socialist programmes in Arab history did not always come from the poor, but from men who had known no oppression and became the leaders of the poor. The Arab nation has never been as class-conscious as other nations. It is true that social differences exist, but today class differences exist mostly between Arabs and non-Arabs. This was not so obvious amongst the Arabs of pre-Islamic times.

I used to have a Communist friend at school. He's dead now, God rest his soul. He spent most of his time reading communiqués and declarations to us, his schoolmates. All we did was make fun of him. We never felt that what he was reading had anything to do with us. The main reason for our indifference was that we knew his theories came from abroad; they had been introduced by a foreigner, not an Arab. Our problems were not simple ones: they were problems of partition, of a struggle against Zionism and against class differences. At the time, the peasants in the northern and southern parts of Iraq felt the oppression of the existing feudal system. In the central parts of Iraq where I come from, the situation was not the same, and we had no feudal class. That is why I never felt at a social disadvantage, even I, a peasant's son. The greatest feudalist amongst us was the cousin of President Ahmad Hassan Bakr, an uncle of mine. If he got angry he beat his relatives, but they gave back as good as they got. As a matter of fact, they hit him much more often than he did them. He certainly was not the feudalistic figure that would make a human being feel oppressed. The feudal authority that invaded so many parts never reached my region, which is why we never lived a life of humiliation. Our heads remained high and we never lost our self-respect.

Besides this, my maternal uncle was a nationalist, an officer in the Iraqi Army. He spent five years in prison after the revolution of Rashid Ali Kaylani. 'He's in prison,' was my mother's constant reply whenever I inquired about my uncle. He always inspired us with a great nationalistic feeling, which is why I never isolated the socialist programme from my national outlook. The nation's problems were part of my conscience and the Party was a part of me before I became a member.

Fuad Matar: As a revolutionary, you are against Marxism. Why? Do you have doubts about the nationalist feelings of Arab Marxists?

President Saddam Hussein: I believe that all human civilisation from the beginning of history is interwoven. This also applies to the revolutionary theories which have emerged in the world: they are connected to, and influenced by, human trial and error over the ages. They cannot possibly cross the current of events without being influenced by some of them. In order for a revolutionary theory, any revolutionary theory, to be human, it must be responsive to fresh ideas. Lenin is one of the world's great thinkers whose books I have most enjoyed because he deals with life in a lively manner. I have also read Mao Tse Tung. I am not against Marxism. I am for responding to human thought, but with spirit and character; the theorist should be willing to give and take, not just to look at a country in terms of what it can offer. Our nation is capable of making Marxism aware that it is no longer equipped to deal with all of the new notions of life today. In addition to my faith and trust in the nation and its capabilities, I am always against the mechanical transfer of theories, just as I am against isolationism and rigidity.

I respect the original programme of Marxism and I respect Marxists. But I have no respect for those Communists who use their association with Marxist theories to drum up followers, in whatever nation of the world. In both my thinking and my programme, I differentiate between the Soviet Union and America and never give both an equal status. The Party has spelt out the reasons for this on more than one occasion. When it comes to adherence, however, I make no distinction between he who follows America and he who follows the Soviet Union. In this I am adamant, using neither courtesy nor diplomacy. It is our Party policy. I believe that people who use their Marxist connections to draw up a programme that means political adherence to any country outside the Arab nation are in the wrong. That is why I differentiate between Arab, African and Asian Communists, for example. I neither blame nor criticise Africans who have adopted Marxism, and I am ready to discuss with any African the true manner of adhering to Marxism. And since neither Africans nor Asians have the traditions or the history of the Arab nation, why should they not adopt Marxism? Marxism is a revolutionary solution and the way to change life. What does an African in Rhodesia have to lose when he adopts Marxism, since he does not have the historical depth or the intellectual heritage of the Arab nation, a heritage which offers all the theories necessary for a life of change and progress? The Arab nation is the source of all prophets and the cradle of civilisation. And there is no doubt that the oldest civilisation in the world is that of Mesopotamia. It is not an Iraqi civilisation in isolation from the Arab nation. It is a civilisation which developed thanks to the strength and ability of the Iraqi people, coupled with the efforts and heritage of the nation.

Fuad Matar: Do you not find that the three slogans of the Baath (Unity, Freedom, Socialism) have been placed in an order that is based more on hope than on practical possibilities, and that the order in which Abdel-Nasser placed them (Freedom, Socialism, Unity) is more realistic? What has the Baath learned from Abdel-Nasser's experience and vice versa?

President Saddam Hussein: The arrangement 'Unity, Freedom, Socialism' was intentional. The Arabs must struggle for a national truth; they cannot achieve true liberty without nationalism and the struggle towards Arab unity. This does not mean that the Party believes that Arabs cannot achieve freedom without Arab unity; it means that the Party's programme is based on the fact that an Arab must be a nationalist to achieve true liberty. This must ultimately lead to unity, and from there to socialism. Let us stop here awhile and talk about Iraq. Is Iraq's freedom today the same as it would be if it became part of a greater Arab nation?

In today's world of blocs and superpowers, where sharks roam the sea around us, it is difficult to say that Iraq's freedom in international politics is what it would enjoy as part of a united Arab nation. At the same time, life cannot consist of pure theory; it is a slow and inevitable process towards revolutionary achievement. Arab unity is like all the other goals of national struggle: difficult to achieve through nothing but theories. Had we all been one Arab nation today, the freedom an Iraqi citizen would have enjoyed would be different, because his liberty today is linked with his relationships and dealings with the outside world. Liberty is linked automatically with the way things stand today. A human being who is capable and self-confident, who is at peace with himself, will grant freedom more easily than a coward. That is why I believe that the order in which our three slogans are placed as goals to be achieved by the Party is correct and needs no change.

We have profited greatly from the experience of Abdel-Nasser. The Party had three historical experiences to refer to when it began to build the nation after the July 1968 Revolution: failure in Syria, failure in Iraq and the experience of Abdel-Nasser. Following Abdel-Nasser's death, and once Egypt had recovered, we could see his efforts as they really were; we used this reality to deal with the problems of our own society, economic, political and social, without forgetting the causes of Abdel-Nasser's failures. The study of the latter is what made Egypt's recovery easier and more complete.

As for the advantages that Abdel-Nasser may or may not have derived from the Baath Party, I am unable to answer this question accurately or at length, since I was not one of the Party leaders at the time of the union between Egypt and Syria. I do wish to say, however, that the programme Abdel-Nasser — God rest his soul — initially set out to accomplish was not the one that he seems to have adopted in the end. Thus one can say that there was some interaction between Abdel-Nasser and the Baath. Abdel-Nasser profited from his experience in that he rose before the Arab nation from a national horizon and not from Egypt alone. This is one of the most important points in the 23 July Revolution in Egypt led by Abdel-Nasser, especially during and after the 1956 Suez war.

Fuad Matar: Can you tell us about the special relationship that exists between you and President Ahmad Hassan Bakr, as well as your relationship with Michel Aflaq? The reasons for the question are as follows. First, it is probably unique for a Vice-President to exercise all the power and authority invested in the president of a republic for ten years without ever deciding to take over the presidency. Secondly, you continue to respect Michel Aflaq, although circumstances have changed since you became President of the Republic. This is also unusual.

President Saddam Hussein: I do not consider respect a sign of weakness; it is more a proof of a strong personality. When someone is said to be polite, this does not mean he is a weakling; it is a proof of strength because he is courteous and diplomatic in his political relationships. This is true strength of character. President Bakr was Secretary of the Regional Command. In our

Party we were always brought up to respect our elders. Besides, a relationship is not a one-way street. A Baathist may be a brilliant thinker; does that mean this is the only image I would want for a Baathist? No. A Baathist is a human being who lives the cause of the people, believes in principles and behaves accordingly in his everyday life, even if his political and intellectual abilities are limited.

Let us go back to our history because it is constantly before my eyes, especially its most glorious and enlightening moments. Let us go back to the relationship between Imam Ali, Omar ibn al-Khattab and Abu Bakr al-Seddiq. What was that relationship like? Was Abu Bakr al-Seddiq stronger than Omar ibn al-Khattab and Ali bin Abi Taleb? When Omar ibn al-Khattab asked for advice from Imam Ali, did that mean Imam Ali had less strength and ability than Omar ibn al-Khattab? And what of the relationship between Imam Ali and Othman, who was by far the weakest? Principles were the basis of the respect between the Rashidi Caliphs. When one of these great men was asked his point of view, he was always accorded total respect and given all the necessary support for leadership and action.

My relationship with President Bakr is one of comradeship; it is also brotherly and paternal. The latter is not meant in the traditional way, but in the civilised sense which involves respect, freedom of thought and opinion, and the full exercise of one's role. It might have seemed that, in an emergency, I conducted myself with the authority of a head of state; this may also have happened in private, but I never turned this 'emergency status' into one that was permanent. When the emergency was over, I became once more the Vice-President of the Revolution Command Council. Constitutionally, I would respectfully return to my place.

Some find it strange that, when President Bakr used to telephone me and ask me to step into his office, I refused to do so until his aide-de-camp went in and announced me. I truly believe in this code of behaviour and it certainly does not make me a weak character or personality; it is a source of strength. As a matter of fact, the Arab nation has deserted its old traditions only to become decadent and weak, especially in moral terms. At this point, what is most wanted of Arab comrades is to stir the Arab nation's conscience by upholding ideal relationships, whatever the sacrifice, since this is nothing compared to the final result, a renaissance in Arab morality.

It is certain that matters would have been accomplished faster had I become the Republic's President five years earlier. This was also President Bakr's conviction. But I used to contradict him because I did not want him to leave his post as President. If I had not behaved in this moral way, what would I have told the people? What would I have had to say about my unique experience? Nothing. My situation would have been exactly like any other revolutionary situation in the world or in the Arab nation, with no clear-cut moral difference. If the one who is better takes over his friend's place and seeks only the reward, then we would be exactly like so many other revolutionary movements, whereas this is far from the truth.

Thus it is Michel Aflaq who created the Party and not I. How can I forget this? How can I forget what Michel Aflaq has done for me? Had it not been for him, I would not be in this position. It is true that Michel Aflaq did not carry out the Revolution and that I achieved my present position because of my own qualities. Yet the spirit in which I carried out the Revolution, the spirit in which the Baathists united, struggled and made sacrifices, and the principles to which I was loyal, were those of the Baath. Baathists carried out the Revolution, struggled and made sacrifices, and the Baath was founded by Michel Aflaq. That is why I must respect him, despite my official position and despite my past and my abilities. It is a unique situation, that is true, but the Party is a unique institution. The Party's principles, morality and goals are unprecedented in the current age.

Fuad Matar: Are the decisions you make based on accurate information? Are they taken after an analysis of the facts with insight and observation? Are you for courageously deciding on a course of action, even if it involves a certain amount of danger, or do you believe that this kind of decision is too hasty and spontaneous? May I ask you for examples of decisions based on analysis and accurate information and what your feelings were if a decision not based on information were challenged?

President Saddam Hussein: I always differentiate between the leader and the expert, the leader and the aide, the leader and the adviser. That is why I believe that a movement cannot achieve historical momentum if it is led by an expert. At the same time, if the race for leadership becomes the leaders' main goal, they tend to forget the presence of the essential experts and advisers, only to make decisions that are hasty, dangerous and spontaneous. That is why I always tend to differentiate between spontaneity and innovation, between calculated temerity and downright risk, between hesitation and consideration. It is on this basis that I make my decisions in leadership. In every decision, I make use of the information at hand but my decision is not a mechanical, automatic action based solely on the information that is before me; it is a birth, a creation based on knowledge and yet distinct from it in that it is a new entity. This not only applies to political and military decisions but also to economic decisions made within the social programme.

Let us take nationalisation as an example. First I collected all the information about our annual resources excluding oil; then I made a study of the possibility of loans from both Arab and non-Arab countries. Next I discussed the possibility of marketing our oil with economic and financial oil experts. All the experts and advisers warned me against nationalisation; not one was in favour. Yet the decision to nationalise was taken. In making the decision, I acted with one thought in mind: the spirit created by nationalisation would turn into hard currency, despite all the traps and failures prophesied by the experts. The latter, in their meticulous study of the matter, never took our spirit into consideration, nor did they think what our life was like in the face of the monopolies, or of the effect of nationalisation on the economic and social aspects of our life. That is why the decision was correct, and was proved so by its success. Had I listened to the experts and advisers, had I listened to the Oil Minister, the decision would never have been made. I took the decision despite the lack of enthusiasm of many of our members.

Great decisions have difficult births. They do not come about as a natural result of tradition but are of a special kind — that is why they are great. Those who make such decisions are special people, special in that they are endowed with rare daring and a particular way of thinking. Often they are the ones ready to take risks.

Fuad Matar: Do you ever take into consideration the particular circumstances of either Arab or friendly countries when you make a decision, or is Iraq your only concern?

President Saddam Hussein: I certainly do. It is one of the aims of our Party. It is impossible to come to a decision related to the outside world without thinking of the effect that it may have on the Arabs, or of the world's reaction to the decisions taken by the Arabs and Iraq.

Fuad Matar: Do you not think that the Iraqi-Soviet treaty casts a shadow on Iraq's independence? And how serious are your intentions on wanting to maintain it?

President Saddam Hussein: It was the Iraqis living abroad who cast a shadow on our independence when the treaty was signed in 1972. I believe that they have changed their minds now that they have seen the nature of the regime in Iraq and observed our political behaviour within the country and abroad after the treaty was signed. We had not deviated from our Party's political beliefs by signing it. It is not a treaty that puts us in chains or strips us of our independence, nor does it make Soviet followers or vassals of the Arabs. We simply look at it as a public announcement to the world that a special friendship exists between Iraq and the Soviet Union. We consider ourselves bound to it and we want it to be so, not just for the benefit of Iraq but for that of the Arab nation and its struggle against its enemies. We want it inasmuch as it serves our national goals and is based on mutual respect and non-interference in internal affairs. I believe this has become clear to all those who initially wrote about the so-called subordination of Iraq to the Soviet Union.

Fuad Matar: But the Baath is in principle against pacts and treaties.

President Saddam Hussein: The Party is against any treaty that is the extension of another country's strategy. However, it is not against a certain degree of friendly alliance. The Baath is against military pacts that are of an aggressive or imperialist nature. These pacts are only part of a strategy that aims at oppressing, annihilating or colonising other peoples and countries, or at turning small states into satellite states. We are against this.

Fuad Matar: You have often spoken of 'direct strategic moments' that may be used against one by imperialism, of moments when expertise has failed to produce the right result, of errors committed in recruitment. What do you mean by this?

President Saddam Hussein: The expressions 'strategic', 'technical', and 'expertise' belong to an encyclopaedia that is part of a revolutionary and military way of thinking. Let us for instance take the existence of Zionism. Zionism exists and so do the Arabs. Imperialism uses Zionism as a strategic arm against Arab unity, progress and development. This is a well-known fact. How can the Arabs deal with this? They are the ones giving imperialism the chance to use this strategy against the Arabs. It is the enemy that benefits strategically so long as the Arabs are divided. As an example, let us take the Palestinians. They differ as to the kind of democracy they want for their state, a state that they do not yet have. This can be used by the enemy, since it has been given a golden opportunity to turn the Palestinians against each other, making them forget the main issue. The enemy has used both strategy and expertise, turning the Palestinians' mistakes to its own advantage. The Palestinians have the right to disagree at times but now is certainly not the time for them to be divided. Only when they have reached their goal can they differ. But since the goal is still far away, even in the eyes of those referred to as the 'moderates', all the division, discussion and disagreement can only produce a golden opportunity for imperialism and Zionism.

Another point to be made is that different tribes and minorities exist in our society and in the Arab world and cannot be ignored. However, how is one to deal with them without giving imperialism the opportunity to use them against our goals? If one deals with them on the battlefield, in a way that is primitive and narrow-minded, one merely turns confessions into confessionalism, tribes into tribalism and minorities into fanatic opponents of Arab nationalism. That is why we always warn the revolutionary to behave wisely and not to commit tactical errors. It is not the enemy's ability, but these errors — errors due mainly to the stupidity of the revolutionary — that benefit the enemy and contribute to his success.

Fuad Matar: What do the following names mean to you: Nebuchadnezzar; Salaheddin al-Ayoubi; Ghandi; Lenin; Gamal Abdel-Nasser; de Gaulle; Che Guevara; Mao Tse Tung; Ho Chi Minh; Tito; Nehru; Castro; Ali bin Abi Taleb; Omar ibn al-Khattab; Mouawiya; Al-Andalus; Jerusalem; Egypt?

President Saddam Hussein: Nebuchadnezzar stirs in me everything relating to pre-Islamic ancient history. I am reminded that any human being with broad horizons, faith and feeling can act wisely but practically, attain his goals and become a great man who makes his country into a great state. And what is most important to me about Nebuchadnezzar is the link between the Arabs' abilities and the liberation of Palestine. Nebuchadnezzar was, after all, an Arab from Iraq, albeit ancient Iraq. Nebuchadnezzar was the one who brought the bound Jewish slaves from Palestine. That is why whenever I remember Nebuchadnezzar I like to remind the Arabs, Iraqis in particular, of their historical responsibilities. It is a burden that should not stop them from action, but rather spur them into action because of their history. So many have liberated Palestine throughout history, before and after the advent of Islam.

As for Salaheddin al-Ayoubi, he was of the same calibre but with the spirit of Islam in him. He was a Muslim Iraqi. This is why, at a Farmers' Congress held in Baghdad in November 1979, I said, 'Do not be surprised if a Palestinian dies a martyr in Palestine without having been born there, or if the martyr is an Iraqi, a Lebanese, a Syrian or any other Arab.' Besides this, I consider Salaheddin al-Ayoubi a great leader because he was able to make use of the nation's spirit; he breathed life into it, united it, and gave it one aim and purpose, and thus won a brilliant victory over the Crusaders.

The greatness of Ghandi lies in that he held power in his hands without the use of arms, an unconquerable power which Ghandi knew was the essence of the personality of the people of India. Ghandi's movement would have failed in a country like Iraq or Syria. Ghandi inspired resistance against the colonialists under the emblem of passive resistance.

Che Guevara's courage and romanticism are attractive, but they are not enough to make a leader out of a man.

Mao Tse Tung's greatness lies in that he was able to liberate China, build up socialism and choose a special road within Marxism, taking into consideration China's particular circumstances, an outlook which certainly differs from that of Lenin.

Ho Chi Minh was a great revolutionary leader. I never met him and I have not read enough about him. Yet I can sense the simplicity of the man and admire him for this and for his relationship with his revolutionary comrades.

As for Tito, he was a great revolutionary leader who, in the face of great difficulties and with the least possible violence, was able to bring different populations together and turn them into one happy, united people. This is what makes him different from all other Communist regimes.

Nehru's name evokes that of Ghandi, the teacher with great respect for the student who became a political leader and a great thinker.

Castro, whom I know well, is characterised by directness and courage. Most revolutionary leaders are daring but Castro is endowed with particular courage.

Ali bin Abi Taleb was a man of principle. What I admire in Omar ibn al-Khattab is his sense of justice and in Khalid bin al-Walid his sense of chivalry. As for Mouawiya, I have no special opinion to give. All I can say is that I have not benefited directly from his history. From what I have read, it seems to me that Mouawiya worked more for this world than for the next, and such people are of no interest to me.

Jerusalem represents the glory of the Arabs throughout their great history and is one of their sacred shrines. The history of Palestine has important links with the history of the Arabs in Andalusia, a fact which has never been given enough credit. The Arab nation is different from other nations: when the latter conquered, they also colonised, whereas the former established constructive relationships based on a deep understanding of nationalist feelings and religions. This is clear in their conquest of Andalusia and their liberation of Palestine. Besides, the Arabs left Spain with a great heritage which the country still uses to attract tourism.

Egypt in the time of Abdel-Nasser was the fulcrum of the Arab nation, a fact of which we must be proud, whatever we may think of Abdel-Nasser's experiment. He was the only leader at the time to express the opinion of the whole Arab nation before the world, no matter how that opinion may have been expressed. And this period in Egypt's history should be the one present in our minds today.

There remains de Gaulle, the knight whose chivalry I most admire. I always remember a conversation between de Gaulle and Churchill, when the former was offered aid. He replied, 'Let it be put on record that France refuses to take unrecorded aid.' This is a great attitude.

Fuad Matar: Is revolution an endless process, or is it an introduction to a flexible situation, as in the case of China? The reason behind the question is your constant warning against the transformation of the revolutionary into a flexible liberal who enjoys the situation and little by little drowns in it, in order to make up for time lost during the revolution. Is not revolution like war, and the revolutionary its soldier? A soldier wages war and, if victorious, automatically takes the spoils. Does this not also apply to the revolutionary when he has taken power?

President Saddam Hussein: Revolution is a process that does not end with the application of its principles. It varies and changes shape according to the changing circumstances of life. That is why one's opinion of a revolution will develop as the revolution does and keep in step with the changes in the revolutionary leader and the revolutionary member of society. It is in the light of society's understanding of rights and duties that one can fully and correctly comprehend a revolution. That is why we find that the definition of democracy and liberty will change in shape and form as the revolution passes from one stage to another, depending on its success. The same applies to the revolution's stand against its enemies. Throughout its progress, a revolution must always remain in the service of the people for whom it essentially takes place. It is true that I always warn the revolutionary against the threats of 'flexible liberalism' and a new settled life that may make him a prey to illegal desires, making him forget his nationalist duties and obligations. However, this does not mean that I forget that the revolutionary is a human being entitled to his rights like any other ordinary human being, as long as these rights and needs are legal.

A Baathist must remember that his duty is not only to safeguard the Party within Iraq; he also has an obligation towards the whole Arab nation. Had we been revolutionaries for Iraq alone, we would not have issued so many warnings. That is why the Iraqi revolutionary must be a light that shines throughout the Arab nation and that is why so much is required of him. If we turn to our ancestors' history, we will see that this matter was always given a very important place in Islam. Omar ibn al-Khattab kept most of his followers within the Arabian peninsula in order to avoid any unwanted external influence. A simple, ascetic life meant that his men were always ready to pick up their swords, mount their horses and go into battle, to emerge victorious. That is why Omar ibn al-Khattab did not distribute the land of Iraq amongst his Muslim followers after its conquest from the Persians.

That is why we warn our people in the revolution against flexible liberalism. We are part of a big nation and would like to be a shining example to it. That is why a revolution has no beginning and no end; it is not like war and its soldiers must not profit from its spoils. It is something continuous; it is a message to life, and the human being is only the bearer of the message.

Fuad Matar: Now that you have achieved revolutionary power, which is the more difficult: working to achieve it, or working to retain it?

President Saddam Hussein: The hardest part is not reaching a position of power; it is rather how to turn this power into a constant means to serve the people. This is the most difficult task, even more difficult than the hardships of the underground life endured by the Party. But I do not draw a distinction between the spirit during the days of struggle and the expression of principles through the means of power. Only true comrades are true revolutionaries and only they can turn power into a means to serve the people.

Fuad Matar: Can you explain your understanding of the difference between a revolution and a *coup d'état*?

President Saddam Hussein: The revolution and the *coup d'état* are technically similar, in that they both change power through the use of force. Yet there is a difference in depth and involvement, as well as in the programme adopted and its outcome. Those who overthrow a regime may be revolutionary human beings who reject what the people have also rejected. Yet if they have come to power without either preparation or understanding of the life that surrounds them, they are simply responsible for a *coup d'état*. Those who carry out a *coup d'état* are to be respected if they overthrow and change a bad leader. Yet if they have no pre-arranged programme in hand, they have achieved nothing but a limited *coup d'état*. That is the difference.

Fuad Matar: What is the role of the Army in Iraq? Is it technical or political?

President Saddam Hussein: Had the Army's role been only technical, the July 1968 Revolution would have been nothing but a *coup d'état*. The Army's role is primarily political. Soldiers in the Army are members of the July Revolution, and primarily Baathists, who make use of their technical abilities for the good of the revolutionary Baath programme. This is the main role of the Army.

Fuad Matar: When can one consider that national independence is a reality? What is your opinion of the Arabs' wealth and how this can be used for the good of the nation?

President Saddam Hussein: National independence can be achieved in stages. One of the most important steps in today's world is to possess a national economy that cannot be influenced by external circumstances. Another is to have a strong army, capable of defending one's sovereignty and beliefs. One must be endowed with power based on a political, economic, social and military structure, built up as a result of one's position within the nation and one's relationship with Arab and foreign countries. This enables one, for instance, to receive arms shipments without pre-conditions or attempts to influence one's programme, one's independence or one's sovereignty; that is, if one is unable to manufacture arms oneself. This is the way for a truly independent and nationalist human being.

We in Iraq have used our resources in order to strengthen our national independence. Had our wealth been less than it is today, our independence would have also differed, since principles and resolutions are not enough for real independence in today's world. Wealth can lead either to enslavement or to sovereignty. We have used ours as a means of strengthening our sovereignty, our independence and our happiness.

Fuad Matar: What made you give the Kurds their autonomy since you feel strongly about unity. Is the Kurdish problem over? What is the relationship between the Iraqi Arab and the Kurd? What would have happened to the Kurds had there been unity between Iraq and Syria?

President Saddam Hussein: There are two main causes for the decision for self-rule: the principles of our Party, and its respect of the desires of the people. It is a fact that our Kurdish people wanted self-rule. Part of the people were incited to act against the Revolution under the guise of seeking self-rule. Yet the latter would never have been established had it not been at the request of the people of Kurdistan. The Kurds wanted self-rule; had we not granted it to them, this would only have led to bloodshed, and division among the people. On the contrary, granting self-rule to the Kurds has brought us together. Self-rule for the Kurds does not stand in the way of Arab unity, and was one of the points that we planned to introduce on the agenda of the union constitution discussed with the Syrian regime. This would always be an essential condition in the event of a union between Iraq and any Arab country since we know that if the Kurds ever feel threatened in their autonomy by Arab unity they will rise up against the Arabs which is certainly not to our benefit. Nor is Kurdish self-rule a threat to our principal aim, Arab unity.

Fuad Matar: It is often said that the Arab nation cannot be a strong and able one without 'a powerful Iraq'. Can you please explain this saying? Does this mean that if Iraq remains strong, the Arab nation will be powerful although many individual states are not?

President Saddam Hussein: First and foremost, I would like to point out that what I mean by a 'powerful Iraq' is an Iraq based on the Arab Socialist Baath Party. It is my right to feel that the road to save the Arab nation is through these principles. Yet this outlook on life does not ignore the actual relationship with the Arab nation. Whatever the nationalist movement, if it exists we must co-operate with it. That is why I believe that Iraq today, with its principles, is an extraordinary power within the nation. Yet its power is not sufficient if it is only surrounded by weak regions. It can most certainly help in the development of the nation, through the power invested in it by the principles of the Party. Iraq can assist in the strengthening of other regions in the Arab nation, both directly and indirectly.

Fuad Matar: You trust the Baathist to an unlimited extent and give him much more importance than others. I remember your saying, 'Iraq cannot preserve its glory, nor can it keep the honour of this land, without the Arab Socialist Baath Party. Moreover, we cannot realise the dreams of our ancestors without the Baath Party.' You also said, 'We could not have reached the correct road without the Revolution of 17 July.' Does this not look as though you are saying that only a Baathist can show loyalty towards the nation and glory in our heritage?

President Saddam Hussein: It is true that you might reach such a conclusion if you take the subject out of context. Yet if you put it in context, you will find that I go on to say, 'All national Iraqis who are loyal to the Arab nation are Baathists, even if they are not members [of the Party].' The meaning now becomes perfectly clear. Moreover, we believe that the Baath is the soul of the nation, and no Arab can progress and develop without believing in the nation's soul. Therefore any Baathist who believes in the principles of his Party automatically believes that his road is the road to save the nation. However, like all other believers, this does not mean that he will reject others. Yet he must have loyalty and belief, otherwise how can he sacrifice himself if necessary? However, in politics, a Baathist should not deny the role of others nor should he be a fanatic. On the contrary, he must co-operate and show understanding, in order to accomplish his chief mission. It is with this belief that a Baathist can become a leader of society.

Fuad Matar: You once said that the Baath experience in Iraq could be studied closely by the rest of the world. Do you mean that it can serve as an example? Have you, in turn, studied the experiences of others in order to profit from them?

President Saddam Hussein: We have studied the experiences of others and their philosophies. We have confidence in ourselves and are against isolationism. We are always ready to learn from humanity's other theories and experiences, as much as we are ready to serve it with our own. That is why I am certain that our Party's experience will be closely examined by Third World countries, not in order to apply it since they would not profit from it, merely to learn from its spirit.

Fuad Matar: Is there a plan to make the majority of all Iraqis Baathists? You have said, 'All Iraqis, whether Party members or not, are Baathists. Even he who holds a grudge against the Party is a Baathist.' Are you talking of the present situation, of what may occur in the future, or of what should exist in effect? How much criticism would you accept from a non-Baathist?

President Saddam Hussein: The essential weight is there, since the vast majority of Iraqis are Baathists, whether within the Party's structure or not. The Baathist is the Iraqi citizen who has faith in the overall programme of the Revolution; the Baathist as such, or the 'technical' Baathist, is he who has closely followed, studied and absorbed that programme. He can discuss all its aspects knowledgeably. That is why I believe that any loyal citizen who believes in the general programme, even if he disapproves at times, is still a Baathist. We believe that we have set a high standard for democracy in the statutes of the National Council and the Legislative Council. And yet this has not stopped criticism of that democracy. Some people offer other alternatives, better ones in their view. We accept and will admit any discussion, as long as the Revolution and its main principles are respected and as long as the Arab Socialist Baath Party remains the leader. This is democracy, and the eventual road that will lead to Arab unity.

Fuad Matar: You talk about the positive aspects of the Baath and of the Baathist as if there were no other. Do you not think that, in the light of your experience, there may be certain negative aspects that should be dealt with, as well as certain negative attitudes within the Baathist that he should rid himself of?

President Saddam Hussein: When we Baathists meet, we put much more weight on the negative aspects than on the positive ones. Discussions are then often heated and harsh; but to mention the negative aspects without pointing out the positive ones would only serve to discourage the Baathist, and that is not my aim. He must feel pride in his accomplishments and those of his Party, rather than feel morally beaten. Yet we do point out errors and mistakes to the Baathist, while encouraging him to go on trying for the good of the Party. We believe one should never break down the morale of a human being.

Nevertheless, I often criticise the Baathist before the people on both radio and television as well as in mass meetings, where we, as Baathists, are often ready to accept responsibility for our mistakes. Leaders must do so. But I wish to point out clearly that I have not as yet discovered a flaw in the premises of our Party. The Party may not have had a set programme for the development of society before the great July 1968 Revolution because the time was not propitious then, and that programme could only be ready and well defined when the Party took over power. Today the Party can truly work towards the betterment of the people with depth and open-mindedness. We are proud of what we have achieved so far. Errors and mistakes may have been committed, but they were not serious and did not touch the major Baath principles and goals.

Fuad Matar: Who is the true comrade? Is the only comrade the one who is a member of the Arab Socialist Baath Party?

President Saddam Hussein: Any human being who lives for the people is a comrade, not only the Baathist. Any human being who abides by principles and does not live by double standards is a comrade — I mean that he cannot cling to the old traditional life and still want the honour of being a comrade. He must be with and for the people, whether they are wrong or not, whether he is far away or close, and he must always be ready to protect the people. This is the true comrade.

Fuad Matar: Are Baathists the only people who embody the true spirit of our Arab ancestry, as you once said?

President Saddam Hussein: I believe that the Party, whether in its principles or in spirit, is the only one of the Arab movements to do so. This does not apply to all Baathists, of course. There still remains a barrier, which we will eventually break down.

Fuad Matar: Twenty years ago the Baath's ideas were a problem for the authorities, yet for the Arab citizen they were a model on which to build the future. Then the Baath came to power, and, wanting to protect and safeguard the Revolution, began to act not unlike the traditional leaders. Then came the divisions within the Baath and the tragedies that accompanied them. Could you give an analysis of the Baath before and after it took over power?

President Saddam Hussein: Social relationships and humanity's basic true principles cannot progress to everyone's satisfaction under the shadow of authority. What the comrade imagines is going to happen after victory does not always take place. Moreover, the circumstances of the authorities may affect the comrade morally or materially, whether in his relationship with the people or within the context of the Party itself. But it is not fair to compare our work, and our endeavours to attain a better world, to the work of the traditional Arab rulers. Occasional failure is natural, so is the erratic behaviour of some comrades, although this is rare. One must not forget the problems faced by the authorities when one condemns their principles. What is most important are the major issues for which we fought and on the basis of which we struggled for a new and better society.

At this point I wish to compare both the Baath's first abortive coup attempt in Iraq and the failure of the Baath in Syria (for which the Party has been blamed) with the present experience of the Baath. The Baath regime has its gaols, although it criticised and fought those rulers who had their own prisons. The Baath also brings people to trial, in accordance with the law . . . although the old Baathists rejected these methods. And yet, let us ask ourselves, who are the people in prison today? Are they the ones who serve the people? Are they the poor? Are they the revolutionaries? In July 1979 we took a decision to free all prisoners. The political prisoners amongst them were few, and they had been convicted because they had taken up arms against the Revolution. After the July 1979 decision had been implemented, only the spies and the economic saboteurs working for foreign agents remained in gaol. We even freed those people who had tried to destroy our economy but were not working for foreign agents. Some of these people had been condemned to death. They are free today.

You may find some Baathists who will accept bribes and others who use their positions for personal gain. A little while ago I was reading about the case of a high-ranking Party comrade in the Ninevah branch of the Farmers' Union. It came to our attention that he suddenly possessed five transport trucks and had built a house costing 30,000 dinars. We formed an investigation committee which first seized all his property and then asked him to account for his income. The committee discovered he was a profiteer. Although he was a member of the Party, he lacked the spirit, principles and morality of the Party. We had no one like him in the Party before the Revolution, but then we were not in power. Had we remained silent in this matter, we would not have behaved like true Baathists. The man appeared before the Revolutionary Court of Justice: he was sent to prison and his property was given to the people. This is the spirit of the Revolution and of the Party. There may still be people like the one I have just mentioned within our midst, but these are not true revolutionaries and they are merely exceptions to the rule.

Fuad Matar: You mentioned once that 'the experience of the Baath is not for Iraq alone but for the nation as a whole. Our ambitions lie even further than the broad horizons of the Arab nation.' This makes me wonder why the seed of the Baath only grew in Iraq and Syria. If so, how can one have ambitions for broader horizons?

President Saddam Hussein: The Baath came to power in Iraq in 1963 and in the Revolution of July 1968, and in Syria in March of 1963 — and yet the seed is present in all the Arab nation. There may be differences between the power of the Iraqi Baath Party and that in other Arab regions. As for the experience becoming the property of humanity, I say so because that is the way I see it. We can be nationalists and humanitarian only if we strive to serve humanity and the nation.

Fuad Matar: What are the special attributes of the Party theories and the Baath theory of labour to which you often refer in your speeches?

President Saddam Hussein: It is the living link that exists between the Party's various aims, in other words, the social, political and national struggle; this is known as the dialectic between social struggle and national struggle. This integration and comprehensive vision are unique to the Baath. I do not exaggerate when I say that, of all the movements in the Arab nation, our Party is the only one which has proved the deep links between its principles and the actual situation it is directing.

In the October 1973 war, Iraq was the only Arab country to fight on two fronts: its Air Force bombed Israeli missile bases in the first air attack on the Egyptian front, and its Army moved to the Syrian front as soon as war broke out in Syria. Iraq left its own land undefended in order to safeguard that of the Arab nation. At the time, our armies had been mobilised on the Iranian frontiers and our relations with the Shah of Iran were at their worst because of our differences over the Shatt al-Arab.

A new period begins in the life of Saddam Hussein: he takes the oath as President of the Republic.

Presidential palace in Baghdad.

Reading a paper and wearing Iraqi peasant dress.

Sharing a meal with the crew of his plane during his visit to the province of Saladin, spring 1979.

His head wrapped in a kefiyeh, the Iraqi President visits the Basra region in 1979.

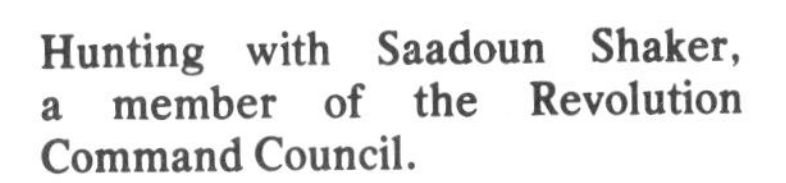

Hunting with Saadoun Shaker, a member of the Revolution Command Council.

A meeting during a public holiday between President Saddam Hussein and his Vice President of the revolutionary council Izat Ibrahim.

With his brother Barzan during the war with Iran in 1980.

President Saddam Hussein accompanied by his family visit a peasant family living in the neighbourhood of Baghdad. Several other families joined them as soon as the Iraqi President's presence became known.

After his accession to the Presidency: President Saddam Hussein carries his little Hala on his shoulders during a walk with his wife, accompanied by the Vice President of the Revolutionary Council, Izat Ibrahim.

With his family during a day off, outside Baghdad.

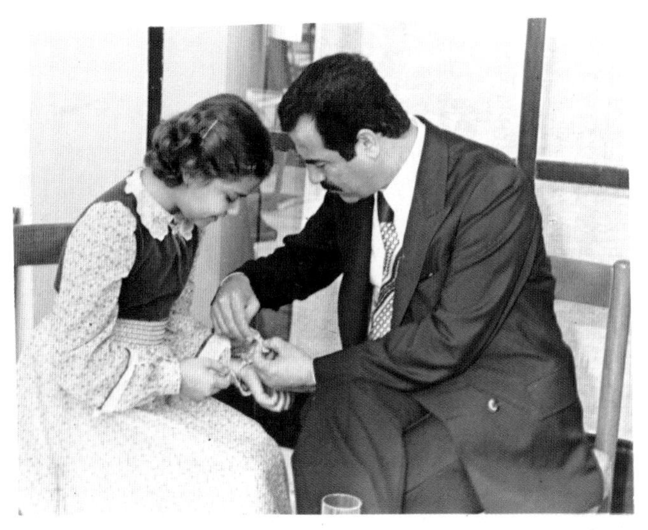

Needle and thread in hand, President Saddam Hussein himself mends the sleeve of his eldest daughter Raghd's dress.

His elder son wanted to be photographed with his father who is wearing a Marshal's uniform (the Iraqi President is also Commander-in-Chief of the armed forces).

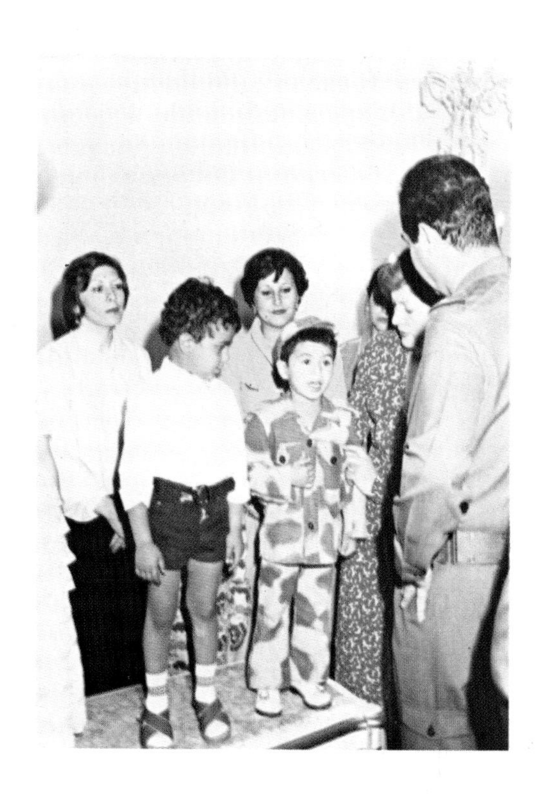

The President receives nursery school children during the war with Iran.

And yet on 7 October 1973 we unilaterally announced, in a Revolution Command Council communiqué, that we were ready to solve all the existing problems with Iran. The general understanding, and what the Shah wanted, was that part of the Shatt al-Arab would be handed over to the Iranians. We then pulled our Army back from the Iranian border, in what was generally thought to be the greatest military gamble, and we moved towards the land of Syria to face the Zionist army that was pushing towards Damascus. There the Iraqi Army fought with courage and honour, to the dismay of the enemy Minister of Defence who had, before the Iraqi Army's arrival on the Golan Heights, stated that he planned to have lunch the next day in our beloved Damascus. That is how we applied the national principles of our Party.

At the Baghdad Summit, Iraq offered sacrifice after sacrifice to stir the nation's conscience, in view of the great danger the nation faced because of the action taken by Sadat.

Fuad Matar: Cuba's primary concern was to improve social conditions, and it has made great strides in this field. What is your view of this issue, and is it your chief concern?

President Saddam Hussein: We make no distinction between one issue and another, whether social, economic or moral, since they all interconnect and influence one another, politically, economically, socially, intellectually or otherwise. That is the reason why no one issue is given more attention than any other.

Fuad Matar: What would Iraq be like today if it had only one nationality, one religion, one sect? Do you think the Baath, in its present form, is capable of resolving the two silent struggles, the confessional and the social?

President Saddam Hussein: In answer to your first question, it is a fact that Iraq would have been stronger. This is a reality which must be faced. Yet this is how our people is formed and it does not worry us; it is not a burden that stands in the way of our progress, nor is it exploited by opposing forces to the extent of preventing us from achieving our aims. The Party can absorb everything which contributes to our people's national unity. Had any power other than the Arab Socialist Baath Party been at the helm, it would have been impossible to solve these problems and to achieve the present national unity of our people. All the sons of Iraq, without exception, work for the good of Iraq, its strength, its aims and its leading role within the nation.

There is no silent confessional struggle in any sect or religion. We do have some people who are confessionist, whether Muslim or non-Muslim, Sunni or Shia, just as we have some chauvinist Arabs and separatist Kurds. But these are simple situations and can be found in any society. The majority of the people are not like that. The people are proud of their Revolution and their Iraq, and of the struggle they waged to achieve the goals and aims of the Revolution. They are happy with what they have achieved. The negative cases just mentioned will not develop into a serious situation, and our achievements so far will eliminate them with the passing of time. A situation comes to the surface when it expresses the opinion of a majority. Therefore, had the majority of the Sunni or Shia been sectarian people, had the majority of Kurds been separatists or had all the Arabs been chauvinists, then we would have failed in our mission. There was a threat that this might happen at the very beginning of the Revolution because of the lack of national organisation at the time, as well as the imperialist and Zionist plans for such disturbances.

Fuad Matar: A revolutionary's dreams usually reflect the plans for which he strives. Do you have dreams of Iraq in the year 2000?

President Saddam Hussein: In general, my dream is of Iraq after 1985, always changing for the better, when things will be more conducive to a happy society and when industry and agriculture will reach their peak.

Fuad Matar: How do you see the role of the private sector within the socialist framework?

President Saddam Hussein: Our Party realised the importance of the historical role of private activity from the very beginning. We do not consider this as a passing phase in the path of socialist action; we believe the private sector and the socialist sector will go hand in hand forever. They are partners in the service of society, working for the betterment of mankind. This is the true road to social change and the happiness of the Arab nation, and this is what we have applied in our programme in Iraq. We are required to transform these principles into a programme of action, what is known in revolutionary thought as the 'theory of labour'. We believe that in certain cases private activity is more capable and useful than socialist activity. In other situations, such as the case of developing countries, this is not so. When we talk about the historical role of the private sector, it is not because we want its investment, as is the case in other regions, but because we want its brains and expertise, and its hard work; this is bound to bring profit so long as this profit does not lead to exploitation. I do not think that we can build socialism with the use of the state apparatus alone while ignoring the need for the private sector.

Fuad Matar: By private sector do you mean the Iraqi one, or could it also be either Arab or foreign?

President Saddam Hussein: Our theory applies not only to Iraq but to the whole Arab nation, which in its turn cannot possibly isolate itself from the world and the rest of humanity. However, our own theory has not been prepared for other nations; they in their turn must choose their own, as we did ours. Nevertheless, socialist beliefs cannot ignore private activity. Human needs are not solely a matter of filling the stomach. In our opinion, anyone who says they can do without the private sector is applying a limited theory. We stress the importance of satisfying human need in all sectors — services, production, and so on — in making it possible for man to use his energies and abilities. What we mean by the private sector is the Iraqi private sector, together with the Arab private sector, in accordance with Iraqi laws, not the foreign private sector.

Fuad Matar: On this basis, does socialist Iraq expect to see the renewed activity of small industries, like tourism, within the private sector?

President Saddam Hussein: Yes. This is not a sudden discovery, it is within an established programme. Today our study of the matter is more accurate and all-inclusive than it was seven years ago. We know that tourism must be taken over by both the socialist and the private sectors. And take garages, for example: we have garages that belong to the socialist sector, yet we cannot force, nor do we want to force, the ordinary citizen to stand in long queues in order to have his car repaired. If the citizen does not wish to do so, he can go to the privately-owned garages which are found all over the country. The state has more important matters to attend to than opening small boutiques, cafés and restaurants, or repairing radios and television sets. This is how we can avoid the errors into which some of the Marxists fell.

However, can the private sector take responsibility for heavy industry? The answer is no; this is not practical in our society. If the private sector were allowed to do so, it would mean heavy investment by that sector, and therefore its increasing influence. This is against our principles, since it might adversely affect the political leadership and change the whole concept of our revolutionary society. That is why we limit private gain. We wish to safeguard our socialist, Baathist and human principles. Practically speaking, it is impossible for private activity to make heavy investments with confidence in a developing country, since no one can predict what may happen or what steps may be taken at a later date. This is why private activity in our country will remain as it is and flourish alongside the socialist sector, as long as it is accepted by socialism.

Fuad Matar: It is noticeable that your calls for a greater interest in agriculture have become more frequent. Are they the result of specific fears or merely a desire to revive the private sector?

President Saddam Hussein: I have spoken of our views on how to make the best use of oil revenues. Yet I am constantly disturbed by one thought: finding ourselves at a point when our reserves are exhausted, without having a flourishing agricultural sector or a sound infrastructure. We would then have condemned ourselves to an eternal state of underdevelopment. That is why we must concentrate on agriculture, not only within the socialist sector; we must also offer all that is needed for the development of the private sector in agriculture.

Fuad Matar: Iraq is a developing country. Do you have any idea when it will move from this stage to the next?

President Saddam Hussein: The word 'developing' is a polite term for underdevelopment. In comparison to the developed countries, Iraq is a developing nation in that it lags behind them in industry, agriculture, culture, technology and education. It is only when we develop and progress in all these fields, and when our *per capita* income as well as our national income increase satisfactorily, that we will be able to leave the term 'developing' behind us. I believe that we will have attained a new level by the end of 1985 because of our programmes. This does not mean that Iraq will then leave all the appearances of underdevelopment behind; it will simply develop in a balanced manner and reach a higher level than that of today.

Fuad Matar: Do you consider the importance given to the private sector as a kind of 'open-door policy', or do you refuse this idea?

President Saddam Hussein: I do not like this kind of terminology because it has come to apply to rightist reactions. We were never 'closed', and so it is impossible to talk of 'opening'. This is our theory; we started applying it and have never regretted it; nor did we ever 'close' in order to 'reopen'. And when I talk of the role of the private sector within the context of its limitations, I also talk of the importance of the socialist sector, its role and its development.

Fuad Matar: Can one consider what you have discussed so far as a new form of socialist action or of socialism?

President Saddam Hussein: This is the first time that our theory has been applied in any country. Before the Revolution, our programme was one of secret struggle for a change in the regime. Today the Party has a historic chance to concentrate on the programme to build a socialist society.

Fuad Matar: I have some questions about socialism and its application:

First, I notice that socialism is not applied absolutely; at the same time, the 'open door' is not fully open. If I may say so, there is a half-socialism and a half-open policy, and the two together have led to a new form of socialism. Is this form an established one and is it the solution?

Second, do you not think that certain gaps in the application of socialism have been exploited by Marxism on the one hand and Islamic ideology on the other; is this why it was important for you to find a new form of socialism?

Third, Abdel-Nasser saved the Baath from committing certain errors in the application of socialism, since he was the first to apply it. Has the Baath benefited from these errors, in that they were not repeated in Iraq?

Fourth, the Baath has succeeded in setting up effective cadres for unity on the political level, yet it has not been able to do the same on the socialist level. Do you not think that these cadres should exist in the socialist sector as well? I say this because I tend to believe that the principal aim of national struggle in the Baath seems to be Arab unity rather than socialism.

Fifth, are the benefits that have been achieved by socialism for the good of the citizen in Iraq, and in the rest of the Arab countries, equal to the sacrifices he has made?

Sixth, is it not strange that, after twenty years of socialism and its application, it is still rejected by the majority in many Arab countries? Is it because socialism is closer to Marxism than to Islam, or is it simply because of an incorrect application of socialism?

President Saddam Hussein: Our socialist programme has never consisted of collecting elements from elsewhere and stringing these ideas and thoughts together into a common denominator for the use of Iraq. We are open to influence. We do not overlook the experiences and theories of others, but we always have the Baath in mind; we do not go to others with empty minds but always with our own principles and ideas in mind. We believe human thought should interact all over the globe; this is the correct attitude. We do not go to Marxism to take whatever small element pleases us in its laws. Marxism is a revolutionary theory, but it is not the only one, nor is it the oldest.

The theory of the Prophet Muhammad applied divine laws on earth, through Islam. The theories of our Muslim Arab leaders and rulers are much older than Marxism, since they are 1,400 years old. Therefore when we study Marxism, we do so in the hope that we may benefit from it in accordance with the Baath system and not in accordance with Marxism. That is why we have no intention of collecting the theories and experiences of others for our own benefit. Even when we study Abdel-Nasser's experience we do so not to copy it, rather to learn from it, to know when to beware of traps and dangers, since Nasser's experience is not far from that of the Baath.

When I talk about the application of socialism, I talk of the Baath and the application of its theories in Iraq. Socialism in other Arab countries is another matter. I do not think that we have fallen into any trap such as is the case in other countries, whereby mistakes in the application of socialism were committed in a manner that repelled people. Some people may have a wrong concept of what socialism means and therefore become rightist as a reaction. A most significant example is Egypt itself. One of the most important weapons used by those who are against socialism is to tell people that the ideology allows for no private activity, or does so only minimally. Saying that the private sector is non-existent in socialism is as incorrect as to say that there is 'free' competition between the socialist and the private sectors without any interference from the State.

This does not mean that we have not made mistakes. Yet there is a difference between natural, human error and falling into a trap. Our mistakes can be treated and resolved. We are capable of correcting them, thanks to the understanding of our people and the Party, our financial resources, and our cadres.

Our dream is not only one of Arab nationalist struggle for Arab unity, it is also the construction of one united Arab socialist democratic nation. And yet, as I mentioned earlier, the Party wanted to place unity before all else, before liberty and socialism.

There is no lack of understanding of socialism among our cadres, although they lack numbers. However, national philosophy has, since the beginning of this century, always stressed the importance of national struggle, giving it preference over the means of using socialism. There should be a dialectic of interaction between national struggle and social struggle. Those Arab countries which attempted to unite, while at the same time building a socialist society, found that the Party, as well as all other nationalist movements, lacked the cadres to which I referred. I can state with certainty that our Party has the cadres capable of understanding and applying Baathist socialism, and yet we can do more by continuing to develop the cultural and intellectual programme among our cadres.

Fuad Matar: You have always stressed the issue of the Arab woman's liberation. Yet it is acknowledged that it is easier to wage a revolution against petroleum monopolies and foreign interests than to go against the traditions that chain the Arab woman. The Revolution hesitates to adopt any forceful measures that go against the inherited customs and the traditions which stand in the way of liberation, which means postponement of the issue.

You have stated on one occasion, 'If the Revolution does not deal with the rights of women on an equal basis, taking into consideration their role in history, then the Revolution will certainly lose a part of its people.' What would happen if this part were indeed lost, although this could be prevented by educating people gently and ending forever the unfair and unjust traditions? If the women are lost, the loss will be permanent, but traditions go on spreading. Can you also tell us about the nature of women's lack of freedom, and what would have happened had you acted with force?

President Saddam Hussein: Whenever I warned against forceful action to liberate women and give them equal status, I always differentiated between this kind of action and that used against foreign companies. We do not lack daring — yet the issue of women is directly linked to the traditions of our society, whereas driving out monopolies is in line with the will of our people, since the companies are foreign parties exploiting our wealth. In using force to deal with the monopolies and in nationalising oil, I placed all the people on the same front, facing the foreign economic occupier. That is why I warn against applying this method in dealing with the social problems of our people. I mention this in connection with a comment made by one of our woman comrades at a women's congress I attended. She said that the leadership which had successfully nationalised oil should also fight against reactionary thoughts and liberate women just as quickly. I answered that there was a difference between the two. Postponing the issue for three years, for instance, was better than losing people from our ranks. Nevertheless, only a year after this comment a law was passed concerning the role of women and the achievement of equality between the sexes.

In this, as in other issues, we do not use the same methods as those adopted by the opposition (even ours) when we were not in power: they thought that solving the problem was merely a matter of issuing a set of laws and applying them. A revolution that does not translate its thoughts into laws remains a verbal revolution. The revolution must become both the law and the tradition if we are to build a new society. Yet we do not look at the woman's situation within the context of law and the study of law. Her situation is different, in that she is a part of the social movement. For instance, we believe that by educating women and making it easy for them to find jobs in both the economic and the social fields, we have partly helped them on the road to liberation. We have also set up children's nurseries to enable mothers to go to work without their husbands objecting and insisting that a woman's duty begins at home.

This is certainly not enough. What is needed is to change society's state of mind. This does not take place in a year, or two, or three, or four . . . It is when one applies a twelve-year plan in one year that one loses part of the people. We do not wish to do this unless we have to. Some socialist revolutions lost followers by the millions in order to apply socialism. We do not want to fall into this trap. This is why we must learn the lesson of others; it also explains why our losses are few. Our programme continues, and the road towards the liberation of women takes its natural course. We do not wish to make only socialist changes, but social changes as well.

Fuad Matar: Discussing Iraqi women in general brings me to a private matter — your wife. Although she has become the wife of the President of the Republic, she still goes to school every day where she is the deputy headmistress. Since this is a unique example, I would like to ask you the following questions:

First, do you personally wish her to remain in this position, as an ordinary employee of the state, in that it contributes to the ultimate goal of women's liberation in Iraq?

Secondly, why is it that the media are silent about this fact, whereas it should be reported as a very healthy attitude and an example of great benefit to both the Islamic world and the Third World? Does your wife receive special treatment as the President's wife?

President Saddam Hussein: My wife is no longer a deputy headmistress. She is now the headmistress of the school. This happened several years after the Revolution, and as a result of the normal procedure of promotion. She is proud of her work and so am I. It is natural for a woman to perform her duties and obligations towards society and the nation. The fact that she is the President's wife should not stop her from doing so, on the contrary. Moreover, who is the President of the Republic? As I understand it, he is a human being who has been given the task of serving the people. He has been put into this position just like a headmaster or a headmistress, or a teacher, whether male or female.

You claim that I have kept quiet about the matter. I do not keep quiet about it, but neither do I publicise it, since I think it is a simple, natural fact of life. It is not a matter for publicity and yet I do not prevent people from talking about it. In answer to the last part of your question, my wife does not receive any special treatment. Her salary is the same as that of her colleagues, and she is called upon to give an account of her actions just like everyone else.

Fuad Matar: There is another question concerning women: you train them in the Iraqi Army; is this due to the fact that Israeli women fight alongside Israeli men, or is it because the Baath's principles call for equality even in this field?

President Saddam Hussein: As a matter of fact, there are two reasons for this: one is based on principle and the other is political. First, we consider that all people in our society are equal within their capacity and abilities, and duties are distributed between men and women accordingly. When it comes to the political side, it is a fact that the Israelis used women in their army to undermine the very spirit of the Arabs. The enemy realised that the Arab suffers from a disease: he has a low view of women. It is as if the Israelis wished to say to the Arabs, 'You who look down on women have been conquered by us through woman.' Both principles and politics lay behind our decision to take women into the Iraqi Army.

Fuad Matar: In the third conference of the General Federation of Iraqi Women, held on 17 April 1971, you mentioned that women had played a major role in building up the Party. You said, 'When the comrades were most cornered, women within the Party played a major role, one that was both constructive and active. They became the link between the High Command and the rest of the Party. They were the link between the comrades in gaol and those outside. They were an active force in the recruitment of the people.' Do you think the time has come to tell us of their achievements and of the role played by some of the heroines? Moreover, why can they not play a more active role today? Why can they not deal with the inherited social problems of Iraq, especially since the position of women in Iraqi society is an exceedingly complex matter and one which deserves serious attention? At that same conference you also talked of 'the total liberation of Iraqi women' as a principal aim of both the Party and the Revolution. What do you mean by total liberation?

Does religion explain the appearance of great heroines in Arab history? In other words, is it faith that can change society rather than theories and inherited traditions? Do you believe that Iraqi women who have followed the Baath's principles have been able to overcome the traditional mentality, or is this mentality too strongly ingrained to be erased by these principles?

President Saddam Hussein: Our women comrades were the messengers during the days of underground struggle. Two of their most important roles were to move equipment from one secret place to another, and to pass messages on to our fellow prisoners. They even delivered equipment which enabled us to escape. This is only one example. The important thing is that they had an active role in our struggle. At this moment the Party is writing a history of its struggle which will include the heroic acts of both our men and women. This is something we did not wish to do until now, since it also included our actions within the struggle and we were not ready to disclose some of these stands. Today the Party is ready to talk about its history in detail and will do so.

In my opinion, it is faith that will change society. No deep changes can take place if man has no faith. As Baathists, we look to life and its beliefs, and yet we do not forget the link between ourselves and our heritage, both national and religious, and, first and foremost, Islam and the spirit of Islam. Islam does not place women in a harem. On the contrary, Islamic society sees both men and women serving one another; it is a society where one cannot do without the other. The division of labour is solely based upon the capacity and the ability of a woman to perform her duties. Women may do certain jobs better than men and vice versa. This is a fact; it was true in the past, it is true in the present and it will be true in the future. That is what I believe and it forms the basis of my programme, of which women's liberation is a part.

Fuad Matar: The West is in the throes of a great crisis, and one of the reasons is that men and women are both forced to work. This has created a sense of emptiness in both sexes, and is resulting in the breakdown of society. So when we talk of women's liberation in the Arab world, do we mean that we want them to be equal to Western women? Does the President not feel that a deeper study should be made, and new theories developed, so that liberation will not create new burdens for women?

President Saddam Hussein: Our Party is aware of this fact. It certainly does not claim that women can work in all fields and under all circumstances. This would only be harmful. Moreover, they themselves do not wish to be treated in this manner. I mentioned at an open session of the Federation of Iraqi Women that legal, practical and theoretical equality between men and women is a weapon against women. We cannot possibly ask women to undergo those hardships endured by men in order to attain equality. In the capitalist West, the end justifies the means. That is why Western women are forced to work in order to help financially and to strengthen family relations. However, the burden and the responsibilities involved lead these women to realise that the spirit of the family has been lost. There is a great difference between a woman working in order to co-operate and one doing so under duress.

In our case, the situation is different because the understanding differs. Salaries are in line with the needs of the individual. Just as we provide jobs for women, we also have laws that strengthen family relationships. As an example, a pregnant working woman is granted leave long before she has given birth and resumes her duties only after she is satisfied with her health and that of the newborn baby. Such a long period of leave is detrimental to our economy, and yet it is granted because the economy should first and foremost serve our socialist society. This is not the only law that we have decreed in order to preserve the family and for women's liberation. Other steps will be taken and become law as soon as they are fully discussed. All these laws will give priority to family relationships.

Fuad Matar: After the developments in Iran, it seems to me that there is a contradiction between Arab revolution and Islamic revolution. Do you not believe there should be a way to make one support the other? Iraq has confronted both regimes, the Shah's and the present one; which Iran did Iraq prefer as a neighbour? What is your analysis of the Iranian situation in general?

President Saddam Hussein: We rejoice at any revolution that takes place with the spirit and goals of Islam, even if it is outside the Arab nation. We see it as a bridge between the Arab nationalist movement, which is working towards a new society, and the non-Arab Islamic nations. Any revolution within an Islamic society which does not abide by the spirit of Islam goes against the Arab revolution. Any revolution that hides behind Islam in order to attain its goals and then confronts the Arab revolution is detrimental to the Arabs, as well as to the cause of Islam, because it is not based on co-operation and understanding.

It is natural for me to welcome any revolution inspired by Islam after 1,400 years, since it can only create a bridge of understanding between the revolutionaries and ourselves: we would then share the same traditions and beliefs, as well as the same feelings towards injustice and oppression. This is why all Arabs rejoiced at the fall of the Shah, not only because he was a tyrannical ruler but because his regime was corrupt; the fall of any such ruler is a proof of the victory of right over wrong, good over evil. The Shah fell in an Islamic society, a society which stands on the borders of the Arab nation. That is why all Arabs rejoiced in the hope that the new circumstances would be a bridge between the Iranian and the Arab revolutions; the Arab revolution is not simply a system of laws on earth, but derives its spirit from heaven.

Yet the Iranians, particularly those in responsible positions, behaved as though they naturally assumed that there were contradictions between their revolution and ours. They were chauvinistic and isolationist in their outlook towards the Arabs, whether historically or as regards their present interests. Moreover, in the case of a confessional movement, conflict is inevitable, since the Arab revolution is by no means a confessional one.

The Iranian revolution is dreaming if it intends to liberate the Arabs. It can help by freeing certain Arab societies from their corrupt regimes, but it certainly cannot be of any assistance through fanaticism and narrow-mindedness in religion. There is absolutely no contradiction between the Arab revolution and one which takes its inspiration from true Islam. We do not wish to force people to accept pre-established ideas or ready recipes. This is why we see the spirit of the Baath in all young people, Baathist or non-Baathist, who work in the spirit of Islam against corrupt regimes, Arab or non-Arab. Any Muslim who stands up to corruption is a revolutionary, wherever he is. There is no difference between people fighting against corrupt regimes, confessionalism and reactionary powers. Yet I would ask them to realise that 1,400 years have passed since the coming of Islam, that people have changed and society has progressed and developed, and all of this must be taken into consideration. It remains to be seen how successful these revolutionaries will be in building a new society.

It is not our business to give advice. Yet we reserve the right to think that the rulers of a society like Iran, composed as it is of five ethnic groups, must face this reality for the ultimate happiness of the people and to safeguard against interference by foreign powers. The Iranians claim that their revolution is based on the concepts of Islam; therefore they must understand that there is no contradiction between the values of Islam and the Persian and four non-Persian groups in their society — the Arabs, the people of Baluchistan, the Kurds and the people of Azerbaijan. As for Arab existence within the state of Iran, that is a fact. The Arab minority does not number thousands there; it numbers millions. It is up to them, and to them alone, to decide their own future.

If it based itself on the principles and truths I have already mentioned, Iran could be a good neighbour to Iraq.

Fuad Matar: How did you become involved with Palestine and when did your view of Palestine change from a romantic to a more realistic one? What do you think you could have accomplished for Palestine if you had been in power at an earlier date? Now that you are in power, what are the barriers that prevent you from achieving these things? What contribution has Iraq made to the Palestinian cause from 1948 to 1979? And for which Palestine are you fighting?

President Saddam Hussein: No movement can create a new society without a revolutionary vision, although it should not base itself on this alone. Through this vision, the revolutionary sees life as he wishes it to be, although he realises its present state. He sees clearly the life for which he fights and struggles, and nothing can separate him from his vision. This is a legitimate dream. Revolutionary romanticism in this sense still exists within me, and I find more pleasure in it than ever. I feel the need for it more than before, in order to be able to face the tasks of practical everyday life. Having said this, it is only natural that I have not yet been able to achieve all my ambitions.

What have we contributed to the Palestinian cause? We would have wished to offer more. We will never be content with our contribution, although we have certainly given more than any other Arab country without exception, apart from the special circumstances of those countries whose territory was occupied. There has been no war in which Iraq has not taken part. We have constantly called for the support of Palestinian revolutionaries. We are in the forefront of this support and will remain so. As for the Palestine that we want, it is a Palestine devoid of the presence of the Zionist usurpers. This is not a call for the existence of a Palestine without Jews. Arabs have never in their history been either religious or racial fanatics. However, the long road to our ultimate goal requires patient planning and optimism.

Fuad Matar: Within this context I would like to ask you, as a revolutionary comrade, the following questions. How can the Palestinian revolution become more effective? Was Iraq's encouragement of a greater number of resistance operations, especially of the kind planned by the late Dr Wadi Haddad, helpful to the cause?

President Saddam Hussein: The Palestinian revolution would be more successful if it rid itself of certain negative currents within the Arab nation and extricated itself from the game of international politics. The Arab nation is its source of inspiration and strength, yet some of its negative aspects may impede the Palestinian revolution. On the other hand, the Arabism of the revolution is also the basis of its strength, its optimism and its success. Although Arabism is sometimes a burden, the Palestinian revolution will never reach its goals without it. Arabism has made the revolution a part of Arab politics and this has laid it open to interference and intervention by Arab rulers, good and bad. The Palestinian revolution could have avoided the negative aspects of Arabism, but it failed to do so. The Palestinian revolutionaries' reasons may have been geographic as well as political, since the revolution had no other base of its own. One can imagine the importance of interaction between the Arab revolution as a whole and the Arab Palestinian revolution. They both have the same goal: the liberation of Palestine.

As for our support of operations, we do so in view of the circumstances. We are in favour of any operations, even suicidal ones, that may serve the Palestinian cause, either within the occupied land or outside it. We will not change this stand — even if we now hold a different opinion as to methods, which may make it appear that we have changed. We are in favour of any method used to express the Palestinian and Arab conscience, as long as this does not set world public opinion completely against it. This is our Party's line.

Fuad Matar: Some of Iraq's heroes have done great deeds for Palestine — I am thinking of Nebuchadnezzar and Salaheddin, for example. May I presume that you too dream of a similar role? Is this possible in your view, or are the circumstances of three thousand years ago different from those of today?

President Saddam Hussein: By God, I do indeed dream and wish for this. It is an honour for any human being to dream of such a role. But like all the revolutionaries of today, Baathists or Arabs, I also realise that the world of today is unlike the world of Nebuchadnezzar and Salaheddin. Today we know that in order to liberate Palestine we must first awaken the nation, liberate it from its chains, and give it confidence. This is understood by all Arab comrades. The genius of any leader should be a reflection of that of his nation. By this I do not mean to belittle any leader, nor do I wish to make comparisons. On the contrary, we must all work together as one nation. There is no more time to be lost by the Arab nation; there are many challenges to be faced and there is too much international involvement in the Arab world. This has certainly limited the advent of great leaders like Nebuchadnezzar and Salaheddin who were in the image of their nation. And yet anyone has the right to dream and try to achieve what these leaders achieved. We may hope to do what they did for Palestine, without ever forgetting that the great powers are trying to threaten Iraq. Iraq will continue to look to its history as an example, and will look forward to the constant advancement of humanity. In any game, even a simple one in the countryside, a would-be winner is always surrounded and stifled so as to prevent him succeeding. I feel that the great powers are behaving exactly in this manner towards Iraq. Despite all this, and despite the limitations, I feel nothing but optimism. I know that one day the nation's spirit will shine, no matter what the trials and despite the moves that will be made against it.

Fuad Matar: I should like to ask the following questions about the Arab-Israeli conflict:

First, how do you see this conflict?

Second, what is the difference between the Soviet Union and the United States, since both believe that Israel is here to stay and since the Soviet Union refuses to send offensive arms to the Arabs which would give them a strength equal to that of Israel?

Third, are there no positive points in the Camp David agreements?

Fourth, did President Sadat's move come as a surprise to you? Why, in your opinion, did Sadat reject all offers made to him to stop him continuing with his separate peace?

Fifth, what strategy do you think would bring about a just solution to the Middle East crisis?

Sixth, do you think that the Palestinian state now acceptable to most Palestinians can bring stability to the region?

Seventh, was your role in holding the Baghdad Summit part of a new understanding? And was your flexibility tactical or was it due to conviction?

President Saddam Hussein: There was both firmness and flexibility at the Baghdad Summit: firmness in that we could not keep quiet about, or condone, Sadat's actions as some would have liked to; firmness in that we stood against this move and would work accordingly and constructively. We told the wavering parties that if we did not stand united against Sadat's move, we would end up fighting one another and would divide into those in favour and those against; there was no middle of the road. This was a firm, clear-cut stand. However, we were flexible in that we wished to find a stand that would include everyone and express the bare minimum of agreement; anything below this would be treason. Had the Baghdad Summit been based on either flexibility or firmness alone, it would never have been able to adopt the resolutions that it did.

Next, we come to the stand of the United States and that of the Soviet Union. It is a fact that, in general, both request the withdrawal of 'Israel' from the occupied territories and the guarantee of secure borders for all countries of the region.

However, the stand of the Soviet Union concerning the enemy's withdrawal is clear-cut and more considered than that of the United States. After all, we use Soviet weapons today, whereas the enemy uses American weapons.

The Soviet stand is flexible in that it does not demand enemy withdrawal from the territories occupied on 5 June 1967. However, it sees no benefit in the Zionist entity holding on to the occupied territories, whereas the United States may find a strategic advantage in the Zionist entity keeping the territories it occupied in 1967. Thus the calculations and strategic considerations of the Soviet Union have placed it on the side of the Arabs, while those of the United States have placed it on the side of the Zionist entity. Both the Soviet Union and the United States insist that the rights of the Arabs should not go beyond recovering all the occupied territories (in the case of the Soviet Union) or most of the territories (in the case of the United States), on condition that the Arabs recognise the right of 'Israel' to exist as a state on the Palestinian land it occupied before 5 June 1967; this includes the Arab Palestinian land of 1948 and before.

How the Arabs should act to prevent the Soviets from seeing the Arab movement and its advancement as opposed to Soviet strategy will have to depend on Arab leaders and on other political and international factors. We believe that burgeoning Arab abilities and strength can change the Soviet stand for the better, as well as that of the Europeans and of other peoples, including those Americans who can liberate themselves from Zionist pressures and interests.

Fuad Matar: What about the Camp David agreements? Do they hold any positive points? And did President Sadat's move come as a surprise to you? Does the acceptance of a Palestinian state by most of the Palestinian parties have your consent as well?

President Saddam Hussein: How can there be any positive points in the Camp David agreements?

Fuad Matar: It brought into the open certain Arab elements that you thought were strong and with which you dealt as partners in the Arab revolution for the liberation of Palestine.

President Saddam Hussein: No defeat can be a victory, and that is why we do not see anything positive in the Camp David agreements. Treason will eventually lead to disaster for the traitor. That is why we warn against flexibility, which is a trait in the Arab mentality.

Sadat could not have taken this action in 1971, for instance. It would have been too much of a risk. What he did — and what was referred to as 'flexibility' — he did according to a plan, with the help and knowledge of the United States and Zionism, and others who fell into the trap through miscalculation or for other reasons. Sadat's move took me by surprise, but not its results. We knew that he had set himself apart before the meeting at Camp David and before his visit to Jerusalem. His treacherous step was the natural result of previous false steps and deviations in Arab politics; these were applauded by Americans, Zionists and some others, excused by others, and explained as flexibility by still others, whereas our stand was seen as rigidity or political immaturity. We knew that what eventually happened was a possibility.

Stability in the region cannot come through the creation of the state of Palestine alone. Real stability will come with the liberation of the Arab nation as a whole. This Arab nation will be self-confident, will rid itself of the foreigner, and will develop all its national capacities in order to defend itself and safeguard its sovereignty and its rights, without the need for aid or support from other nations.

Fuad Matar: I have the following questions to ask you about Arab unity and understanding:

First, when shall we reach the stage when each Arab state will feel the need for unity with other Arab states?

Second, what are the barriers that stand between us and this unity? Is it because of a lack of conviction, or is it a fear of losing our identity?

Third, do you not think that it is impossible for the Arab nation to unite as long as there are problems of minorities? Could there possibly be another intermediate step before complete unity?

Fourth, do you feel optimistic about Arab unity? When, and under what circumstances, can it take place? Since you believe in flexibility, is there not a way other than unity in order to reach understanding?

Fifth, how do you explain the fact that traditional regimes get along better with one another than the revolutionary ones do?

President Saddam Hussein: Reactionary and rightist Arabs have one plan and one political line, although they may differ in the application of their principles; this explains their stable relationships. They share the same interests, the same capitalist and feudal outlook, whereas progressive regimes are still on the way to building a dual existence: one based partly on tradition and partly on new laws and a new way of life which have to be accepted by the people. The ambitions of reactionary regimes are more realistic than those of progressive regimes. Many progressive regimes find that the greatest challenge to their existence comes from other so-called 'progressive' regimes.

Thus we find that differences become open conflict, rather than remaining differences. There are many reasons for this, mainly the lack of maturity and depth in the general outlook and behaviour, as well as a lack of self-confidence. One can also add to this the effect of international currents, which are now affecting progressive regimes as well as reactionary regimes. We would work better and more effectively if only we could all realise that there is enough space within our region for several different progressive movements (as long as they are not influenced by foreign powers), with no danger of one encroaching upon the other. Had there been enough understanding of joint Arab action, we could have found a vast field for Arab action, and for co-operation between all the national and progressive regimes and organisations.

Now we come to the subject of unity: twenty years ago we believed that unity could be achieved through a common constitution, and that it was a political act, as in the case of the unity between Egypt and Syria in 1958. Today we who fight and struggle for unity see it differently. We consider it an honourable goal, and we strive for a constitutional and political union between two or more Arab regions, in order to reach the ultimate goal: complete unity. This can only be achieved through a common constitution and policy. We also try other methods that would bring us closer to unity. For instance, we believe that economic ties may serve to promote unity, but are not in themselves unity. The problem is that people either have their gaze fixed on the future and neglect to do anything for the present, or they work only for the present and reach a form of Arab co-ordination which they see as unity.

We must not belittle the importance of any links between the Arabs; they may all contribute to unity on a constitutional and political basis. Yet we must not think that these steps will necessarily lead to unity, since sometimes they do not have unity as their aim. After the year 1958, co-operation between one Arab region and another was often incorrectly referred to as unity or union. I can give several examples of this: 'unity' between Syria, Egypt and Libya; unity between Egypt and Libya; unity between Egypt and North Yemen at the time of the late Gamal Abdel-Nasser; talk of unity between Syria and Jordan. It is only when the Arabs are convinced of the importance of uniting that they will do so. It is only when they realise that they must unite in order to be truly effective in society that they will do so. It is the Arab belief and faith in unity that will make them reach the ultimate goal, always bearing in mind that they must rely on themselves.

Fuad Matar: During the days leading up to a revolution, democracy comes first and foremost on the agenda, and it is believed that democracy will spread once the comrade comes to power. But then the concept of democracy changes so that it is no longer an issue. Do you believe that the concept of democracy is unsuited to the Arab world or do you have a practical definition of it? As a leader who has fought for twenty years, half in the Revolution itself and the other half in power, can you not install a democracy that would be peculiar to the Baath?

President Saddam Hussein: I do believe that we can establish a form of democracy in Iraq that can be imitated in the Arab nation. If we are not able to do so, then what is the use of my believing in the Baath and why does our Party struggle in the entire Arab nation? But if you ask me whether Western democracy is suitable for the Arab nation, my answer is no. Let us go back in history to the time of the early Arab Muslims. Their democracy never followed a Western pattern, and they relied on consultation rather than a parliament. That is why our own understanding of democracy should be based on the particular characteristics of our nation, as well as of our Party. Democracy has to develop and change with the times, while taking into account the political and legal rights of the citizen and his role in building the nation, together with his relationship with the Party. We cannot automatically apply democracy through imitation; this would only be detrimental to us as well as destructive, whether the source of imitation is Western or Eastern. How can our society, which is less developed than some, adopt the patterns of a very advanced society?

What is the right way of introducing a developed democracy within a traditional society? This is what we have been implementing in stages since 30 July 1968. If you were to ask the Iraqi people today who 'Abu Dolof' is, they would immediately answer, 'He is Karim al-Jassem, the head of the General Federation of the Farmers' Unions.' Karim al-Jassem is a farmer's son and a farmer himself; an Iraqi who can barely read or write, he has become an important social figure in Baath society, a personality who is the leader of millions of farmers. How could he have reached this level of leadership in his relationship with the farmers if there had been no democracy in revolutionary action? This is an active expression of the will of the people, applicable since 30 July 1968, and yet always changing with the times.

We have not yet dealt directly with the exercise of democracy on a constitutional level. Until now the Revolution Command

Council has been the only body to adopt higher constitutional resolutions directly. However, the draft laws for the National Assembly and the Legislative Assembly for the Autonomous Region, which the people are now discussing, will ensure that the people's representatives participate in constitutional decisions and in shaping the higher policy of the nation. We do not believe that the liberal democratic experience is suited to our society because it was founded and developed on the basis of a capitalist society. Its context differs from ours, which is mainly based on our Revolution. According to the Western concept, for example, a society must have a free economy, even at the expense of other freedoms; yet one cannot possibly isolate the economy from life itself.

Fuad Matar: You know more than most people about Arab human rights because you faced difficult social circumstances in your childhood, because this stage was followed by one just as difficult, and because you were willing to make sacrifices, to the point of martyrdom, in your stand against a regime which had no use for human rights. In view of this, I would like you to define minimum and maximum Arab human rights. Under what circumstances will the Arab attain his political and social rights? What are the rights the Arab has attained in Iraq? What rights has he not yet attained, and how will he be able to attain them?

President Saddam Hussein: First we must agree that the matter of human rights is dynamic, not static. If we go back to early Arab Islamic history, to which I attach great importance, we find the Arabs' concept of rights was not rigid. It adapted to the times, from the coming of the Prophet and throughout the era of his followers until decadence set in. Rights changed with each new circumstance but were always based on principles. Even at the beginning, divine laws were based on the conditions and circumstances that prevailed at the time. That is why the advent of Judaism, Christianity and Islam came in that order, by the will of God, to be carried out by His prophets and their followers according to the times and circumstances . . .

Was preaching the only means that the Islamic religion used, or did it also make use of knowledge, education and the sword for its conquests? The answer is well known: Muslim Arabs used both, the Quran and the sword. But did they later use the sword as fervently as they did at the beginning of their mission? Did the Prophet Muhammad make as much use of the sword in the eleventh year of Islam as he did in the first years? The answer is no. That is why we say that human rights will depend on the time, the conditions and the circumstances. They will always be in step with the Revolution and its principles. The concept of human rights today is different from what it was four years ago, for instance, because the Revolution has progressed in the last twelve years.

Yet the basic principle of human rights remains the same: man was born to be free but not to be alone in his freedom; he must also take society's rights into consideration, as well as the freedom and rights of others. The interests of man and society are interrelated. Our view of human rights is different from that held by capitalism, which is based on the assumption that the individual's freedom and interests are equal to society's freedom and interests . . . Human rights outside society's rights are based on self-interest alone. So Americans can talk of human rights in the Soviet Union when they themselves are killing human beings in other societies, and we find Communist societies discussing the same subject when they, too, destroy human rights in their own lands and in another people's territory.

We must always remember our history, although I do not wish to do so in order to imitate it. Each Arab must learn the lessons of our heritage and our past. Some of the sons of our nation have a firm belief in our history, its greatness and its depth, and, finding themselves unable to follow in the path of their ancestors, decide to leave history well alone. This is wrong.

Fuad Matar: Yesterday I spent some time with your children to see how they live, and what sort of relationship you have with them. When I talked to your eldest son Adi, I saw he was wearing a military uniform and that he is being trained in the use of weapons despite his youth. It occurred to me to ask him the standard question: what do you want to be when you grow up? His answer reminded me of an important question I had prepared earlier for you. Your son said he wanted to become a nuclear scientist. My question to you was the following: is Iraq planning to procure a nuclear bomb?

President Saddam Hussein: Science must always be based on solid foundations. I do not believe nuclear weapons can be used for peaceful, scientific purposes in an underdeveloped, bedouin society. Money alone does not mean that a state possesses the key to the correct use of nuclear weapons for peaceful purposes. The use of such a weapon has its own conditions, circumstances and demands. It cannot be separated from the rest of life, society, international politics, the state's interests or the people's demands for a better life. However, I think that if you ask any person in the world whether he would like to possess a nuclear bomb, he will tell you that he would. A nuclear bomb is not a child's toy. It is a heavy responsibility, although it may not seem so. And if you asked countries such as Djibouti, India,

Dubai, Nepal or Japan — all countries which have entered into special treaties since the Second World War — they would tell you that the nuclear bomb is definitely a burden. However, there is no doubt that within our essential programme we attach great importance to the peaceful uses of nuclear power, both technologically and scientifically.

Fuad Matar: Where do you think the axes and poles of power will lie in the last quarter of this century? What are your strategies to face the balance of power that may arise? Have you ever considered an alliance for the future between the Soviets, the Arabs and the Europeans, or an Arab-European-Japanese alliance capable of settling certain issues for which the United States is responsible?

President Saddam Hussein: In 1975 we told our ambassadors which countries we thought would exercise particular influence in world affairs in the next twenty years. These countries would be independent of the two blocs which divide them or bring them together according to their own interests. They included Japan, Europe and the Arab nation. The discussion also involved the circumstances that may either bring us together or set us apart. This is naturally connected with the strategic changes of interests according to necessity. That is why we cannot talk today of one particular pole of attraction as opposed to another. We would like to add that there are so far no contradictions between China and the Arab nation, or between Japan and the Arab nation, that stand in the way of their meeting, although there may be differences. This also applies to all the great powers, as well as most of the smaller states on an individual basis.

Fuad Matar: Do you believe that the two superpowers enjoy such stability that it is impossible for them to suffer the débâcle experienced, say, by Great Britain, which is no longer great after the tripartite aggression of 1956 against Egypt? And if the same were ever to happen to the United States, under special circumstances, is it possible for one superpower alone to reign over the whole world?

President Saddam Hussein: I do not think it is possible for one great power to rule the world on its own. Never in the world's history has this happened, nor will it do so now.

Fuad Matar: Had you been in a position of responsibility during the Cold War, how would you have acted?

President Saddam Hussein: It is not possible for me to speculate on what I would have done in the past. However, I can say that the reason behind the delay of Arab unity is that many international conflicts are taking place on Arab soil. This is not the only reason, of course, and it is to be hoped that Arab maturity and development will deal with all factors eventually.

Fuad Matar: It is well known that you think it necessary to co-operate with all the blocs of the world, with the exception of the United States. Why is that? Do you not think it is in the interests of the Arabs to lean on one bloc only, as Israel does?

President Saddam Hussein: We do not reject alliances in politics. Temporary alliances for a definite goal existed even in the time of the Prophet Muhammad. I fully realise the power and the capacity of the United States, and I am not against establishing an honourable relationship with that nation if it will serve our interests without the USA exploiting our region for its purposes alone. A united nation is in a better position for such a relationship than a divided nation. When we talk of the United States of today, we find it impossible to make either a friend or an ally of that country, because of its own alliance with the Zionist entity. The United States acts against our nation and harms it; we would be fooling ourselves if we thought otherwise. In time, and if the United States decides to serve its own interests rather than other interests, then we will co-operate with it.

We are also against an alliance with one power and one power alone. This would only be possible if that power accepted the unity of the Arab nation and saw in this unity a guarantee of its own interests and strategies; this is impossible as such a power does not exist, nor will it.

Fuad Matar: Your special treatment of France looks as if you are predicting a greater role for it. Am I right?

President Saddam Hussein: I believe that to this day France is acting, whether out of conviction or out of necessity, within the context of de Gaulle's programme: this demands a European unity that is distinct from the United States. Some Frenchmen have gone even further, as can be seen by the statements issued by both Gaullists and non-Gaullists. They believe that colonialism does not serve their interests, but that the development of industrial and economic relations with the Third World nations does. We favour this, as we favour any commercial exchange that serves our economy and our interests, if this exchange is on the basis of honour and respect. That is why we encourage the French policy which believes in these factors; it will eventually be followed by the rest of Europe, as France has influence and weight in Europe and its international politics. That is why we distinguish France from other European nations.

Fuad Matar: Gaullism looks as though it might be a French form of Baathism.

President Saddam Hussein: I do not like to look for similarities, and yet I do find a bridge between their policies and ours.

Fuad Matar: Is France capable of meeting Iraq's economic and military ambitions?

President Saddam Hussein: Certainly not. This would be most difficult.

Fuad Matar: It is impossible to breathe new life into a union once it has broken up. For example, Syria and Egypt were never able to reunite after they separated, despite all the attempts made to do so. The same now applies to the Baath, which is divided into two countries as well as two movements despite the attempts at reunification. Do you believe that the Syrian-Egyptian union was spontaneous, and arose from force of circumstance rather than conviction; was there any way it could have been saved? Can the Baath become one again, or will it remain divided?

President Saddam Hussein: In the light of our study of the Syrian-Egyptian union, and based on the analysis of Party leaders, non-Baathist political thinkers and the leaders who had a role in setting up this union, it is clear that the reasons for it were goodwill, nationalism and ambitions for a broader horizon, rather than practicality. That is why the union broke up. It occurred without any serious attempt to stop it from happening, and in a dramatic manner not suited to the concept of Arab unity.

As for what you refer to as unity between the two Baaths, we do not consider what is in Syria as the Baath, and I am sure that Syria would say the same of Iraq's Baath. And yet we have not issued a single judgement concerning the power bases of the Party in Syria, or commented on the ills that have befallen all levels of organisation there. When the people realise that their interests are not served by division and corruption, unity will prevail again.

Fuad Matar: What were the reasons that led to the resumption of parliamentary life in Iraq after twenty-one years? And are you sure that a political life will not lead to contradictions with the concept of political work as the Baath understands it?

President Saddam Hussein: What made us act in this manner is the Revolution's development and the implementation of its programmes on all levels; the people have been awakened to their rights and duties. We know today that such a step will serve the Revolution's path.

Fuad Matar: Can one say that your frequent impromptu visits to ordinary citizens for lunch or tea are influenced by ancient Arab traditions?

President Saddam Hussein: Let me say that I am as proud of our shining Arab history as I am of our Muslim Arab leaders, and I try to learn lessons from our glorious past. It is no shame to want to walk in the shadow of their work, although I know that we are still far from their accomplishments. However, we have tried to teach and lead our people, not through our history in general but through our outlook on the Baath and its humanity.

Fuad Matar: I have noticed that you seem to be somewhat in awe of the Cuban experience, and the Cuban revolutionary flexibility *vis-à-vis* the existence of American bases on Cuban soil. You excuse this fact although it goes against Cuba's independence and sovereignty, and when you have never allowed such a thing in Iraq and have not resumed diplomatic relations with the United States. What aspects of the Cuban experience do you most admire, and do you wish to follow their example in wiping out illiteracy?

President Saddam Hussein: In my answers I have consistently stressed the importance of all human experience. I am proud of the Cuban revolution and feel nothing but respect towards it and its leaders, particularly Fidel Castro. That is the reason behind Iraq's special relationship with Cuba. Yet we do not wish to become Cuban Communists nor do we wish to make Baathists of the Cubans; to each his experience. We exchange our experiences, our views and our opinions without trying to imitate one another.

It was not Cuba's experience that influenced us in our plan to conquer illiteracy, but our Baathist programme based on our own history. What was the greatest concern of the Islamic call in its early days? Is not the first verse of the Quran, 'Read, in the name of your Lord and Creator'? It is our own history and heritage that teach us great lessons.

What we most admire and respect in the Cuban revolution is that it was created by Cubans, with a Cuban spirit, based on a realistic outlook and on Cuba's own interests. That is why it will always be victorious. It is this that all revolutions in the Third World share, and we are part of it; these revolutions resemble one another when they are carried out by the nation itself. No one else made the Iraqi or the Cuban revolutions and presented them as a gift to either nation.

Fuad Matar: But why is it that the revolution and the application of socialism in the Arab nation do not bring about the feeling of joy that they do in Cuba, for instance, or in other socialist countries in the world where the citizen seems more reassured and content? I bear in mind that most socialist states are not wealthy and have limited incomes.

President Saddam Hussein: In which part of the Arab nation has socialism been applied in its true, serious sense? Even in our own country we are still attempting to apply socialism through a clear-cut programme and the application of firm measures. As for other Arab countries, socialism has taken on another form, one of nationalisation and of full state power over certain economic activities, rather than an overall change in life itself. Socialism cannot limit itself to one form. It must be based on a new and developed society where justice and democracy prevail, rather than socialism for its own sake.

What do you think of our society in Iraq? Is it a happy one? You, as an Arab, have been in contact with it: have you found it distressed or disturbed by its own experience? Our society is proud of its experience. Whether in a socialist experience or otherwise, it is the people who choose their own route to happiness. Iraqi society is happy with its experience so far, and we plan to make it happier year after year and to avoid any path that our people will reject. If our people believe that one form of socialism is better than another, we will respect their views and take them into consideration even if this may mean a major change in our original plan.

Fuad Matar: Do you not think it is time to evaluate the Baath's principles now that it has been in existence for thirty-five years, especially as regards its view of Islam? We are living in the midst of an Islamic awakening or, if one may say so, in a state of Islamic 'baath'. The reason behind this may be that the generation of the seventies is suffering from the failure of nationalism. The Baath has always stressed the importance of secularism. You are in the best position to judge this analysis: you are in power, and the Islamic 'baath' stands a good chance of attracting a generation of Arabs whom the national Baath appears to have failed to attract.

President Saddam Hussein: The Party's outlook on religion is not only based on the inspiration it derives from Islam, nor is it neutral before faith and apostasy; the Party is for faith. When we say that we are not neutral between apostasy and faith, we mean that Baathists are like all other believers, free to worship as they wish. They pray, fast and carry out their religious duties towards God. They have a direct relationship with their religion, whereas those who have a scientific outlook on life may stand on the borderline between faith and apostasy, or may even have a materialistic outlook on life. Yet, although we may be inspired by religion and its laws, we do not deal with life by following a religious path. Today, after 1,400 years, religion has taken many new paths, new meanings, new conduct, new schools of thought. We do not believe in dealing with life through religion because it would not serve the Arab nation. It would only serve to divide the nation into different religions and numerous sects and schools of thought. We discussed this point before the Iranian revolution took place and we find that our predictions have come true: differences have arisen amongst the believers in everyday religious matters. What I wish to point out here is that we have two relationships with religion: an inspiration stemming from the main principles and lessons, and the fact that, like all ordinary citizens, we are believers who worship without any interference from those in power. That is why I do not see the need for an analysis of the Baath's attitude towards religion.

However, we must pause here and analyse the reasons behind the politicised religion of some of the young men who use religion as a weapon in their struggle against corrupt regimes, instead of using the Baath as a way of achieving their goals. We all have the same aims. The Baath is not operating in a limited field; on the contrary, it is spreading, and so are the religious movements of these young men. They deserve our attention, not because we are afraid of them, but because they are in the image of the Baathists in that they are fighting against corruption, injustice, confessionalism and reactionary movements. Whether they will succeed — and they have not yet done so — is another matter.

We believe in religion and it is ever-present in our daily life and in our Party. Therefore we do not find any contradiction between these young men and us, inasmuch as they struggle, often under the seal of secrecy, against injustice and without foreign aid for the unity of the Arab nation. Yet we still believe that the road taken by the Baath is the best one to deal with injustice, in that it has greater experience and is more capable of bringing happiness to Arab society. In our struggle it is just as important to find a way to build a better society within the framework of religion, its principles and traditions, as it is to erase corruption.

We follow the dictates of Islam fully, as we are people who come from a religious society; yet the manner of worship is free of any state interference, since each human being practises in accordance with his religion, his sect and his customs.

We are content, although not completely, with our calculations and our programme. We are content in that the application of our Party's principles has taken the right road in the Iraqi region, and we find Baathists fighting against corruption and injustice and dying for their honourable cause wherever the need arises in the Arab world.

How long is it since the revolution took place in Iran? Eleven months. Has it taken development into consideration, its circumstances and its demands? If it does not do so, then it must explain each development which may lead to the creation of a new school of thought, and even to a new sect. We believe that if the Iranian revolution continues on its present path, it may split from the Shia sect and become a new sect. This is why our Party and its early leaders looked upon Arab life as they did, believing that the Baath was the right way. This is also our view of the matter. We do not deal with life through religion, but at the same time we are linked to religion through worship, which takes into consideration freedom of worship. Had the Arab world been one nationality and one religion it would have been easy to resolve this. However, it is surrounded by new and hostile currents which seek to exploit the weak points in the Arab nation and thus prevent its development. We truly believe that the Baath's road will save the nation from dangers and bring about a new and flourishing civilisation, free from corruption and injustice, where happiness and justice will prevail.

As for the religious awakening you mentioned earlier, I would like to point out that it is not the first time that our young men have rebelled against injustice, taking the principles of Islam as their inspiration (whether they succeed in their call or not is another matter). For example, the Muslim Brothers used their religious beliefs as a weapon to resist the British in Egypt. Religious movements flourished in the Arab nation in the forties and fifties. This was the case, for instance, amongst our own young men in Iraq before the Revolution of July 1958.

The explanation for this recent awakening is that corruption is more widespread in the Arab world today than ever before. Some regimes are the image of corruption itself. The presence of mosques has been a great help towards the creation of such movements, since mosques are sacred places on which assaults and attacks would be strongly discouraged, although some rulers have taken such steps. Mosques, if I may say so, are the ideal headquarters for underground activities in the context of a religious direction of the struggle. We rejoice and feel deeply with any young man who believes in the Islamic call and is ready to die for it in his struggle against corruption. In the past this has only occurred in Egypt and Algeria; today, it is more widespread. However, the Baathists fight for the same causes and are ready to die for them.

Fuad Matar: The religious movements you have just mentioned came into existence in order to fight colonialism, whereas today's religious awakening stands vehemently against the misuse of wealth and the misconduct of the ruler, both on the public and the private level. In Iran the issue may be a religious one for the ayatollahs and religious scholars, but it is a national one for the ordinary citizen.

President Saddam Hussein: It is primarily an Iranian national and social cause which came into existence in answer to the widespread corruption, not only among the Shah and his entourage, but also on many levels of Iranian society. Before the Shah's fall, Iranian society was an example of corruption incarnate. The Iranian state knew corruption at all levels, as well as poverty and class differences which were unique among all the other Islamic states.

Fuad Matar: First came the incident when a naturalised Iraqi threw a bomb at a packed crowd at the Mustansiriyah University on 1 April 1980; many Iraqis and Arabs died and a member of the Revolution Command Council, Tareq Aziz, was injured. Two days later another bomb was thrown at the funeral of those who had died in the first incident. Even at the time, the manner in which you dealt with both incidents seemed as if you were preparing the people for a confrontation with Iran. You visited the wounded in hospital and talked to each and every one. Am I right, and if so, did you take into consideration the fact that many Arab powers were quite happy for you to enter into a confrontation with Iran so that Iraq might be weakened?

In the last eleven years you have shown goodwill towards the Gulf states although you could have altered the map of that area. What is the stand of the Gulf rulers in relation to your problems with Iran? Are they with you or are they neutral? Have you consulted them over the dangers of Iranian hegemony and the way to deal with it?

President Saddam Hussein: It seems that the Arabs do not realise the depth of the changes brought about by the Revolution in the psychology of the Iraqi citizen. The Iraqis are easy-going and tough at the same time. They are easy-going because they are emotional and they are tough for the very same reason. This is why they gave their loyalty for short periods in the first years of the new era. They either gave or took, they were never neutral. They were either staunch supporters or became confirmed enemies. For the first time in history, our people have shown their loyalty to a regime — that of 17 July 1968 — and this loyalty still exists some twelve years after the regime came to power. This proves the depth of their feelings. Any people can be sentimental and admire a ruler. His looks may please them, his behaviour, some decision or other, some word; all of this may lead the people to trust him, carefully awaiting what the future may bring. But when trust is given gradually and after twelve years, it becomes deep, stable and infallible, and this is something out of the ordinary. The Iraqis are never restrained in their attitudes; they have never been spectators in history, whether before or after Islam. They have always been either the victors or the vanquished, either on top of the mountain or at the bottom of the valley. Life has its ups and downs, and in order to reach the top one must start at the bottom. No ruler is without enemies from among the people and the surrounding nations.

As for what you said about our having mobilised the masses, this is not so. We behaved naturally in view of the circumstances; the only thing that may have been out of the ordinary was my visit to the university and my addressing the students. This was in answer to what happened. Moreover I have visited the hospitals more than fifty times since July. This was not in the context of mobilisation, but rather a duty towards the citizens. Any planned action of this sort cannot possibly have the same effect on the people.

Our enemies continue to fool themselves because they do not understand the Iraqi people. All that is said by the rulers of Iran are lies. Read the Iranian daily papers and you will clearly see the lies. When I visited the university I swore three times that the bloodshed would not go unavenged. The Iranians claimed that I had sworn three times to divorce my wife, implying that Saddam Hussein does not believe in God. Some Iranians are still under the influence of the Shah's actions and mistakenly believe that Saddam Hussein is the Shah of Iraq and that they are the ayatollahs of the Iraqi people. This is because they cared only for their cause; they never paid attention to Iraq, a neighbouring state, although Khomeini could have helped them to understand Iraq. But Khomeini is a man of religion; he is eighty years old, his seat is in Najaf, and he sees only a narrow path and hears from those who do not come from the people. He listens to some religious men since he has enemies amongst them: for example, Al-Khouti in Iraq, and others with whom he does not feel at ease. When a man has lived in Iraq for fifteen years without mingling with the people, it is difficult for him to know the truth and easier for him to believe the stories of oppression and injustice.

We now come to the Arabs. It would be shameful to ask anything of the Arabs; their burden is heavy enough as it is. We would be demanding too much even if we asked them to try to understand the nature of our struggle with Iran. The Arabs need a regime that will assume all responsibilities without asking them for anything. We cannot burden them with a request for analysis, since analysis sometimes makes them psychologically uncomfortable. Are we supposed to discuss the nature of our struggle against Iran with Shaikh Zayed [of the United Arab Emirates]? Are we supposed to ask him why Iran chose

Iraq [as its enemy]? This would be shameful, not for Shaikh Zayed's sake but for the sake of the land he is in. This is our general view of the [Arab] rulers, be they dear to us or not. As for the cause of the people and the land, it is our cause and we shall not abandon it, even if a ruler decides to do so.

If you made a quick analysis of the situation, you would know why [the Iranians] chose Iraq. The operation is purely Persian, Persian in its sick imaginings and in its underdevelopment. And if you made a survey of the different [Arab] regimes and the nature of their relations with Iran, you would find many strange factors. It has reached a point where Libya is used to train pseudo-commandos who will put their training into effect in order to destroy parts of the Arab nation. [Iran] talks of wanting to apply the Islamic religion in its true sense, and yet it has dealings with regimes like that in Syria, which Islam has rebelled against. [The Iranians] know perfectly well that they cannot reach Abu Dhabi before they have broken down the great barrier of Iraq. Abu Dhabi seems to know this too, and is reassured by this fact. Iraq is a barrier which stands in the way of those Persians who give way to their imaginary hatred of the Arabs. And they are no better than the Shah. They have kept all the Shah's profits and believe that, as long as they have not conquered Iraq, they cannot conquer the other [Arab countries]. Their good relations with any Arab regime are simply intended to weaken Iraq.

Fuad Matar: On 8 February 1980, on the anniversary of the Baath's coming to power for the first time, you proposed a National Charter to organise relations between Arab countries and put a stop to the use of arms against one another. You also called for economic co-operation. The Charter seemed like an answer to the role played by the Soviet Union in Afghanistan. It also sounded like a decision to place less emphasis on spreading your Party's principles in other Arab countries. May I presume to say that such a Charter places you among the rulers of today rather than among the revolutionary ones? What are the reasons behind such a Charter?

President Saddam Hussein: Every image can be applied in a different manner, and each situation has two sides: the way you imagine it, and the way you plan to achieve it. Our Party talks of one nation, one Arab nation. In order to achieve this aim, the land must not be divided. How can we develop and progress if our land is divided into several parts? In our analysis of the present situation it would be fair to say that, as long as there are great powers, there will always be a danger of their wanting to divide and influence regions for their own interests.

China will expand its borders as soon as it is sufficiently

developed. The same applies to the Soviet Union, Japan and the Americans. The Arab nation's land may be parcelled out in this redistribution. Thus a decision on Arab unity is no longer in the hands of the Arabs alone. Some countries react with fear because of their feelings of weakness. For instance, if they feel that the Soviet Union is coming nearer they turn to the Americans for help. The United States then sets up a base; the Soviet Union wants to do the same. We talk of unity because of the present dangerous situation in the Arab nation, not because we are in full control of the nation — we are not.

This brings us to a further question: how do we see Arab unity? We see it having a specific constitution and being established through specific economic and political relations. Is this possible? At the time of the advent of Islam many people remained within the Arab nation without becoming Muslims. No religion has covered the whole world, whether Christianity, Judaism or Islam. What I mean by this is that we are capable of reaching our goal and are willing to die for it. At the same time, we must not look on time as something frozen; it may bring an opportunity closer or it may take it further away. This means that there is a great danger that, if the Arabs do not take giant steps technologically and scientifically in the next twenty years, their golden opportunity will be lost. All these factors lead us to say that we must find things that the Arabs, any Arab, can agree on and work for; when the Arab thinks a little, he will see that there is nothing to be gained by selfish regionalism and that in unity he will gain rather than lose. If countries such as Egypt, Algeria and Iraq cannot reach the level of Brazil in comparison with the United States, or that of Rumania in comparison with the Soviet Union, then we will be nothing but slaves, whether we like it or not. The price of oil in twenty years' time will be similar to that of coal today, since the world will have turned to another source of energy, a source that is inexhaustible such as solar energy.

The principles of my Declaration are very simple: we must not kill one another; this energy must be diverted elsewhere. If an Arab country does not have a foreign country on its borders, it must not go to a foreign state for aid as Tunisia did when it requested France's help against Libya and Algeria. We ask all of this, because we have one important cause: facing Zionism. We also must help certain countries, like the Yemen for instance, to improve their economic status so that in twenty years' time they may reach the level of Iraq. The Charter was also announced to plug the gaps through which the foreigner enters. This we can achieve through peaceful relations and non-interference in the internal affairs of any state. The Arabs have understood the importance of our statement, but this is not enough to achieve the goals for which it was announced.

Fuad Matar: Do you sometimes wonder why the Arabs were greater in the past and why they have changed so drastically? And why is it that the Arabs are now only good at poetry and imitating others, whereas the whole region was once a shining light for other civilisations? And why were the Arabs an example of chivalry in the past, unlike today? Why are they living through a religious crisis when they were the very source of religion? Why are they facing a crisis of legislation when they were the source of law? They were pioneers in medicine, yet today they send their patients to be treated abroad. They were the masters of philosophy, but have become the followers of Western thought today. They were the source of history and are now given a fleeting reference in history books. Why?

President Saddam Hussein: It is natural for me to wonder about all this, but I still believe that our nation is capable of a renaissance. There is no nation that has given as much to humanity as the Arab nation has. There is no other nation that has risen, fallen and risen once more, without being colonialists or aggressors, and with only human interests in mind. A nation goes through life just as a human being passes through different stages: infancy, childhood, youth, middle age, old age, then death. There are reasons behind this which I do not wish to go into. Decadence sets in when man loses faith and its incentives. There are other reasons which account for the decadence of the Arab nation at certain points of its history.

But let us also ask ourselves the following question: where were the other nations when the Arab nation was at the height of civilisation? They were then at the stage of receiving knowledge. We must point out that the Arab nation is not made up of a single civilisation but of many — civilisations that were unique in their humanity. Non-Arab nations were still living in darkness when the Arab nation's civilisation shone throughout the world.

When the nation starts to weaken and becomes decadent it is the fault of those in power, because they have lost their belief in the principles of life and forgotten the importance of a nation's role, its message and its values. We can state without hesitation that our nation has a message. That is why it can never be an average nation: throughout history our nation has either soared to the heights, or fallen into the abyss through the envy, conspiracy and enmity of others. Any rising nation attracts enemies who have only one wish, to stand in the way of its development.

If one asked whether the Arab nation today is on the ascent

or in decline, the answer would have to be that it is on the ascent as compared with the previous ten years; indeed, it is experiencing a renaissance. Do we have the necessary means today for a new renaissance? The answer is no. However, our young people have faith, and believe in taking the necessary steps to save the nation. We are reaching a crucial stage in the struggle for the nation's renaissance. Your questions are natural and meaningful, yet the state in which we find ourselves today as compared to that of our ancestors will not sap my energy, nor can it prevent me from stating that the nation can and will rise again.

There have been many opportunities of which the Party could have made use. However, they did not do so. This does not mean that the Party was incapable of doing so, but rather that the Party would not at that time have been able to emerge as a popular leader over the whole Arab nation rather than over Iraq alone, as is our ambition. It is not only the difficult moments the Party has lived through which are responsible for this, it is also a lack of the right opportunities. There were shortcomings in the use of the Party's capabilities, as well as a certain neglect in the way the Party's beliefs were explained. This could have been done better. The Arab nation would be in a stronger position today if the February Revolution in Iraq and the March Revolution in Syria had both taken our same Baathist path.

Although we recognise our mistakes and try to learn from them, we do not stop to cry over the negative aspects. We must consolidate our struggle and strengthen our purpose to push ever forward. Ours is a great nation, and it will be even greater in time. This is the solemn pledge made by all our comrades.